COUNTRY LIFE

100 FAVOURITE HOUSES

COUNTRY LIFE
100 FAVOURITE HOUSES

Candida Lycett Green

B◈XTREE

This book is dedicated to the
memory of David Vicary.

First published in 1999 by Boxtree, an imprint of
Macmillan Publishers Ltd, 25 Eccleston Place,
London, SW1W 9NF and Basingstoke

Associated companies throughout the world

ISBN 0 7522 1333 4

Title page photograph – Lower Brockhampton
Manor House
Opposite photograph – Mapperton, Dorset

9 8 7 6 5 4 3 2 1

A CIP catalogue record for this book is available
from the British Library

Design by DW Design, London

Printed by The Bath Press, Bath

Country Life is published by IPC Magazines Ltd,
King's Reach Tower, Stamford Street, London SE1
9LS. For subscription enquiries and overseas
orders call 01444 445555 (fax 01444 445599).
Please send all correspondence to: IPC Magazines
Ltd, Oakfield House, 35 Perrymount Road,
Haywards Heath, West Sussex RH16 3DH.
Alternatively, you can call the subscription credit
card hotline (UK orders only) on: 01622 778778.

CONTENTS

INTRODUCTION

The photographic archives of *Country Life* contain records of several thousand houses and gardens throughout the British Isles. From the magazine's first beginnings under the inspired leadership of Edward Hudson, the presentation of architecture has been consistently brilliant and evocative, and has appealed at every level. The *Country Life* architectural correspondents have been and remain exceptional, in both safeguarding a reverence for the best of the past and celebrating the best of today: they have contributed to making *Country Life* the national institution it is.

I feel honoured to have been asked to select the 100 favourite houses, but in fact for the most part the houses have chosen themselves. I have merely balanced things out, both geographically and stylistically. Firstly, to whittle down the choice I haven't included any castles in the real sense of the word because they were built as necessary defensive structures and thus tend to be repetitive. In praise of our architecture I have tried to include as wide a panorama of styles as possible, from the unassuming fourteenth-century Gothic of Markenfield to John Outram's polychromatic Wadhurst Park of the 1970s. The styles which predominate are what people have liked the best – the ancient jumbles are clear favourites, with the eighteenth century a close second. As for modern 'favourites', this is a matter for conjecture for they have not yet stood the test of time. I have chosen my personal top four and I have also included Meols Hall because it represents the neo-Georgian taste, still prevalent among new house builders.

I have tried to present a wide geographical spread, to show the great diversity of building materials used over the centuries, in this the most geologically complicated country in the world. The surrounding landscape of each house is therefore part of its point. Its materials are often dug or cut from it, and its surrounding farmland often its *raison d'être*. I have been at pains to describe the place in which each house lies because for the creators and certainly for me, the house and its setting are a single conception. The place often shapes the house, as at Castle Hill and Baggy House in Devon. I have never been able to see houses out of context, just for their architecture alone.

I realize that Ireland, Scotland and Wales are not as well represented as England, but this is because I live in the latter. I have covered every county in England. Some are richer in great and good houses than others. Norfolk, for instance, presented dilemmas. It had to be Houghton *or* Holkham, and the latter lost on the flick of a coin.

The late great Christopher Hussey, the mainstay of *Country Life* for so long, wrote, 'The English home, while not laying claim to supreme artistry, yet represents to our sight a complex of facts and traditions and aspirations that are the very essence of our consciousness as Englishmen. The home is a 'work of living', an expression of the deepest instincts of our forebears through the ages.' Many of the houses in this book tell of lives well spent, some more elaborately than others. Through writing about each house I have followed families through historical upheavals and been moved by the loyalty of some to their particular cause and surprised at the fickleness of others. I have watched owners ruining themselves to impress a member of the Royal family like Mr Howard at Audley End or to outdo a neighbour like Lord Belmore at Castle Coole. The Victorians took the biscuit with their swank: look at Harlaxton. Yet only a few decades later, armed with the moral philosophy of William Morris, the bright new Fabian socialists like James and Margaret Beale of Standen showed an altogether different way of bringing their domestic aestheticism into the light. In the 1930s the modern movement proponents took the art of living still further into the realms of quiet reserve, as at The Homewood.

In the end I am interested in the people who have fashioned these houses and why. In why they wanted a window here or a house sited there; I like to imagine conversations they had with their architects or their wives and what they thought when they looked out at the view. I am interested in the builders and craftsmen and the pride they must have taken in their work, and wonder what they thought of their clients. I do not pretend to be a scholar, but have enjoyed following in the footsteps of the greats. In particular Christopher Hussey, Howard Colvin, Avray Tipping, John Julius Norwich, Harold Nicholson, Mark Girouard and Hugh Massingberd. We have been travelling over the same terrain and have often been moved to the same reactions. From the sidelines I have occasionally witnessed little scholastic one-upmanships. Ramsbury Manor for instance has involved much postulating over its authorship. Four articles in *Country Life*, over a period of seventy years have come up with more and more learned articles suggesting different possible architects. In 1961 Hussey plumped for Roger Pratt, but by 1975 Howard Colvin is concluding that it is *almost* certainly by Robert Hooke. I would not presume to hazard a guess.

GODOLPHIN

Cornwall

Towards the very edge of the West, a few miles short of the end of England, there is a magical lost domain. It lies hidden in this doleful stretch of inland Cornwall, where warring Danes never bothered to penetrate, where depression still hovers and strange chimneys above redundant mine shafts strike up through the brambles. Past Cambourne, the tin-mining boom town, through the long straight Methodist chapel-ed street of Praze-an-Beeble, and out along treeless telegraph poled lanes, Godolphin's dark woods of soaring lichen-covered beech and sycamore begin. Somewhere in a patch of light the great seventeenth-century granite house stands calm, once one of the grandest in Cornwall and still as remote as ever it was.

There is such a settled air here, such a sheltering peace that it makes you want to stay. Perhaps this has to do with the fact that there has been a settlement here for five thousand years. There can be nowhere in Britain which better shows the unbroken thread of human life

RIGHT
The courtyard, looking west past the façade of the Elizabethan great Hall (pulled down in 1804) towards the early seventeenth-century King's Room.

continuing in one place – from the prehistoric hut circles, pillow mounds, and Celtic and medieval field systems on the bracken-covered heights of Godolphin Hill, to the remnants of tin mines in the woods around the house – evidence of the Godolphin family's wealth.

Walking back from the hill which still dominates the spirit of the place, the track leads down under a wide avenue of sycamores, bowers of honeysuckle clinging to bent hawthorn trees and fern-smothered granite-block walls edging the fields. East of the house the stables and rambling barns, cart sheds, cow houses and piggeries are speckled with gold lichen and there are secret doors in high walls, campion and penny royal everywhere,

swallows swooping under the eaves, dozens of brown hens scratching around and cats stretched along wall tops in the sun.

The house once had 100 rooms and forty chimneys. Now little more than the strange and haunting seventeenth-century front remains, with its eleven mullioned windows along the first floor and an open colonnade beneath supported on great silvery columns of sparkling granite. A huge oak doorway leads through into an inner courtyard where wisteria swamps castellated walls and the vestiges of lost rooms. A perfect sycamore towers over the inner lawn.

The Godolphins were here since the fourteenth century, rising in fame and fortune – romantics and Royalists to the end. Sidney Godolphin was a famous Elizabethan poet, his nephew Sidney a famously honest treasurer to Charles II who became the first earl. Francis Godolphin, who died in 1766, was the last. He bred racehorses at Newmarket and imported the legendary Godolphin Arab, a formative bloodline of the English racehorse. His daughter, Mary, married Thomas Osborne, the fourth Duke of Leeds, and the estate thus remained in the Leeds family. Let to tenant farmers, the woods became impenetrable and rats ran through the mouldering rooms of the house.

Godolphin was brought back to the state of gentle perfection it is in today by Sidney, the visionary son of an American impressionist painter, Elmer Schofield (friend of Julius Olson and the arty St Ives set), who bought his long-dreamed-of idyll in the 1930s. He and his wife Mary (sister of the renowned painter Peter Lanyon), spent forty years restoring it, finding lost doors in neighbouring farms and Godolphin portraits in sale rooms, including a John Wooton painting of the Godolphin Arab. The Schofields have overlaid the place with the perfect degree of quiet, ungrand calm.

The untouched Elizabethan garden layout – nine rectangular terraces with raised walkways on tree-sprinkled walls and huge fish ponds now filled with rosebay willowherb – is unutterably romantic. Mary Schofield gardens near the house. In June she had picked lupins and arranged them in jugs in the faded blue library with its swirling seventeenth-century plaster work. In August there were bunches of scarlet sweet peas and crimson dahlias among the Staffordshire china in the panelled breakfast room. It is her spirit which keeps Godolphin so well.

ABOVE
Looking out from the house southwards across the courtyard through the Colonnade.

RIGHT
Brunel's railway viaduct over the St German's River, seen from the Battery.

BELOW
Port Eliot from the east, showing the entrance front designed by Sir John Soane in 1804–6. Behind the house to the left is the priory church, a Norman foundation.

PORT ELIOT

Cornwall

The winding drive which follows the banks and slow bends of the River Tiddy has not been used for fifty years. You can walk its sinuous, two-mile length under bent trees and come out from the dark to see the languorous park before you: beyond the wide sweep of pasture, scattered with oaks, the long grey house lies low under the towering Norman church behind, with the village clustered on the hill above. The estate's Edwardian châtelaine, Lady St Germans used to say that if you had a problem, then you should walk along the Tideford drive and by the end of it the problem would have gone. Port Eliot's situation is as near to Arcadia as England gets. It is the pastoral ideal – a seductive and secret kingdom of lichen-covered oak trees encircling ivy-covered temples, with towering beech woods, and sheep grazing on gentle hills strung along the great, wide, tidal river. Downstream Isambard Kingdom Brunel's dramatic viaduct strides in gigantic arches across the river, dwarfing the cottages around St Germans Quay.

The chain across the short front drive from the village of St Germans is padlocked. Port Eliot, in this soft Cornish valley, has long been protected from the world in its own cocoon – it even seems to have its own micro-climate. There are palm trees beside the orangery, and if it is raining in Saltash it may not be raining here. Outsiders speculate; passers-by are sceptical. Only twenty years ago a guidebook writer, annoyed at being unable to gain access, wrote: 'A heavily feudal air hangs over the place.' He had glimpsed the walled gardens through cracks in the door on the village street and heard tell of the summerhouses among magnolias and camellias. For generations its Eliot owners have been unconventional. Perhaps the ghost of Montague Eliot, the eighth Earl of St Germans, still walks. He laughed a lot and built a sundial in the 1920s, in a north-facing garden which never sees the sun. On the dial is written 'Ni Wor den Vithey an er', which is old Cornish for 'No man knoweth the hour'. The present tenth earl is true to Eliot form. He loves the place and seldom leaves it. The writer Heathcote Williams came here for a week and stayed ten years, such is its sway.

The Eliots, who were worthy Cornish yeomen, bought Port Eliot in 1564. It was a crumbling priory surrounded by rambling medieval buildings and overshadowed by the most majestic, and much the grandest, church in Cornwall. Over the centuries, the house grew organically around the early monastic vestiges and reached its architectural peak when the genius architect Sir John Soane was brought in at the end of the eighteenth century. He built reserved and elegant stables, a warehouse and lime kiln on the Quay and radically remodelled the interior of Port Eliot, giving it the graceful proportions it lacked. He added castellations to the exterior (which Humphrey Repton referred to as 'Islington Gothic'), to harmonize with the noble Norman church tower. But still the St Germans wanted a bigger house and added a large west wing in the 1820s. Today Port Eliot has eighty-two chimneys and eleven staircases. There is half an acre of roof which has not once, in living memory, been entirely watertight. Until the end of the seventeenth century water came to the door, and boats sailed past on the river inlet giving the house its name of Port. The scene was not always idyllic: at low tide there was a wide expanse of mud which stretched before the house.

By the middle of the eighteenth century Richard Eliot had risen in politics and decided to pull the Eliot family out of their Cornish parochialism and put them into high society. He married an enormously rich thirteen-year-old heiress, the illegitimate daughter of Mr Craggs (who had hoodwinked the nation over the South Sea Bubble) and the actress, Hesther Booth. Richard became intent on improving the estate in the grandest manner. He made an extraordinary and gargantuan quarry garden on the distant hill, referred to as 'The Craggs' and diverted the vast tidal river. When Sir Humphrey Repton, the landscape gardener, was called in by Richard's newly cultivated son Edward, who had been on the Grand Tour, to enhance the plantations, he was mightily impressed by what had been already done at Port Eliot. The 'judgement, taste and preserving energy' of Eliot astounded Humphrey Repton, who described how he had 'not only clothed the naked hills with flourishing plantations but also moved the waters of the neighbouring ocean, converting into a cheerful lawn what was occasionally a bed of ooze'. That 'cheerful lawn' is now this verdant park.

After Edward Eliot, 'there then followed' wrote Heathcote Williams 'a series of tall spare Victorian and Edwardian earls and countesses moving up and down the corridors of Port Eliot fairly silent to history. One insured that the Kitchen was 110 yards from the Dining-Room, so that the smell of boiled cabbage could be kept to a minimum. Another insisted that the newspapers were ironed in winter so that they were warm enough to read, but would then refuse to read them "for fear of ill news". One was prone to summoning servants simply to inform him which room he was in.'

The present earl has made the most spectacular clearings and landscape restorations, recovering the Craggs from a tangled jungle. He has also laid out a maze and sold his grandfather's Packard car to pay for the 52,000 bricks which make the paths. Gates across these can swing in two directions and thus create millions of different combinations of ways to enter the heart of the maze.

COTEHELE

Cornwall

The best way of all to approach Cotehele is by the River Tamar a few miles up from Plymouth Sound. You arrive at the slaty quay under the soft woods just as Queen Charlotte, the wife of George III described in her diary in 1789: '. . . [We] landed at the woods of Cotehill half hour after 10 where we found Lrd and Ldy Mount Edgecombe ready to receive Us. We went in their Coach up to this Old Family seat of theirs . . . At Breakfast we Eat off the Old Family Pewter, used Silver knives Forks Spoons which have been Time immemorial in the Family have always been kept at this place . . .' The family pewter is still in the kitchen and a tall masted boat is still moored at the quay.

Cotehele was the first house to be taken on by the National Trust in lieu of death duties. It came lock, stock and barrel with everything in it. Jim Lees-Milne, who worked for the Trust at the time, describes finding Cotehele in December 1946. 'Very showery but beautiful day. After breakfast motored across the Tamar into Cornwall, up and down steep hills and descending narrow lanes till I reached Cotehele . . . the situation is romantic, wild and wooded . . . It is uniformly old, late medieval with pointed windows, all of granite. The great hall is as fine as any I have seen, with curved windbraces in the roof and plastered white-washed walls, hung with armour.' In May of the following year Lees-Milne returned to Cotehele with a view to making an inventory for the Trust. His diary reads, 'Lord Mount Edgcumbe is in bed with a temperature, but his Countess, a little, gentle, sweet and pathetic old lady, was about. Their story is a tragic one. They inherited during the war, and their only son was killed at Dunkirk. They are now packing up to leave Cotehele which, since the thirteenth century has been in their family.'

Cotehele feels ancient, secure and peaceful. It is the sort of house you want to come home to. It has a comfortably intimate scale, even the hall – its great showpiece with the massive moulded granite fireplace –

feels full of light and warmth. Rooms lead off one another at angles. There are beeswax-polished wooden floors, tapestries, winding stairs, tiny squints into the chapel and hall, and in every room little windows giving views over sills tufted with ivy-leaved toadflax into the courtyards or across prospects of the garden. Cotehele stands on an east-facing shelf high above a sweeping bend of the river. Woods fall away below the house, and downstream in the distance the village of Calstock is scattered down another steep hill and a grand viaduct marches loftily above the disappearing river.

The Edgcumbes first came to Cotehele in 1353 when William married its heiress, Hilaria de Cotehele. The family was to play an important part in politics for four centuries, holding a West Country seat in almost every parliament. It was Richard Edgcumbe, however, who dared to put his head highest above the parapet. He declared himself in league against the crown, probably because he had heard that Richard III had murdered the two sons of Edward IV in the Tower of London. He was pursued by the King's local agent, Sir Henry Trenowth, a fearsome man who was hated by the Cornish and who eventually encircled Cotehele with his men with a view to capturing his prey. Richard slipped the net and scrambled down through the steep woods to the river's edge. He threw a huge boulder into the water followed swiftly by his hat. His pursuers assumed he had drowned while all the time he was hiding in the undergrowth. After a spell in Brittany he returned to Cotehele when the coast was clear and, to thank God for his life, he built the chapel in the wood in the late 1480s. Richard, followed by his son Piers, transformed the ancient de Cotehele house into the house which stands today, with its three courtyards, high chimneys, covering of pale grey lichen and garlands of wisteria.

In the latter half of the sixteenth century the Mount Edgcumbe family removed themselves to their then modern house at Mount Edgcumbe overlooking the Sound. None the less Cothele was kept in good order and 100 years later Colonel Piers Edgcumbe moved his family and household back. He was a Royalist supporter who felt that Mount Edgcumbe was uncomfortably close to the Parliamentarian stronghold of Plymouth. He replaced the winding staircase with a great wide wooden flight of timber steps. His son Richard, who had married Lady Anne Montague in 1671, was residing at Cotehele four years later when his wife mysteriously 'died'. Her body was placed in the family vault and while it awaited burial a greedy sexton who had noticed her rings, went down to the vault and attempted to pull one of them off. On pinching her finger, she sat upright, scared the living daylights out of him, and lived happily at Cothele for many years thereafter.

BELOW
*The courtyard, looking
back to the granite-
vaulted passage of the
entrance tower.*

ABOVE
*Prideaux Place's
Elizabethan entrance
front is screened from
the road by
eighteenth-century
mock fortifications.*

16   100 FAVOURITE HOUSES

PRIDEAUX PLACE

Cornwall

Nicholas Prideaux was a brilliant and sharp-witted Cornish lawyer. He advised the Prior of Bodmin to pre-empt Henry Vlll's seizing of priory lands, and together they sold off leases so that the Royal exchequer could only appropriate the freehold. Nicholas then engineered a marriage between his nephew and heir, William Prideaux and the Prior's niece, Joan Munday, who owned a lease for the manor and the thriving port of Padstow. After a complicated legal action which Henry Vlll lost, the property was secured for, and still remains with, the Prideaux family. (The present Prideaux incumbent has followed the family profession and is also a lawyer, 450 years later.) Nicholas' great nephew, also Nicholas, built the grand E-shaped house at the end of the sixteenth century and was knighted by James l in 1606.

Prideaux Place looks out over castellated garden walls and turrets to a deer park which slopes down towards the Camel estuary. Across the water, speckled with coloured sails in the summer, the strange hump of Bray Hill rises beside Daymer Bay. Like most Elizabethan houses it is on a road, small and unimportant now, which turns into a rambling farm track where wild mint grows. This leads to Tregirls beach and the grim heights of Stepper Point, facing out into the Atlantic Ocean. From the sand dunes beyond Rock you can catch a ferry across to Padstow and walk round the harbour of slate-hung houses, past souvenir and fake flower shops, past the small, ancient Abbey House, made of glistening granite with madonna lilies on its balcony, past tarted-up pubs, and thread your way through to a back street which as it ascends the hill, grows empty and quiet. Georgian and Victorian houses with geraniums stuffed in their front windows line the way towards the gigantic ilex and beech trees which secrete Prideaux Place from the town.

As you turn the corner and walk under the trees there is the house on a wide grassy plateau as discreetly open to the public as could be. There is hardly a sign up – it is almost as though the Prideaux family have just left the door open for you to walk in. The house is built of the local rag slate which over the centuries has been smothered in the palest lichens. Various members of the Prideaux family have impressed their taste on Sir Nicholas' Elizabethan house, most notably Edmund who returned from the Grand Tour in 1739 full of the romance of Greece and Rome. He built temples in the garden, removed the pointed gables on the front of the house, put in sash windows and replaced the open fires with Georgian grates. The next radical change came with the Reverend Charles Prideaux who gave the house a Regency Gothic veneer at the beginning of the nineteenth century with crenellations, and he transformed some of its chief rooms into 'Strawberry Hill Gothic' (see page 73) confections. He left the hall and its Elizabethan panelling alone and the glorious barrel-shaped and voluptuously plastered ceiling of the Great Chamber remained hidden by a false ceiling hung below. The chamber had been made into four bedrooms in the eighteenth century and was only reinstated to its full glory in 1987.

Prideaux Place boasts some exceptional Art Nouveau light switches – it was the first house in Cornwall to go on electricity. In the drawing-room there is an amusing picture of four Prideaux daughters and their companion Miss Shaugnessy rowing a boat through a storm towards the treacherous 'Doom Bar' in the estuary on their way to rescue two men from a shipwreck. They were awarded the silver medal of bravery in 1878.

A large sunken garden, once lost in the undergrowth, has just been restored, with the voluntary help of the Cornwall Gardens Trust, the National Trust and the Cornish Nurserymen's Association. If you walk under the ornamental bridge beside some of the best walls in England, built of wafer-thin feathery rag slate set upright in tight packed rows, bursting with ferns and valerian, you will find a path called Trictroll which leads across fields and the cliff walk back to Padstow.

ABOVE

A detail of the screen in the great hall. The inlaid panels may be Spanish craftsmanship of the late sixteenth or early seventeenth century.

CREEK VEAN HOUSE

Cornwall

BELOW
'Even as I cook, I can enjoy the view,' says Rene Brumwell of her kitchen.

Creek Vean is already in the architectural history books. 'In our opinion this small building is a work of outstanding quality' read the jurors' report of the 1967 RIBA award. 'The architects have achieved an imaginative and highly original building without resorting to clichés or gimmickry. The design is carried with commendable consistency using a self-imposed discipline in the choice of colours and materials. The general impression is that every arrangement in this design is an essential and significant part of the concept as a whole.'

OPPOSITE
The young architects Norman Foster and Richard Rogers designed Creek Vean in the mid-1960s. It looks south towards the sea, west to the Creek and north up a valley.

Norman Foster, one of Creek Vean's architects, had left school at sixteen to join the City Treasurer's department in the Town Hall at Manchester, the place of his birth. After serving as a radar technician in the Royal Air Force for his National Service, he decided to pursue his interest in architecture and resolved to find a related job. He paid his way through his five-year course at the School of Architecture at Manchester University by a mixture of part-time and holiday work as a freelance architectural perspectivist, as a bouncer in the local cinema and as a labourer in an industrial cold store. He won a fellowship to study at Yale University in the United States, where he met Richard Rogers and their friendship was cemented.

Back in London, in 1963 Foster joined Rogers and two architect sisters, Georgie and Wendy Cheeseman, in establishing Team 4. Norman subsequently married Wendy, from whose small Belsize Park flat the practice operated. 'None of us appreciated the difficulties of running a practice without experience' Richard Rogers later recalled. 'I remember episodes such as crying under a tree on Hampstead Heath and thinking "I will never be an architect" . . . unplanned-for springs of water bursting into beautifully conceived living-rooms . . . and our precious unopened drawings being used by contractors to wrap up their fish and chips . . . We worked fifteen hours a day, seven days a week. No one invited us to dinner as we would invariably fall asleep during the first course. It took the team three years to build the Brumwells' Creek Vean House . . . This slowness of production when related to the National Housing Shortage stimulated us to reconsider our architectural direction. Looking back, the fifty or so different designs we prepared for the house under the kind eye of the Brumwells [Rogers's then parents-in-law], gave us the opportunity to work through a wide range of approaches and ideas.'

'The house looks south towards the sea, west towards the creek, and north up a valley' Norman Foster later wrote. 'The rooms fan out towards three different views. The house is built along two routes. One is external and splits the house in two, leading from the road access across a bridge to the front door. The other is internal, in the form of a top-lit picture gallery which at night is floodlit from the outside. It connects all the rooms, starting at the highest roof terrace and ending at the path to the underground garage.'

In a lecture in 1978 Foster said 'The building attempts to fit more snugly into its waterfront surroundings by generating a garden on the roof. As this starts to become overgrown the house will recede into its creek-side Cornish setting.' Thirty years later, Creek Vean feels well and fully anchored to the place. The steep winding steps which lead down to the boathouse are grown all over with grass and valerian, the bedroom roofs are thick with ivy and the house's flowing form has become part of its surroundings.

Rene Brumwell finds the house inseparable from the sea. '. . . Even as I cook I can enjoy the view. One important thing is you don't feel shut in . . . Delivery boys who come to the front door, they look at it and say "This is a marvellous place!" They really like it and I don't think it's put on. And what have we spent on decoration? Local people are always doing up their places. We haven't spent a penny on decoration.'

RIGHT
An eyecatcher in the grounds, laid out by Lord Clinton in the 1730s and remodelled in the second half of the eighteenth century.

BELOW
Castle Hill's spreading south front, seen from the road.

'"North Devon" is still a name for the nearest thing we have in the West Country, and maybe in England, to wilderness . . .' wrote the poet laureate Ted Hughes, 'to a native of north Devon, Cornwall is a crowded holiday land, south and east Devon a garden for the affluent and retired, and England itself is a crowded modern place somewhere away east beyond Bristol.' Castle Hill is buried deep into north Devon. A public road has always cut through the middle of this, one of the greatest landscaped parks in all England, and affords a spectacular view of the house in its midst. All around is a great wide bowl of encompassing hills on whose tops there are copious woods – Dark Lane Wood to the north and belts or plantations along the high edges. The house sits on a parallel with the road, perched on tiers of mown terraces above a tributary of the River Bray. The nature of its site, cut back into sheer rock face, has dictated Castle Hill's elongated shape. Although its central block was gutted by fire in 1934 it was restored almost immediately and looks with its golden colour wash as it must have done for the last two centuries. On the exact same spot stood a sixteenth-century house which was rebuilt in 1684 and then extensively remodelled between 1730 and 1740 at Lord Clinton's behest by Roger Morris, under the direction of Lord Burlington and Lord Herbert.

It is the scale and ambition of the landscaping which astounds, and all the more because of the wild beauty of this bit of north Devon. Directly behind the house, a mile up the steepest hill of all, is a sham ruined castle – hence the name of the house, Castle Hill. A precipitous drive winds up through trees to this castellated folly from whose first floor, through arched openings, you can see out across the bracken-covered hills of Exmoor on the northern horizon. To the south, you look clean over the top of the house which is hidden by trees below, to the great triumphal arch dead in line on the brow of the opposite hill a mile away, then on to the distant heights of Dartmoor. The extraordinarily grandiose scale of things was the brainchild of Lord

CASTLE HILL

Devon

Clinton whose family, the Fortescues, had owned the estate at Filleigh from the fifteenth century. It was he who had dressed up the earlier house with the long Palladian front we see today. For a West Country squire in the 1720s, Lord Clinton had made a speedy and spectacular ascent into intimate Royal circles and had been made a Lord of the Bedchamber by the Prince of Wales, later George II. He was in with the foremost Whigs of the day and was attracted by that fashionable artistic group of dilettantes who deemed Palladian architecture the only acceptable style and who marvelled at William Kent's experiments with landscape gardening. In this remote Devonian outback Lord Clinton resolved to create a West Country paradise. On the horizon of High Bray, at the south-east axis from the house a mile away on top of the ridge, he built a sham village – today only the sham church tower remains. To the south-west at Filleigh he rebuilt the church on a new site as a Gothic eye-catcher and also Spawood Cottage with a façade in the form of an arch. His hermitage, Chinese temple and other adornments have unfortunately disappeared.

Lord Clinton's son continued with the landscaping from the 1760s onwards, transforming the formal canal below the house into a series of thin winding and connected lakes spanned by a series of beautiful bridges. He built the Holwell Temple in 1772 during the very height of England's Picturesque Movement. Viewed from the house and the hill behind, it was designed to evoke a painting by Claude Lorraine. Standing on a bluff a mile away it formed a romantic focus for idle eyes to gaze upon from the special viewing terrace before the house. A lake was created below the temple from the marshy mere and furnished with boats and trees, shredded to look like ships' masts to 'favour the deception of a port'. This maritime aspect of the design has long since disappeared. It was originally intended to be a banqueting house but was eventually converted into two cottages.

Today Lord Clinton's descendents Margaret Fortescue, her daughter Nell Arran and her husband have done much to restore whole tracts of this magical landscape. They have cut out vistas and views from temples which were forgotten and lost in undergrowth; they keep the wide terraces in front of the house with their huge stone sphinxes and urns immaculately mown for public view. They have restored the arch, the sham village tower and the sham castle and re-built the hermitage. They have redredged the ornamental water in the valley and made good the dams and cascades and, with the help of English Heritage, have replanted much of the original structure of trees.

ENDSLEIGH

Devon

Endsleigh is lost in the deep Devon of dark steep valleys and huge dumpling-shaped hills, of wooded coombes, twisting lanes between high fern-filled banks. Here beyond the village of Milton Abbot the great River Tamar winds extravagantly in huge loops around Wareham Wood and on down towards Plymouth. Just upriver towards Launceston it forms the division between Devon and Cornwall.

The drive at Higher Edgecombe leads off the road down a laurel and rhododendrum-shaded tunnel to the huge Endsleigh 'Cottage'. It sits on a high plateau, trees rising behind it and below, down a 200-foot bank, are the black waters of the wide Tamar in this most beautiful hidden and secret of all stretches. Endsleigh is a ducal idea of a cottage. It was begun in 1810 as a holiday retreat for the Duke and Duchess of Bedford. The Duke was a fresh air fanatic, a keen farmer and a collector of sculpture (he bought Canova's notoriously naked *Three Graces*). His second wife Georgina was Scottish and boisterous, and together they had twelve children. It was her energy and her desire to be ahead of fashion during the Regency burgeoning of taste towards the picturesque, particularly in the seaside resorts, that made Endsleigh such a wonderful place. The 'Cottage', built to catch the best views, was designed on a bat's-wing plan by Sir Jeffry Wyattville. It was almost like three separate little houses joined together by rustic verandahs and patios some of which are paved in sheep's knuckle bones laid close together to form a rustic farmyard mosaic.

It is the views from and the surroundings of Endsleigh that are its *raison d'être*. Humphry Repton, the landscape gardener, was employed to add excitement and interest to this already idyllic place. By 1818 it was described as 'the garden paradise of the West'. He planted the thickly wooded slopes, made arbours, shell grottoes, cascades and miles of sinuous paths leading up into the woodland heights and down to the wide level sweep of pasture which runs beside the river. There is a 'dairy dell' complete with a tiled and marble-slabbed dairy, and high on the skyline is a thatched Swiss cottage with a wrap-around double-height verandah all clad in crisscross wood bark and built with great silvery oak timbers. The ground and top floors were lived in by estate workers originally and on the middle floor the Duchess of Bedford had picnics and kept a collection of Swiss furniture and crockery. Outside was a separate privy which was kept for the use of the Duke and his guests if they got caught short on one of their long walks.

The Bedford family continued to use Endsleigh for holidays until they sold it in 1953 to a fishing syndicate. Happily it has hardly changed and now, as a private hotel, it still resembles a rather shambolic country house. It has not been tarted up and remains a place where fishing friends gather together in the book room for a drink at the end of the day and look down at the breathtaking view below.

RIGHT
The Swiss Cottage, designed to be a summerhouse on the first floor and a labourer's cottage below.

OPPOSITE
The view west, along the south side of the house, gives some sense of the superb landscape in which Endsleigh is set.

John Heathcoat, a brilliant young entrepreneur from Derbyshire, had by the age of twenty-five set up a lace-making business and designed and patented a machine that revolutionized the manufacture of lace. His success was meteoric but, on the 28 June 1816, his Loughborough factory was attacked by a mob of Luddites and within half an hour all fifty-five of Heathcoat's new machines were destroyed. Rather than rebuilding he decided to move to the safety of Tiverton and the majority of his workers walked the 200 miles to begin again in his new lace works. Heathcoat had no son but his daughter married a Mr Amory from Taunton who inherited the business which grew to become by far the largest lace factory in the world. Heathcoat's grandson, John Heathcoat-Amory, decided that he would rather live the life of a grand squire than run the works in Tiverton and he left the day-to-day affairs to his brother-in-law. He became the Liberal MP for Tiverton and in order to provide an appropriate background for his new status he bought the estate of Knightshayes in 1860. Above the wooded valley, the winding lanes and chocolate-brown fields, the park spreads out on a south-facing slope and the drive curls upwards between gigantic oak trees to the astonishing house Mr Heathcoat-Amory built to replace the modest Regency one which had stood there before. Knightshayes commands, down its terraced gardens and lawns, a perfect view of Tiverton on the other side of the valley with its church on a little hill and the tall chimneys of the lace factory rising from the town – the source of the Heathcoat-Amory wealth.

He had employed, probably through his wife's recommendation, the avant-garde architect and decorator William Burges to build him a brand-new house. Burges had already begun St Finbar's Cathedral in County Cork by 1862 and also the remodelling of Cardiff Castle for Lord Bute. 'I was brought up in the thirteenth-century belief', said Burges, 'and in that belief I intend to die.' He proceeded to design a medieval fairyland made of the deep red Devon Hensley stone with golden Ham stone dressings. Knightshayes is grandly ecclesiastical in front and presents a startling and wonderful symphony of medieval symbolism behind. The fantastic gargoyles and turrets seem to attract the rooks which sit in the evening cawing from the chimneys and roof ridges, with tall Scots pines towering above. All the woodwork is painted red, which suits the stables to a tee; set away up a rise of parkland, they resemble a little French castle with a turret, studded doors and Virginia creeper, which is scarlet in autumn.

The designs Burges created for the interior in a fifty-seven-page book of meticulously painted watercolours scared the Heathcoat-Amorys to bits and, although they had stuck by him for the ten long years it took to build the house, by the time it came to the inside they had second thoughts. They dismissed Burges and

employed a far more conventional designer called John Crace. Any of Burges' work which had already been executed was painted over or ceilinged off (the National Trust is at present restoring it).

The gardens were originally designed by the great municipal designer of the day, Edward Kemp, who had worked with Paxton on designing the Victorian park at Birkenhead in the 1840s. He had written a handbook on how to lay out a garden and John Heathcoat-Amory deemed him appropriate for Knightshayes. He designed the terraces and the immediate garden around them. In 1930, Sir Ian Heathcoat-Amory, who lived for hunting,

had created a topiary of fox and hounds to the east of the garden which is still crisply cut to this day. He died as a result of an accident in 1931. It was the latest incumbent Sir John and his wife Joyce who transformed the garden into what it is today and carried it away into the woods and all around. Joyce continued to live at Knightshayes until her death in 1997. She was described in the 1920s as the 'greatest lady golfer of all time' and won the British Ladies Open Championship on four occasions and the English Ladies' Open on five.

LEFT
A corbel in the billiard room, carved with a fox in a monk's habit, illustrating the story of the fox and the geese.

OPPOSITE
The house from the garden. Burges's richly modelled forms are enlivened by the contrast of colours in the red Hensley and Ham stones.

BAGGY HOUSE

Devon

Baggy Point juts out from the Bristol Channel into the face of the Atlantic Ocean and shelters the wide sandy sweep of Wollacombe Bay. In 1799 over 100 men drowned when *HMS Weazle* was wrecked on the rocks below. This is a treacherous piece of coast and at Morte Point on the north side of the bay five ships went down in the winter of 1852. On the south side of the point the white blocks and slate roofs of Baggy House with their solid, buttressed safety rise triumphantly from the ashes of an Edwardian hotel.

The founder of the *Birmingham Post* had built on the

BELOW

Baggy House from the east, showing its spectacular site, overlooking Baggy Point.

OPPOSITE

The view from the sitting-room across the dining-room to the pavilion at the front of the house, which can be enclosed by glass screens. The structural column of polished maple acts as a pivot for the flowing, open-plan design.

site originally in the 1890s and his house had been enlarged over the ensuing decades. Gavyn Davies, a London banker, and his family wanted a summer seaside home and having bought the site had first thought to convert what was by then an existing hotel. The cost to do this made no sense and they decided the best and bravest thing to do was to start afresh. With the enlightened North Devon County Council on board and the National Trust who own Baggy Point a little apprehensive, the Norfolk-born young architect Anthony Hudson took on the task of creating this triumphant

house. He had a head start because the site faced south across the most spectacular coastal views towards Hartland Point. Croyde Bay curved in below where huge Atlantic rollers pound in, carrying surfers and sometimes seals, and where, at low tide, the currents are terrifyingly dangerous. On a clear day you can see fifty miles to Lundy Island. The wind-cropped turf slopes precipitously away from the site to the north coastal path below which winds on out to the point.

Despite his East Anglian upbringing Hudson fell in love with the north Devon coast immediately, and the design of the house grew out of the nature of the site rather than straight off a drawing-board. Driving through the long networks of lanes as often as he did to visit the site, Hudson was imbued with a feel for the local styles and materials. He had studied architecture at Cambridge and at the Westminster Polytechnic and was, like all his peers, taught to believe in the three icons – Le Corbusier, Frank Lloyd Wright and Mies van de Rohe – but he knew there was a common ground between old and new architecture whose magic centre is tradition. Baggy House, at every turn, respects its setting and in the very best Arts and Crafts tradition uses local materials and local craftsmen. The cream rendered walls are like Devon cob but beneath the render lies the latest technology of external insulation – a new invention akin to a person putting on a mackintosh. The original blockwork is covered in a polystyrene coat and then a thin layer of acrylic waterproofing which never cracks, unlike ordinary cement render or lime mixture. The saltwater, which storms bring with relentless regularity, has to be sprayed off with a power hose. 'We thought of fixing enormous windscreen wipers to the windows', said Hudson, 'but they would have had to have been so big it seemed easier just to hose down the windows after each storm.'

Inside the house is a mixture of cubism and a curvaceous cob cottage, blending harmoniously with the wonderful materials. There are slate floors in the hall, oak floors in the sitting-room, creamy limestone floors in the dining-room and traditional elements such as oak panelling refined by Hudson into his own style. A Devon organ-maker turned the maple column supporting the roof above the sitting-room. Hudson designed the cast glass table top on its oak base for the dining-room and a young student of the Central St Martin's College of Art and Design, whom the Davies' had spotted at a degree show, was commissioned to paint the silk curtains in the dining-room. The open-plan layout has the kitchen at its heart from which leads off the children's playroom, the dining-room and then the sitting-room. The guests' quarters are in a separate wing up the sculptured staircase where the building hugs the hill and rises up at the back.

FORDE ABBEY

Dorset

Forde lies in dim, low-lying dairy country on the Dorset and Somerset borders, where Tess of the D'Urbervilles came upcountry to escape her past and fell so disastrously in love with Angel Clare. Across from the deep-cut River Axe, Forde Abbey rises serenely above the willows – the most complete Cistercian monastic building to survive as a home in Britain. It is built of deep golden ironstone, from the famous Ham Hill quarry, which soaks up the sun and is etched all over with the palest grey lichen. The glory of the building's south side on a high summer's day is hard to beat.

The Abbey was founded 800 years ago and its church has long since disappeared, but the monastery the monks knew then still stands, transformed by the architecture of the sixteenth and seventeenth centuries into a beautiful country house. The last abbot, Thomas Chard, beautified the place greatly, reconstructing the cloister and refectory, which remain as he left them. When Henry VIII ordered the dissolution of the monasteries in 1539, the Abbot of Glastonbury was hanged from the gates for refusing to surrender, but Chard and his twelve monks handed Forde over to the King. It remained empty and forlorn for 100 years, until in 1649 it was bought by Sir Edmund Prideaux, Attorney General to Oliver Cromwell, who set about transforming the Abbey into a sumptuous house. He made private family quarters at the east end and added state apartments over Chard's elegant cloisters. The whole is wild and imaginative and was created before our own indigenous architecture became completely influenced by foreign styles. The south front combines the last of our own Gothic with the first of English baroque, pulled together by a castellated parapet. Forde remains unique: it has nothing to do with Palladianism which transformed so many of our eighteenth-century buildings into a tidy measured essay.

The back of the house is ghostly. It is a jumble of centuries, with turrets and towers and steep grey roofs – almost like a photographic collage of myriad bits of buildings. In late summer swarms of swallows fly around the eaves and up above the chimneys. The cloistered undercroft is sprung over with Gothic arches of white- and gold-striped stone.

In the saloon are the most exquisite tapestries woven at Mortlake from Raphael's original cartoons for the Sistine Chapel in Rome. They were ordered by Sir Edmund Prideaux and made for the room, but delayed in their delivery by his death and then by the arrest of his son for helping the Duke of Monmouth against his uncle, James II. Eventually they were presented to Sir Francis Gwyn, who married Prideaux's granddaughter, by Queen Anne in recognition of his services as Secretary of State for War. The brilliance of the colours is said to be retained by the Dorset air.

Wide terraced lawns climb the mild rise on the south side of the house to merge over a ha-ha with the oak-sprinkled park. A number of huge stepped pools, the top one made by the monks and the rest constructed for ornament by Sir Francis, are joined by a series of waterfalls which end in a huge final pool reflecting the abbey. The herbaceous borders beside it march into the distance with Irish yews rising from them every so often. The walled gardens contain a rampant mixture of all good things, from every conceivable summer vegetable to lush agapantha and a flashy bed of scarlet gladioli, orange mombretia, yellow dahlias, orange and red Iceland poppies, hollyhocks and love-lies-bleeding. Around the backs of the steading towards the river are acres of head-high pink balsam, and still beyond the occasional train from Waterloo whizzes through the meadow towards Exeter.

ABOVE

A detail of Abbot Charde's richly decorated gatetower, built in the 1520s, not long before the Abbey was dissolved.

MAPPERTON

Dorset

Mapperton is remote. A few miles back from and 400 feet above the sandstone-cliffed sea, it hides beyond unadopted lanes. The country around is like an English Tuscany – with small hills stretching away into the distance. It is green and scattered with small woods, and beloved and immortalized by Dorset's great pastoral poet William Barnes. Whether you approach Mapperton up Storridge Hill from the pretty market town of Beaminster or winding up Mythe Hill from Melplash, its position at the head of a sudden and secret valley is a complete surprise. You approach the ancient manor house down a short straight drive which leads you to the west front. The entrance courtyard is like a hamlet huddling around the house, with barns, a dovecote, a small chapel and two eagle-topped gate piers. A little apart are two ravishing Renaissance stable blocks which continue the courtyard effect and lead your eye out over a ha-ha to level fields. The whole composition in stone of various shades of gold is an English idyll.

It is only when you walk through to the eastern side of the house that you first glimpse Mapperton's miraculous position – from the plateau on which the house stands, a dramatic valley falls steeply away winding in a long slow curving descent towards thick woods and the unknown pastures of blue, distant Dorset. From the house and down the first slopes of the valley there stretches a magical garden. It was created in three completely different stages but rolls into one wonderful whole. Like the house the garden has evolved over time – the same local stone has been used throughout and topiary yew trees blend the varying dates of building.

At the head of the valley there is an elaborate Italianate garden which was made in the 1920s by the then owner, Mrs Labouchere, who was following the fashion of the day. Wide shallow steps lead down between gently banked lawns to terraces of early crazy paving. There are stepped octagonal rose beds, statues, a pond choked with lilies, Roman columns, yew rooms and other secret places, and an inordinate number of stone storks. One huge step below is the seventeenth-century terrace where an Elizabethan garden house looks down on to two rectangular carp ponds. The topiary yews have gradually been added over the years. Below this is the latest garden of shrubs and trees started by Victor Montagu in the 1950s and still being added to by his son and daughter-in-law. Through young woodland a path straggles on and on down the valley. An old and long-abandoned drive leads away from Mapperton winding on down for over a mile through lost parkland and then past a ruined mill beside a stream, past clumps of yellow flags and patches of bright pink vetch until it eventually reaches the road to North Poorton.

Until this century Mapperton has a long history of unbroken occupation in the continuous descent from the family of Brett or Bryte, who owned the manor in the

time of Edward I, to the Morgans, Brodrepps and Comptons, each inheriting through the female line. Robert Morgan of Mapperton was granted a licence by Henry VI to sit in his presence with a hat on because of 'diverse infirmities which he hath in his hedde . . . cannot convenyently, without his grete daungier, be discovered of the same'. His grandson Robert built the present house in the middle of the sixteenth century, but it has since had the layers of time laced in and around it and it is much changed from the original manor house. Richard Brodrepp built the exquisite stable ranges and remodelled the church in the seventeenth century, and a fourth and last Richard Brodrepp classicized the north front in the eighteenth century. The church was linked to the Tudor house in the Edwardian period by the Comptons.

CAME HOUSE

Dorset

Came is exquisite. It is a grand mansion distilled into a small house. Everything about its detailing, from the swags in its tympanum to its richly decorated ceilings, is of the highest quality. Built in the palest of pale Portland stone and arguably the finest building stone in Britain, quarried over the down a few miles towards the sea. It is the obvious masterpiece of its Dorset architect, Francis Cartwright. On his monument in Blandford St Mary Church are carved a T-square, dividers, a rule and a scroll in which is incised an elevation of Came House.

The quiet park, sometimes speckled with hefty Simenthal cattle, lies just out of sight and sound of Dorchester. The house – perfect countrified Palladian, built all of a piece in 1754 – sits on a small hill looking out over the descending pasture across the River Winterbourne to cornfields beyond. A line of chalk hills rise between Came and the sea and Maiden Castle, the greatest earthwork in Europe, tops the neighbouring hill. Sir John Damer, whose family had moved to Came from Devon in the early eighteenth century, and whose father had been MP for Dorchester, could well have afforded to build a much bigger house on the site of an earlier manor house. He probably wanted to keep a low profile after the gigantic rumpus his elder brother had caused with his enormous building programme near Blandford. (Viscount Milton, first Earl of Dorchester, had razed a village to the ground in order to make a lake and build the model village of Milton Abbas, with its uniform thatched cottages spaced well apart up the ascending village street. Today it is considered to be the epitome of picturesqueness; at the time its sterility horrified its inhabitants.)

If Came is of modest proportions compared to the huge pile beside the river at Milton Abbas, Sir John Damer certainly didn't skimp on employing the very best craftsmen from London. The present drawing-room, which runs the length of the three central ground-floor windows and used to be the entrance hall (until the 1840 addition on the west side was made), must have stunned the neighbours with its sumptuousness. First impressions were all-important to the cultivated Georgian gentleman – the long meandering drive to display the land, the rich pedimented pillars to display the learning and quality of the owner, and then the entrance hall. A fine gold garland of flowers winds wildly in plasterwork around geometric patterns on the ceiling, gold and white Corinthian columns flank the grand double doors, and paintings of Greek friezes by Cipriani surmount the overdoors. The central chandelier hangs from a cluster of white plaster clouds from which the eagle of Jove shoots shafts of lightning. An account for the decoration of the room in 1761 still exists, and reads: 'For a gilder's time 26 weeks, 3 days in the country. Gilding and painting a room £27 16s 3d.'

The Damer line has carried on at Came through a series of unusually complicated inheritances and transactions which seemed to peak when Lionel Seymour Dawson-Damer became fourth Earl of Portarlington on the death of his cousin in 1889. Came was then bought by his daughter-in-law Lady Portman who made the property over to Lady Christian Martin, daughter of the fifth earl who lived here until 1959. Her husband, Mr F W Martin, describes first coming to Came from their home in Sussex on 15 December 1919. 'We travelled down in an old Packhard car. Came at that time was in the charge of a caretaker and had been unoccupied during the war. We brought down all our servants from Buxted, while all our belongings came by road in a pantechnicon, including a prize lot of poultry . . . No electric light . . . Water had to be pumped up daily by hand – two men on the wheel pump . . . Christian's daughter, Rosemary Bowes-Lyon aged four, with Fraser, her nurse, arrived later.' Until the outbreak of the Second World War Came then boasted eleven indoor staff and six gardeners. The present owner is a grand-daughter of Lady Christian Martin carrying on the Damer line.

Below the house, hidden in the trees near the great walled kitchen garden, is the simple fifteenth-century church with a barrel-vaulted ceiling where Came's famous son, the Reverend William Barnes, was rector. He is buried in the churchyard. Thomas Hardy and Mr Gosse visited the Dorset poet on his deathbed in the rectory in 1886. 'It is curious that he is dying as picturesquely as he lived,' wrote Mr Gosse. 'We found him in bed in his study, his face turned to the window, where the sun came streaming in through flowering plants . . . He had a scarlet bedgown on, a kind of soft biretta of dark red wool on his head, from which his long white hair escaped on to the pillow; his grey beard, grown very long upon his breast . . .' On walking home it is doubtful that the companions gave a second glance at Came House, described ten years later by Sir Frederick Treves in *Highways and Byways of Dorset* as 'an unattractive mansion in which is called the "classic" taste'.

OPPOSITE
A mansion in miniature: the north front of Came House.

BRYMPTON D'EVERCY

Somerset

The great Christopher Hussey wrote: 'Nearly every country-house has some quality about it whether of architecture, sentiment, historical associations or scenery that makes it, in the narrower sense of the word, incomparable. But Brympton has them all and unites them so perfectly that the whole cannot be surpassed. There are greater, more historic, more architecturally impressive buildings in grander scenery; but I know of none of which the whole impression is more lovely. None that summarizes so exquisitely English country life.'

Brympton d'Evercy is in a lost pocket of farmland on the outskirts of Yeovil. Although the town suffered a disastrous fire in the fifteenth century, its spirit remained undaunted and it fast became a centre of the leather trade and is now the home of Westland Helicopters. As you drive past an outlying trading estate you could well be in any suburb of any town in Europe, then suddenly, down a hawthorn-hedged lane, unadulterated Somerset begins. Past a golden-stoned seventeenth-century thatched farmhouse surrounded by straggling buildings, the short drive to Brympton leads round a steep bend to this unexpected glory. Swathes of lawn backed by flowerbeds and balustrades herald this most perfect of English scenes.

All is built in the local Ham stone, now lichen encrusted, and the varying dates of the ensemble present delicately differing shades of gold. The small, rambling church of St Andrew flanks the southern side of the entrance square, with its top-heavy belfry like a large lantern and its rich monuments to the Sydenham family, the early owners of Brympton. Just beyond the church is the fifteenth-century Chantry House, or perhaps the dower house of Joan Sydenham, whose staircase within a polygonal turret leads to a hall and chamber. Opposite, beyond a higher terraced lawn are the beautiful late-seventeeth-century stables with a grand pedimented doorway, a little Vanburghian garden house and then straight ahead the archaic jumble of the house itself. The north end of the west front is early Tudor, the main central section is mid-sixteenth century and the southern end, half hidden by a *Magnolia grandiflora* is seventeenth century. The whole effect is utterly harmonious and settled.

Few documents record the building of Brympton, but it is known that the d'Evercy family bought the land in the thirteenth century. The Chantry House could possibly have been part of an original manor. In 1434 Brympton passed to the Sydenham family. The south front, built in the late-seventeenth century by John P Sydenham, is one of the most beautiful façades in England. Countrified baroque to the hilt. Its appeal has an instant and magical effect on the viewer. The ten tall windows on ground and first floors are topped by alternate pedimented and segmental arches. Before the wing there is a wide gravel walk which looks out over a balustrade to a small lake and the gentle slopes of lush cattle-strewn pasture beyond. A faint hum of traffic wafts across from Yeovil but the atmosphere of Brympton is protective, the ivy-clad, brick-walled gardens all-encompassing.

The Sydenhams had run out of money by the early 1700s and in 1731 Francis Fane bought Brympton. A colourful Victorian inheritor through the female line was Sir Spencer Ponsonby, a nephew of Lady Georgina Fane, who was a co-founder of the I Zingari Cricket Club and began a strong tradition of cricket which is still upheld today on the field below the lake. Mrs Violet Clive, who was the châtelaine in the 1940s played hockey for the West of England, rowed for Leander and was a very good carpenter and gardener. When Alec Clifton Taylor visited her in 1947 he described her as being 'somewhat casual of dress'. On numerous occasions she was mistaken for one of the gardeners. Her grandson, Charles Clive-Ponsonby-Fane and his wife kept the house open to the public throughout the 1980s, as their own custodians, curators, administrators, public relations officers, gardeners and upholsterers, but eventually sold up. The new owners have restored and maintained the house as a happy family house.

RIGHT
A view of the church and dower house from the terrace.

OPPOSITE
One of Country Life's most celebrated country house photographs: the late seventeenth-century south front, seen from the garden in 1927.

MONTACUTE HOUSE

Somerset

Montacute is probably the most romantic Elizabethan house of all. First, it is built of that irresistible honey-brown stone which comes from the strange steep hill close by – the *mons acutus* from which the village name is derived – and, secondly, because the local master mason, William Arnold, who almost certainly worked on it has given it an individual beauty which renders the house a work of art.

Successful Elizabethan lawyers made gigantic amounts of money and Sir Edward Phelips was no exception. He ended up being Master of the Rolls and Chancellor to Henry, Prince of Wales. He opened for the prosecution at the trial of Guy Fawkes in 1605 and was said to be 'over-swift in judging' and, being violently anti-Catholic, he once condemned a man to death for entertaining a Jesuit. The modernity and flamboyance of his new house must have astonished the locals when it was built as they craned their necks ever upwards at the eastern front. Here nine statues stood in niches between the windows representing Hector, Alexander, Julius Caesar, King Arthur, Charlemagne, Godfrey of Bouillon and the biblical Judas Maccabaeus, Joshua and David. The long gallery on the second floor stretched for 172 feet and at each end boasted a generous oriel window both of which commanded wide views of Somerset, with its orchards and willow trees, which women could admire as they walked from end to end taking their daily exercise during bad weather.

No member of the Phelips family ever made so much money as Sir Edward, who died in 1614, but a fierce loyalty to the family name and to hanging on to the house and its estate fired every successive owner to stay. By the end of the seventeenth century Montacute's future looked uncertain. The fourth Edward Phelips married his cousin, Ann Phelips, whom he thought had been left the estate and, after she died, he then married her sister Elizabeth. They appeared to be a scheming and unattractive lot until the fifth Edward Phelips took over in the eighteenth century and is revealed through his diary as being a kind man, and happiest of all at his beloved Montacute or hunting in the neighbourhood with local friends. He decided to build a new front of Ham stone on to the western side of the house. In May 1786 he went to the sale of the materials of a house called Clifton Maybank which was being pulled down near Yeovil. The house, which had been built by Sir John Horsey in the middle of the sixteenth century, was of the same golden Ham stone and its porch, arms, pillars and ornamental stone blended in beautifully to the western front of Montacute and added an extra layer of local craftsmanship.

In 1845 William Phelips at last married a rich woman, something that Montacute was desperately in need of, but by the 1860s William's compulsive gambling had brought ruin. Once on a wet afternoon he staked a bet on one of two flies that were crawling up the window pane to reach the top first and, when his friend's fly reached the wooden plinth which marked the winning post first, he heard William say: 'There go Sock and Beerly!' – the names of two outlying farms on the Montacute estate. The luckless William's son did not have the wherewithal to remain at Montacute and, although he delayed his departure by selling the pictures and the family silver, by 1911 he was forced to put the house up for rent while the remains of the estate, which had not been sold by his gambling father, was slowly dismembered.

In 1915 Knight, Frank Rutley let Montacute on behalf of the Phelips family who had owned it since the late sixteenthth century for £550 a year to George Nathaniel Curzon who was at the time Lord Privy Seal in Asquith's coalition cabinet. Llewelyn Powys, whose father was vicar of Montacute in the 1880s, comments in appropriately melancholy moralizing vein on this decline: 'I do not think any occurrence I have observed in my life has given me sharper understanding of the insubstantiality of all temporal values than the separation of this house from the Phelipses.' Curzon set his mistress to redecorate the house, the legendary authoress Elinor Glyn, infamously commemorated in the clerihew:

> *Would you like to sin*
> *with Elinor Glyn*
> *on a tiger skin?*
> *Or would you prefer*
> *to err*
> *with her*
> *on some other fur?*

By 1929 'the world-famous Montacute House' was advertised as such on the open market and described as being 'of moderate size only and comparatively inexpensive to maintain'. Apparently it had twenty-five bedrooms and dressing-rooms, six bathrooms and additional servants' quarters. This seemed an ambitious boast. Nobody fell for the seductive copy-writing and by 1931 Montacute was valued at £5,882 'for scrap'. At this point the philanthropic Ernest Cook who was grandson of Thomas Cook, founder of the travel agency, rescued Montacute for the nation and presented it to the Society for the Preservation of Ancient Buildings who subsequently passed it to the National Trust.

OPPOSITE TOP
Statues of soldiers in parade along the east front.

OPPOSITE BOTTOM
The approach to the house from the west. This is the façade embellished in 1786 by Phelips using fragments of another Elizabethan house, Clifton Maybank.

LACOCK ABBEY

Wiltshire

Lacock Abbey is a sylvan dream of a place in low-lying land on a slow sweep of the deep-cut River Avon. Since its first beginnings in the early thirteenth century it has more often than not been the

stronghold of women. It was started as a nunnery for Augustinian canonesses by Ela, Countess of Salisbury in memory of her husband. Her eldest son William was killed on the Crusades, her youngest Nicholas became Bishop of Salisbury and left his heart to be buried at Lacock. Two of her granddaughters became nuns here. The large village which grew beside the Abbey has wide streets and little twisting lanes stuffed with pretty buildings of every period, half-timbered cottages, smart little Georgian houses and inns, a tithe barn and a wonderful light and airy perpendicular church.

During the property developer's nirvana which Henry VIII brought about through his dissolution of the monasteries, William Sharington, an arch political intriguer within the Court circle, was quick to lay down a deposit of £100 on Lacock Abbey. He ended by paying £783 altogether to own it outright in 1540. Unlike many of his fellow developers throughout the kingdom, he evidently appreciated Lacock's beauty and didn't pull it down – the additions he made were enlightened. He vaulted the tower chamber with pendant scorpions and the Sharington crest.

Although William married three times he had no children and was succeeded by his brother Henry who had no surviving male heir. However his daughter Olive fell famously in love with Worcestershire-born John Talbot (coincidentally, a descendant of Ela, the Abbey's founder). The love-affair made her father furious because he deemed Talbot to be highly unsuitable and the celebrated diarist and historian John Aubrey described what ensued: 'Dame Olave a Daughter and co-heir of Sir Henry Sharington of Lacock being in Love with John Talbot (a younger Brother of the Earle of Shrewsbury) and her Father not consenting that she should marry Him: discoursing with Him one night from the Battlements of the Abbey-Church; said shee, "I will leap downe to you": her sweet Heart replied, He would catch Her then: but he did not believe she would have done it: she leap't downe and the wind (which was then high) came under her coates: and did something breake the fall: Mr Talbot caught her in his armes, but she struck him dead; she cried out for help, and he was with great difficulty brought to life again: her father told her that since she had made such a leap she should e'en marrie him.'

The next Sharington descendant who made a significant change to the face of Lacock was John Ivory Talbot who followed the very latest fashion of the mid-eighteenth century. He commissioned the architect Sanderson Miller to rebuild the great hall in 'Strawberry Hill Gothic' (see page 73) style – a startlingly and wonderfully brave innovation at the time. He swept away the formal flowerbeds and relandscaped the grounds to display a casual informality.

Towards the end of the eighteenth century there were again no male heirs and the estate passed to John Ivory's granddaughter who was married to the Reverend William Davenport. Their son married Elizabeth Fox-Strangways whose son, William Henry Fox-Talbot, was one of Britain's pioneers of photography. His calotype process laid the foundation for myriad later developments. He was also a prominent botanist, mathematician, Egyptologist and astronomer. He planted American black walnuts, tulip trees, swamp cypresses, a nettle tree and a Judas tree in the grounds. By 1916 the male line had petered out again and the Abbey was inherited by Fox-Talbot's great-niece Matilda, thus continuing the Sharington family bloodline which stretched over 400 years. She presented the Abbey to the National Trust in 1944.

ABOVE
*The east front. The tower
added by William
Sharington is on the left.
In the distance on the right
is the stable court.*

THE SOUTH-WEST   39

LONGLEAT HOUSE
Wiltshire

Longleat is set in the big bold county of downs and great dark wooded hills of westernmost Wiltshire. From Heaven's Gate high above, the first sight of it on the level green below is unforgettable. The four-square house amidst its laked park, its huge bluebell woods and its lions' terrain, remains England's greatest Renaissance house. It was built as an expression of power and riches by an alarmingly single-minded and overbearing man, John Thynne. He was an astute and brilliant businessman. He had been the Protector Somerset's protégé and was imprisoned in the Tower of London together with his employer who had been accused of embezzlement and was eventually beheaded. Thynne somehow managed to escape and went into property development, as did many astute men at the time. As the old rhyme goes

> *'Homer, Paget, Patman, Thynne*
> *When the monks stepped out and you*
> *stepped in.'*

Following the dissolution of the monasteries in 1540 John Thynne bought a small priory built by the Austin friars. It had a mill close by whose watercourse from the village ended in a long leat – hence the name. He adapted the monastery buildings, added a wing and made a twenty-seven-room dwelling – modest for him – and so began his unending and determined quest for the perfect house.

By the 1550s Thynne had got the bit between his teeth and began to employ skilled craftsmen to redesign his original building completely and turn it into a model of modernity, but in 1567 it was almost entirely destroyed by fire. Undaunted he began again, building more and more ambitiously around the wreckage. In 1572 he wrapped yet another house around his ever-evolving mansion. At this stage he employed the great master mason Robert Smythson and the Frenchman Allen Maynard for the next twelve years, and though it was they who produced the effervescent splendour of Longleat, it was the merciless Thynne who was the driving force. He was a famously difficult employer who changed his mind endlessly, gave everyone a very hard time and was never satisfied. He upbraided all his servants and to his son wrote: 'I have received your letters . . . so scribled as I can hardly rede them wherefor seek to mend your hande in some reasonable sort as men may rede it besides you have the worst frase of speche in your letters as ever I red in any mans as though he had never gon to scole.' If those surrounding him had a difficult time, it is nothing to what his house had of it. His neighbour, William Darrell of Littlecote, wrote describing its restlessness: 'But now see him that by these thirtie yeares almost with such turmoyle of mynd hath byn thinking of me, framing and erecting me, musing many a tyme with great care and now and then pulling downe this or that parte of me to enlarge sometyme a foote, or some few inches, upon a conceyt, or this or that man's speech, and by and by beat downe windows for this or that fault here or there.' It seems amazing that Thynne had any time left for making enormous amounts of money, which he did, or for entertaining, which he took extremely seriously. It was his idea to build the little pavilions on the roof called 'banqueting houses' which were in fact for entertaining small numbers of guests to dessert. From the windows they could see the huge tracts of land he owned. Although the house was done over by Wyatt and modernized at the beginning of the nineteenth century, and still more lavished upon by its end, its outward and glorious exterior is still very much that of the original John Thynne. Subsequent Thynnes have added to Longleat's cultural richness, sometimes through inspiration and sometimes through clever marriages. Today there are seven libraries at Longleat housing more than 40,000 books.

No Thynne has ever lacked style. The last Marquess had the prescience to see that the only way to hold on to Longleat was to open it to the public on a modern commercial basis in 1948, the first private owner to do so after the Second World War. The present Marquess, whose modern murals dance around his private apartments, is forever adding colour to his lionized inheritance.

OPPOSITE

Longleat set a new style for the Elizabethans with its rippling bay windows around the compact four-square plan.

LEFT

Part of the Victorian decoration in the Saloon, the chimney piece is by J G Crace – part-copied from one in the Doge's Palace in Venice.

WILTON HOUSE

Wiltshire

Nothing in the land surpasses the south façade of Wilton House. Although it was built as a contrived set piece, none the less it has a completely fresh and innocent air. Perhaps this is because it was built in the early 1630s before too much academicism had crept in to deaden the design of houses. 'King Charles I did love Wilton above all places and came thither every summer' wrote the diarist John Aubrey. 'It was he that did put Philip First Earl of Pembroke upon making the magnificent garden and grotto and he need build that side of the house that flanks the garden.' Inigo Jones, who was just finishing the Queen's House at Greenwich, was certainly consulted and could be said to be Wilton's architect, but being busy at the time may only have sketched the outline. The detailed work was passed on to his assistant, a Frenchman from Dieppe called Isaac de Caus. The original plan was for a south front over double its finished length but with the advent of the civil war and a slight falling out between the First Earl and Charles I, it was never actually built. This made Wilton all the more glorious, for it retained its four-square compactness which somehow contains and personifies its beauty.

The town of Wilton had been perhaps the most important in the whole county in Saxon times and by the time an abbey was built on the site of the present Wilton House, it had twelve parish churches. The Black Death wiped out two-thirds of the town's population and none of the original twelve churches now remains. The abbey, and the nunnery beside it, was famous not only for being founded by King Alfred, but also for the extraordinary number of abductions which its nuns attracted. First Wulftrude was abducted by King Edgar and bore his daughter who became St Edith (famous for the many miracles which were worked at her tomb). Then Osborne de Giffard from Dorset carried off two nuns but was apprehended and was sentenced to be 'whipp naked with rods three several Sundays in the church of Wilton and also in the Market Place at Shaftesbury'. When Anne Boleyn wanted to make a friend of hers the Abbess of Wilton her husband King Henry VIII said, 'I wolde not for all the golde in the world clog your conscience nor mine to make her the ruler of a house which is of so ungodly a demeanour'. He then proceeded to dissolve the monastery and give it to his friend Sir William Herbert, a Welshman who by 'making good use of his opportunities during this eventful period managed to secure continued accession of power and wealth'. William wasted no time; he pulled down

RIGHT

One of England's most celebrated seventeenth-century buildings, the south front was built after consultation with Inigo Jones. It was designed to face on to a large formal garden.

everything including the church which St Edith had built and only left a block of storehouses standing. He then built a mansion using the old stone on the four-square lines that still exist today. The central portion of the east block still stands and is known as the Holbein front. It was in this Tudor house that Shakespeare performed *As You Like It* for the first time and where the poet Sir Philip Sidney, whose sister was married to the Earl, wrote part of his *Arcadia*.

Barely eighty years later the fourth earl had pulled down the south block and built the present house. Within it were a set of seven state rooms including the single- and the double-cube rooms which rise to roof height and to this day are unrivalled in their perfection. Their flamboyance is astounding and in contrast to the quiet, gentle outward appearance of the façade. Inigo Jones, who had concentrated all his efforts on the state rooms, following the fire of 1647 wrote: 'Outwardly every wise man carries a gravity, yet inwardly has his imagination set on fire and sometimes licentiously flies out.'

There has been an unbroken line of male Herberts at Wilton until today. The eighth earl was responsible for collecting many of the paintings and statuary, and also for starting the Wilton carpet factory by smuggling Huguenot weavers from France hidden in barrels. The ninth earl built the Palladian bridge which he designed entirely by himself and was helped by his clerk of the

works, Roger Morris. James Lees-Milne describes it as 'one of the most beautiful buildings in all England'. The tenth earl, an expert horseman, was responsible for writing the British Army's manual on riding. The eleventh earl, perhaps unwisely, employed the architect James Wyatt who did so much to try and stamp his mark on various great houses in England when he should have gone more quietly. However, he did build an internal corridor around the central courtyard which meant that you could walk from one room to another without disturbing people and today it provides a brilliant children's bicycling circuit. The present Earl is a remarkable film director and producer who has done much to enrich the garden. He commissioned David Vicary to create the now mature forecourt garden with its pleached limes, lavender and dramatic fountain – all in memory of his father – and Xa Tollemache to create a box parterre in the internal courtyard.

ABOVE

The Palladian bridge, designed by the ninth Earl of Pembroke in a collaboration with Roger Morris.

RAMSBURY MANOR
Wiltshire

From Marlborough, below the fringes of Savernake Forest, the chalk-bottomed River Kennet winds along a shallow valley to the prosperous village of Ramsbury with its long curving streets of thatched cottages and brick houses. The church contains Anglo-Saxon remains and also, next to the altar, the elaborate tomb with a reclining effigy of Sir William Jones, the Attorney-General to Charles II. He died unexpectedly at the age of fifty-one in 1682 only a year after he had begun to build Ramsbury Manor, today one of the most coveted houses in the land.

Jones, a successful lawyer from Somerset, had built up a profitable practice in the King's Bench keeping out of the political forefront. After the Restoration he was befriended by the Duke of Buckingham and knighted in 1671 to become Attorney-General four years later. He was reputed to be 'the greatest lawyer in England and a very wise man'. He successfully prosecuted Titus Oates and was about to embark on a still more glittering career when he died. After much legal wrangling he had procured Ramsbury and its surrounding lands from the fifth and inglorious Earl of Pembroke who was 'chiefly known for deeds of drunkenness and manslaughter'. He proceeded to raze the four-square stone Tudor house to the ground and build in its stead this reserved, dignified and most beautiful of Carolean houses. Today it stands exactly as it did when it was built, unaltered but for the weathering of the rich red brick and golden limestone dressings. Inside, the glorious Grinling Gibbons decorations are as crisp as the day they were carved. From the elegant five-arched bridge across the river, widened to form a lake, the view of the house on its upward slope of park with towering trees behind is unforgettable. The stables beyond are as grand as can be with their *oeil-de-boeuf* windows.

Ramsbury Manor was built at one of the high points of English domestic architecture when builders possessed an inadvertent sense of proportion which, through the eighteenth century, was often lost on the drawing-board. Because of Ramsbury Manor's undeniable beauty it has, for the whole of the twentieth century, been a favourite topic of surmise between architectural historians as to its architect. At the beginning of the twentieth century it was deemed to be by John Webb who was employed by Inigo Jones, which seemed a natural progression from Inigo Jones working at Wilton for the Earl of Pembroke. In the 1920s Avray Tipping wrote of Ramsbury that it had 'so delicate a feeling for detail, and [also] so free and personal a touch within the limits of the prevailing style, that failure to identify its designer is a matter [of] regret'. Christopher Hussey in the 1960s went round its brother and sister houses like the lost Coleshill in Wiltshire, Clarendon in Surrey and Berkeley House in Piccadilly and flirted with the idea of it being by Sir Roger Pratt. A decade or so later the great architectural historian Howard Colvin came up with the latest and 'almost certain' supposition that it is by Robert Hooke, an associate of Wren who was known to be a friend of Sir William Jones. The latter had noted in his diary that he had visited Ramsbury. However, he never mentioned that he actually designed it.

It wasn't until Sir William Jones' granddaughter took over Ramsbury a century later that the house underwent any change. She had married a Mr Langham who, because she was the heiress, took on the name of Jones and was made a baronet in 1774. Lady Jones supervised the elegant landscaping of the park by damming the Kennet and creating the artificial lake at the end of which she built the beautiful bridge, to be viewed from the eastern windows. She built the most elegant orangery with high arched windows and a large new walled garden which was approached through a grove of tall trees among which was set a 'cold bath' fed by the Kennet. She redecorated and ornamented much of the interior and built delicate Adam-style lodges at the park entrance.

After Lady Jones died Ramsbury Manor went to her sister's family, the Burdetts, and in 1800 was passed to the radical MP Sir Francis Burdett whose still better-known daughter was Baroness Burdett-Coutts. In 1837 when she was only twenty-three, she inherited £2 million from her banker grandfather. She paid little attention to inevitable pursuit (although she developed an unrequited passion for the aging Duke of Wellington) and instead devoted most of her time and money to alleviating the plight of the poor of London either through housing or education. She had little time for Ramsbury Manor as had her family who chose to live most of the time at their Derbyshire home of Foremark. By the end of the nineteenth century, the gardens had been considerably reduced and the house was let. In more recent times, the house and grounds have since been lovingly restored to deserved glory.

ASHDOWN HOUSE

Berkshire

It is Ashdown's setting which stirs the soul as much as the perfection of its architecture. Near to the site of the battle of Ashdown, scene of King Alfred's glory in 871, the house lies enfolded in unending downs. There are skylarks and peewits, racing cloud shadows, dew ponds and sarsen stones; there are ash tree-filled dells, beech-shaded barrows, turf castles and strings of racehorses on early morning gallops and never far away the ghosts of early Britons, Roman soldiers and warring Danes passing the same way along the archaic Ridgeway, the oldest track in Europe, which rides the crest of downland just north of Ashdown. On Kingstone Down where two centuries ago there was a racecourse, two lonely beech trees stand sentinel to a perfect dead-on view of this utterly magical chalk-white beauty of a house below you: stranded, remote and alone.

Ashdown was built away from the world, in the early 1660s, when the Plague was rife in London. There were four-inch gaps under all the doors so that draughts would blow any germs away. It was commissioned by a Yorkshireman, William, first Earl of Craven, one of the richest and most chivalrous figures of the seventeenth century. His father had become Lord Mayor of London and had, in his lifetime, made a lot of money, but it was William's mother who as a widow had converted the money into some astute land purchases starting in 1610. She had bought Coombe Abbey in Warwickshire, Hampstead Marshall in Berkshire and in 1625 she bought wide tracts of land at Ashdown, twenty miles from the latter, with a view to hunting it.

William was a staunch supporter, if not an unrequited lover, of King Charles I's sad sister, Elizabeth, Queen of Bohemia. He had first encountered her as a young soldier in the service of Prince Maurice of Nassau while she and her husband were in exile in The Hague. Later, during the English Civil War, when she was being pursued by creditors, she wrote to William: 'I have no more to eat, there is no money, no credit for any; and this week if there be none found, I shall have neither meat,

nor bread, nor candles.' He came to her rescue, and when eventually the 'Winter Queen' returned to England as a widow during the Restoration he put his London house at her disposal. The Plague, by then, was beginning to take hold. It has always been surmised that William built Ashdown to offer her a refuge. That she would have felt at home with its looks goes without saying, for Ashdown was most probably designed by William Winde, a soldier and amateur architect who had been brought up among the exiled Royalists in the Low Countries. The tall, ethereal building looks like an unutterably beautiful foreigner, as though plucked from beside a canal in Holland and placed in these isolated chalk uplands. Tragically, the Winter Queen never lived to see Ashdown. She died in William's London house and, in an obvious show of her deep affection, she left him her papers and pictures and the stags' antlers she had brought from Bohemia, some of which hang in the house today. William lived for another thirty years and died a bachelor at the age of eighty-eight.

From its parapeted roof with the huge cupola-topped lantern in its midst, flooding the wide stairway with light, you look to every horizon on infinite downs;

it would have commanded a fine view of the Ashdown Hunt, for hunting was a consuming passion of the Cravens. Elizabeth, wife of the sixth Baron Craven however found another consuming passion in the reigning Margrave of Brandenburg-Anspach and Bayreuth. She left Lord Craven, having borne him six children and went to live with her lover in Germany in 1780. She wrote to her husband that she was to be regarded as Margrave's sister. The following year Lord Craven died. Elizabeth married the Margrave who sold his principality and the couple came to live for a short time at Ashdown where she wrote plays.

The Craven family owned so much land and William, the first Earl, had built so many houses, most famously Hampstead Marshall (now vanished, but for some of the grandest gate piers in England), that Ashdown was hardly ever their primary residence. It has a long history of emptiness. During the Second World War it was occupied by the Army and became derelict. In 1956 it was given, with an endowment, to the National Trust by Cornelia, Countess of Craven. It is now a loved family home, on lease from the National Trust, and has been beautifully and fittingly put in order.

DEANERY GARDEN

Berkshire

Edwin Lutyens' career as one of England's greatest Edwardian architects rocketed through a series of lucky meetings, not least one with the great man himself, Edward Hudson, who created the magazine *Country Life* and who was to commission Deanery Garden. Hudson, who owned the family printing firm, was playing golf one day at Taunton Heath in Surrey with George Riddell, the firm's solicitor. They discussed general business and how *Racing Illustrated*, one of their latest ventures was doing badly as a weekly. Hudson had the idea of relaunching it as a new magazine about the 'countryside' – a whole new world which new commuters, brought into the country by railways, were just discovering. It was the most perfect timing, for *Country Life* had a waiting audience. Although Hudson did not edit the magazine he none the less exercised control and sought the highest quality in everything. He met Gertrude Jekyll the famous gardener at the beginning of his magazine venture and it was she who introduced him to her protégé Edwin Lutyens, who had already designed her much-admired house at Munstead Wood in Surrey. Now before he was even thirty, Edward Hudson was asking the young architect to design a house for him too.

Lutyens had been brought up at Thursley in Surrey and had a love of that county's local styles and materials, heightened through his endless excursions with Gertrude Jekyll in her trap pulled by her pony Bessie. Tile-hanging, so typical in these southern counties, was thus deeply embedded in his heart and he used it often. He was an extremely independent character from the outset and after spending two years at the South Kensington School of Art he went for a year to the office of the architect Sir Ernest George when he was still only eighteen. It was the only formal architectural training he was to have and towards the end of his life he told Osbert Sitwell: 'Any talent I may have was due to a long illness as a boy, which afforded me time to think, and subsequent ill health, because I was not allowed to play games and so had to teach myself my enjoyment, to use my eyes instead of my feet.'

Deanery Garden was both wildly innovative and romantic. Lutyens was keen that it should belong immediately to the village of Sonning and left the ancient wall almost intact which guarded its privacy along the village street. One of the two arched doorways in the wall leads into a vaulted passage and the courtyard with its inner pool. Christopher Hussey, who wrote Lutyens' biography in 1950, describes Deanery Garden as 'a perfect architectural sonnet compounded of brick and tile, in which . . . handling of the masses and spaces serve as rhythm: its theme a romantic bachelor's idyllic

afternoon beside a Thames backwater'. As Gertrude Jekyll had no doubt taught Lutyens, the garden was part of the house and, if planned as such, immediately became part of the landscape. Casement windows could be opened on to lilies growing below whose scent would waft in to the room; a pergola, archways and a cloister all laid out by Jekyll become part of the house and standing in the huge wonderful wood mullioned bay window with its hundreds of leaded lights is like being in the garden. The great double-height hall and the long gallery upstairs are both reminiscent of Great Coxwell tithe barn with huge silvery oak timbers lending security and 'the reserve and repose that reigns throughout the house' – so wrote the anonymous describer of Deanery Garden when it first appeared in *Country Life* in 1903. 'It is a superb instance', the article continued, 'of what can be accomplished in a very short space of time. Not more

than three years ago an aged and ruining wall was the only building here and eighteen months ago this fair garden was little more than a waste overgrown with rank docks and metal.' As a result of Edwin Lutyens' assured brilliance and efficient professionalism he became the apple of Edward Hudson's eye and through him got many a commission including most aptly one from George Riddell, now a Lord, who had been Hudson's partner on the golf course when *Country Life* was first conceived. Riddell commissioned Lutyens to build Dormy House on Walton Heath golf course in Surrey in 1906. Later Lutyens was to restore Lindisfarne Castle on Holy Island for Edward Hudson and ultimately to remodel his last country house, Plumpton Place in Sussex.

MOTTISFONT ABBEY

Hampshire

Overhung with high trees all along its far bank, the trout-filled River Test marks the eastern boundary of the magical garden at Mottisfont. In the 1930s Geoffrey Jellicoe laid the foundations with a lime walk – carpeted in spring with an electric-blue mass of chionodoxa – and the rose garden within the high brick walls of the kitchen garden, now one of the greatest in Britain. Looking towards the Test, the sunny side of the house with its receding façades cocooning the elegant central perfect doll's-house face is ravishing and unlike any other. On first glance, it is a Georgian house but as the architectural historian Henry Thorold describes: 'Walking round the east end, the sudden appearance of a monastic pillar here, an unexpected medieval archway there, will reveal more. Indeed the north front reveals all. Here is the long, buttressed aisleless nave of the church, a fragment of the tall archway which led into the vanished north transept, with the truncated arch above, and the long line of Tudor mullioned windows below and Georgian sash windows above it is an exceedingly attractive composition.'

Mottisfont tells the same story as so many other monastic settlements in Henry VIII's reign: the Court acolytes hovered around like vultures awaiting the distribution of land following the dissolution of the monasteries. William, Lord Sandys who lived at The Vine, an already enormous house up the road, swapped his villages of Paddington and Chelsea on the edge of London for Mottisfont. He determined to build another residence around the ruined church beside what was only a priory. A large and impressive house evolved around two courtyards and although William did not finish the building, his son seems to have made it his primary seat in Hampshire and must have given it its final touches.

In 1684 Mottisfont passed to a nephew, Sir John Mill whose son Richard, an MP, transformed the Tudor house into a modern one during the 1740s. He created a brilliant and symmetrical composition exemplifying the different heights and levels of the land and combining the rose-red brick of the centre with flanking stone bays like little half pepper pots. Although the monastic remains were not more than a

OPPOSITE

Mottisfont from the south-east, seen across the River Test: a Georgian remodelling of a Tudor rebuilding of half a medieval monastic cloister.

ABOVE RIGHT

A detail of Rex Whistler's 1938 Gothic murals in the saloon.

priory, he aggrandized Mottisfont's name by adding 'Abbey' and so it has remained. The Mills family died out and when Mrs Vaudrey inherited the house in the 1880s she decided to let it to a London financier called Daniel Meinertzhagen.

The Meinertzhagens loved the house to distraction and to their ten children it was a paradise. Richard and his brother Dan, 'knew every inch of the Mottisfont estate, every coppice, hedgerow, chalk pit and almost every tree'. Sadly they were only here for sixteen years, from 1884 to 1900. In 1942 Richard returned to Mottisfont which had been empty for some time. 'So unfrequented was the duck-pond by inquisitive humanity that when I visited a favourite little dry island in its midst . . . picking my way carefully along the overgrown track amid tussocks and fallen trees, I found at the base of the old maple tree an old rusted saucepan, two tins of sardines and a pot of jam just as Dan and I had left them in 1897.' Mrs Meinertzhagen's sister was the famous Beatrice Webb who, with her husband Sidney founded the Fabian Society. Mottisfont in those sixteen years of the Meinertzhagens' reign saw many high-minded visitors such as Bernard Shaw and Cecil Rhodes. When Mrs Vaudrey Barker-Mill finally returned to her house in the 1900s, she had the central heating, which had been installed by the Meinertzhagens, taken out and she refused to have electric light put in. By 1922 the house was empty and gradually over the next five years the contents were sold. In 1934 Gilbert Russell bought the property and he and his wife Maud proceeded to lavish their self-conscious 'good taste' throughout the house. Maud was a great beauty. She was friends with William Orpen, John Singer Sargent and William Nicholson, and she sat for Matisse. She bought drawings by Picasso, Degas, Derain and Modigliani, and commissioned Rex Whistler to decorate the saloon at Mottisfont in the Gothic style, about which the historian John Julius Norwich rhapsodizes. He was lucky enough to be asked to Mottisfont by Mrs Russell who lived here until 1972: 'Many is the sunlit summer afternoon, with the tea table set out on the east lawn under one of those magnificent trees beside the swiftly flowing Test, on which I have reflected, helping myself to another cucumber sandwich, that here at Mottisfont I could happily live and die, and that earth, almost certainly, had not anything to show more fair.'

THE HOMEWOOD

Surrey

Buried in the expensive wooded suburbs south of Esher, near the ghost of Vanburgh's house at Clarendon, The Homewood's first floor sails out among the silver birches. 'We danced like mad' remembered its designer Patrick Gwynne. It was he who planned that the maple-wood drawing-room floor be sprung for dancing – its joists resting on rubber pad clips. The furniture he designed for the room was light and easy to push back. Patrick was a keen twenty-four-year-old architect when he persuaded his parents to allow him to design a brand-new house for them. They had already decided to pull down their Victorian house around which Commander A L Gwynne, an amateur horticulturalist, had created a sumptuous garden. Armed with Patrick's plans The Homewood was built in 1937.

Patrick had just left the office of Wells Coates who was part of the burgeoning modernist movement. Wells Coates was chairman of MARs – the Modern Architectural Research Society – and had already built the Lawn Road flats in Hampstead which were considered highly progressive at the time. Patrick had travelled extensively in Europe looking at landmarks of modernism including the Weissenhof Siedlung housing estate in Stuttgart by all the leading modernists including Mies van der Rohe, but his favourite of all was the renowned Villa Savoye just outside Paris which had been completed in 1931 by Le Corbusier. Corbusier's book *Vers une Architecture* had revolutionized British architecture. 'A house is a machine for living in . . .' he wrote; 'an armchair is a machine for sitting in and so on.' Patrick was able to use the latest technological innovations. The Homewood's reinforced concrete frame made it possible to create huge expanses of uninterrupted floor space, something which hitherto had been impossible. His parents found themselves thrown into this easeful open-plan living which all took place on the first floor. The three large windows of the living-room overlooked the garden and made them feel part of it. Wells Coates had helped with various details but most importantly had supplied the provenly reliable builders who knew how to achieve the latest techniques in construction. Patrick's young colleague in the office, Denys Lasdun, who was to build the National Theatre on the South Bank in London, was enthusiastic throughout.

The house adheres to a system of units designed to work for the human scale – they measure four foot horizontally and one foot eight inches vertically. 'We were always getting out our set squares then', remembered Patrick. He had worked out variations on these proportions, and they constituted all the major elements of the house – the windows, door widths and ceiling heights. Just as Andrea Palladio had laid down his set of golden rules in the eighteenth century, so the modern movement were creating their own set, which were more modest in their proportions. Certainly the effect at The Homewood is calm and elegant, both from outside and looking out from within. The ground floor contains the garage and boiler house, the principal rooms on the L-shaped first floor are joined in the centre by a spectacular circular staircase, bathed in light from the large windows. A balcony runs in the long arm of the

'L' facing west. 'Since its completion (on the eve of the Second World War), The Homewood has held a quietly influential position in British modern architecture,' wrote Neil Bingham in *Country Life*. 'Generations have appreciated its rationale, sophisticated and poetic beauty.'

FIRLE PLACE

Sussex

Coming off the crest of the South Downs west of Alfriston, where the sea is glimpsed on one side and the Weald of Sussex on the other, a chalk track leads down low and diagonally through ancient wind-cropped pasture to the Bloomsbury mecca of Tilton and Charleston. Here, beyond the straggling farm, a path leads on towards Firle; it takes you past the flint tower rising from a cornfield, past Gothic-windowed flint and brick cottages and into the ancient oak-scattered park. Gradually this pale grey beauty of a house unfurls – graceful yet not grand – its stone the colour of a watery sky. Though the stone came from Caen in France it seems to belong in this chalk country. There is an inexplicable rightness about the house in its setting. It is the old home of the Gage family, and is Tudor beneath a Georgian face. It nestles under steeply hanging beech woods which cling to the 700-foot backdrop of downs, well sung by Rudyard Kipling:

> The Weald is good, the Downs are best –
> I'll give you the run of 'em, East to West.
> *Beachy Head and Winddoor Hill,*
> *They were once and they are still.*
> *Firle, Mount Caburn and Mount Harry*
> *Go back as far as sums'll carry.*

At the far gates the village breathes an air of settled satisfaction. In the early 1900s its straight little street boasted a butcher, baker, bootmaker, tailor, miller, blacksmith and harness maker. There is still an excellent Post Office-cum-shop. The church is packed to the aisles with Gage memorials: Gages in long gowns with fur collars and cuffs, bearded Gages in armour. Gerard Johnson designed the grand altar tomb of John Gage and his wife whose effigies lie stiffly on top, their hands together in prayer. The Gage family had come to Firle from Gloucestershire in the fifteenth century but it was not until Sir John Gage, a soldier and courtier who died in 1556, that they made their name. By all accounts he was an extraordinarily kind man and perhaps would have needed to be considering the troubled times he lived in. He managed to be the trusted friend of Henry VIII, Edward VI and Mary I. He was also a constable of the Tower of London and was the friend as well as the jailer of Princess Elizabeth and Lady Jane Grey. He was a staunch Catholic yet, although he disapproved of the King's divorce, managed to stay in favour with Henry VIII. He also commanded the expedition which ended in the defeat and death of James V at Solway Moss and shared the command at the Siege of Boulogne for Henry VIII. Despite his remarkable career he was able to build a substantial house which, at his death, boasted an inventory which included forty feather beds. Some of the Tudor house can be detected in the façade which faces up to the South Downs, and the great hall has a surviving sixteenth-century hammerbeam roof above its plaster ceiling. Perhaps Sir John acquired the superior Caen stone during the dissolving of so many monastic glories along the south coast which were built of this famous material.

All through Sir John's long life he loved Firle with a passion. He left it to his eldest son but only if he wanted to live in it and had enough money to do so; if not to his second son, if not to his third. He was keen that his descendants should love it as he had done and he became the role model to whom the Gage family still adhere. He left money to all the poor people who came to his funeral and in his will asked that his gold Order of the Garter should be sold in order to give alms to forty neighbouring

parishes. He was the most popular man of the sixteenth century in the county. His grandson, Sir Edward, courted the beautiful Lady Penelope D'Arcy who was also being courted by Sir George Trenchard and Sir William Hervey at the same time. She promised to marry them all in turn and did so. First Sir George who died when she was only seventeen, then Sir John Gage with whom she had nine children, and when he died she became the wife of Sir William Hervey.

During the seventeenth century the Gage family suffered through their Catholicism, but by the middle of the eighteenth century the seventh Baronet, Sir William had become a Protestant. He was one of the earliest devotees of cricket and in August 1735 captained eleven Sussex men against eleven gentlemen of Kent. He had also brought a kind of plum back from France in 1725, planted it in his kitchen garden and produced what is now known as the greengage. It was Sir William who began the radical alterations at Firle, giving it its wonderful Palladian hall and its plasterwork and broad staircase in the manner of Roger Pratt. By the time he had finished, the Tudor house was almost completely hidden. When his first cousin, Viscount Gage, succeeded him and married the heiress of Sampson Gideon, he carried out still more mid-Georgian improvements.

The most celebrated of the nineteenth-century Gages was Sir Thomas, who was Governor of Massachusetts at the outbreak of the War of Independence and on the losing side of the Battle of Bunkers Hill. The twentieth century saw the Gages as a worthy county family, as great patrons of the Bloomsbury Group of writers and painters who lived, for peppercorn rents, on the estate, and as custodians of one of the great art collections. The present Gage incumbent loves the place no less than the original Sir John did in Tudor times, and has kindled the tradition of cricket at Firle: in 1998 the Firle eleven were top of the Cuckmere League and won the highly prized Thomas Lusted Cup.

LEFT
From this viewpoint, to the north-east, Firle's Tudor history is largely invisible behind Georgian remodelling. The entrance front dates from about 1745.

GREAT DIXTER

Sussex

The virtuoso gardener Christopher Lloyd, who has written his famous weekly gardening column in *Country Life* for the last thirty-six years, has been responsible for making Great Dixter a place of horticultural pilgrimage. The cosy demesne is tucked up on the Kentish-looking side of Sussex, where oast houses, apple orchards and huge oak trees abound. The 'wooded, dim, blue goodness' of the Weald, which Kipling loved so, stretches away in every direction. Beyond Newenden, watery meadows spread beside the River Rother. Over the bridge, past the chocolate-box railway station and on up the hill, is the village of Northiam where there was once a giant oak on the green – now only the hulk remains. The manor, buried in its garden, grows organically in its setting. The heart of the house, well

BELOW
The Hovel, an outhouse dividing the Topiary Lawn from the Exotic Garden.

years later, on his retirement (aged forty-four), he bought the dilapidated 'Dixter', later adding the 'Great' to distinguish it from 'Little'. Lloyd was adamant that the restoration and enlargement of the house should reflect local traditions. Lutyens, his chosen architect, and he travelled assiduously round the nearby villages examining buildings. At Benenden, nine miles away, they found the remains of a Wealden house which was under threat of demolition. They bought it for £75 and Lutyens meticulously grafted it on to the manor house at Great Dixter using the line of the down-sloping land and a deep, deep tiled roof to create a seamless join between the two houses.

The way that he has welded together the house and garden is magical: he laid shallow steps, and used the site of the farmyards and original farm buildings as loggias and summerhouses. Lloyd himself designed a sunken garden with an octagonal pool in the early 1920s. Yew hedges, topiary, brick paths, pools and orchards encompass and almost bury the house beyond which, over Dixter Wood down across the marshy valley to Bodiam Castle, the view reaches on to Bedgebury Forest and blue hills of Kent and Sussex beyond.

When Nathaniel Lloyd's son Christopher took over the house and garden it was already a part of him. He was born here and today has lived here for seventy-eight years. Each day he uses those enviable Lutyens latches, with their soft smooth clicks, on the oak doors and moves from parlour to solar to great hall and out into the garden, his life's work.

His garden is a true artist's canvas – he paints different pictures all the time within the framework. It is ever changing, always fresh, always inspired. The fat bird-topped pyramids of yew topiary have become as much part of the architecture of Great Dixter as the timbers of the house. 'It has a presence, especially when shadows are long and it appears to inhabit, rather than grow' writes Christopher Lloyd. The 'bones' of Great Dixter had the making of the epitome of the archetypal English idyll – the half-timbered manor, oast house, great barn, the blue distance.

OPPOSITE
The picturesque qualities of Lutyens' enlargement of the medieval house is especially apparent in this view of the roofscape from the garden.

settled and contented since the fifteenth century (with earlier beginnings), was so skilfully added on to by its Edwardian owner Nathaniel Lloyd and his architect Edwin Lutyens that you could never tell where the joins and additions begin and end.

Lloyd was a successful businessman, a master printer and the owner of a bleaching business in Manchester. His colour printing business was in Blackfriars, London. In 1905 he and his wife Daisy leased a house in Rye where Lloyd could play golf at weekends. (So keen was he on the game that he redesigned the course at Rye.) Four

What he actually planted among the bones were not the predictable romantic rambling roses, scrambling up rose-red garden walls, nor lavender spilling on to paths; instead there are strange exotic climbers like the lilac annual *Cobaea scandens*, there are startling giant dahlias of red and shocking pink, and vast patches of orange and scarlet cannas and black-striped acanthus. Different worlds unfold constantly; at one moment you are in a Sussex meadow, at the next you could be in Africa among giant shiny leaves like small canoes and sumptuous and exotic rustling grasses as high as an elephant's eye.

STANDEN

Sussex

Standen is reservedly elegant. It reflects the quiet characters of its builder James Beale and its enlightened architect, Philip Webb. Beale came from a famous Birmingham family, the sort that formed the backbone of industrial England: he was non-conformist, hard-working and philanthropic. The family's main business was as solicitors and during the nineteenth century they specialized in railway affairs. In the 1860s The Midland Railway (created by George Hudson, the 'Railway King') employed Beale and Co. to bring about the complicated deals involving buying the site for a main London terminus at St Pancras and land for the line towards it. James Beale was chosen to run the newly opened London office. By 1890 he and his wife Margaret Field (also from a family of Birmingham non-conformists) had seven children between the ages of five and nineteen, and a considerable amount of money. Beale decided to turn his money into a country house. Because he liked playing golf (rather badly) and because the Oxted to East Grinstead line had recently opened, he plumped for a beautiful patch of land in the Sussex Weald. Down a narrow high-banked lane stood an old farm looking south across a beautiful valley to Charwood (now a huge reservoir) and on to Ashdown Forest. The site nestled well back into the hillside and even before the building began the Beales were terracing and planting a garden to envelope their future house.

Unlike many Victorian house builders they were socially unambitious and were not out to show off. They chose the architect Philip Webb because they knew he would understand what they wanted and for his reputation for keeping within budget. The twenty-five-year-old Webb had met the twenty-two-year-old William Morris in 1856 for the first time. 'We understood one another at once,' Morris had said and their firm Morris Co., which came out of their friendship, transformed interior design and formed the nucleus of the Arts and Crafts Movement. Webb built the Red House for Morris three years later which for a long time was deemed to be the first seed of the modern movement in England – it did not appear to be built in any revival style but in a fresh new one of its own. (Later Webb said he was fed up with the Red House being dragged out of his past the whole time and that no architect should be allowed to build a house before he was forty.) When he came to build Standen he was in fact fifty-five, and when he wrote his specification for Standen it read: 'The whole of the work is to be done with the *best*

materials and workmanship of their several kinds . . . The term *best* means strictly what is implied thereby notwithstanding any other trade acceptance.' The perfection and level of finish which remains to this day is remarkable (restored imperceptibly by that great lover of Webb, the architect John Brandon Jones, who was responsible for the restoration of Standen in the 1970s). Though Webb took the local styles and materials of the Weald very much into his palate, he none the less brought invention and an inimitable gracefulness. The chimneys sail high, but not in any sort of exaggerated fashion, and the tiles hang discreetly.

Inside, the whole house is light and airy, and a hymn to Morris Co. Its papers, chintzes, hand-stitched embroidery, stamped velvet, woven textiles, carpets and tapestries, its light fittings all have the vision of Morris or Webb. The latter's chimney pieces are perhaps the most wonderful things of all – minimal elegance personified. Webb got on famously with the Beales and when the job was finished they presented him with a silver snuff box with the inscription: 'When clients talk irritating nonsense I take a pinch of snuff.' There was no irritating nonsense at Standen.

The Beales' children – Amy, Maggie, Jack, Sydney, Dorothy, Sam and Helen – were brought up here from the 1894 onwards, and when the older ones began marrying and moving away they still came back for holidays and Christmas. Nineteen grandchildren gradually appeared and there were always some of them around the house. James Beale had retired from Beale and Co. by the early 1900s and in his leisure time enjoyed a game of golf. His obituary in *The Times* records: 'He was president of the Royal Ashdown Forest Golf Club, a position he owed not so much to his skill in the game as to the fact that he was a prominent and highly respected resident in the neighbourhood of the course.' He loved riding and was apprehensive about buying his first car to whose radiator he fixed a horseshoe.

In the early years, when all the children were at home, there were nine or ten indoor maids, a cook-housekeeper and a butler with other servants brought down from the Holland Park house for special occasions. The servants' rooms at Standen were cheery, light and airy. (Webb's former client Mrs Wyndham of 'Clouds' had written to a friend after a fire which had necessitated retiring to the attic floor: 'It is a good thing that our architect was a socialist, because we find ourselves just as comfortable in the servants' quarters as we were in our own.')

Maggie and Helen stayed on at Standen as spinsters. Maggie died in 1947 and Helen left the property to the National Trust in 1971 and died the following year.

WADHURST PARK

Sussex

Way beyond the pretty village of Wadhurst with its long street of tile-hung cottages, Wadhurst Park lies in a lost pocket of Sussex, through which a stream meanders forming a lake in its midst. There are mile-wide woods and small coombes and hills. It was here that one of the three famous Murietta brothers from the Spanish banking family, who figured so prominently in Edward VII's life, built a substantial house for himself in the 1870s. It was pulled down in 1950 leaving a solid arched conservatory, a walled garden and one of the most idyllic ready-made sites imaginable on which to build a new house. Dr and Mrs Hans Rausing bought the 600 acres of park and the vestiges of the Victorian house in 1975. It had been Dr Rausing's dream to own a park where he could keep a herd of deer. They were in no hurry to build at that point because they were still living in their native Sweden with children at school, but their long-term plan was to build a new house which would be comfortable and convenient. Mrs Rausing was keen that it should all be on one floor and after visiting Peter the Great's beautiful summer palace in Leningrad they were convinced that a single-storey building was the answer to the site.

Mrs Rausing began to make inroads on the lost garden and, on a visit to the local nursery at Tunbridge Wells, she was advised to employ a landscape gardener. Anthony du Gard Pasley began a planting scheme and it was through him that the Rausings were introduced to John Outram. In commissioning him they made a brave and brilliant choice. Outram's structures have always been sensational – the Stormwater Building on the River Thames in the Isle of Dogs, Addenbrooks Hospital in Cambridge, the Rice University in Texas.

Outram did not fail them; the house he built is strong and bright, and the Rausings love it. 'It is built like a factory and finished like a palace' said Outram. He admires architectural traditions in the grand manner. He likes taking ancient traditions and modernizing them. 'I like to freshen things up' he says. The result is this extraordinarily happy mixture of materials used in completely unconventional ways. The house is modular – on factory lines – and the ceilings inside are vaulted in a massive and elegant way. Outram developed a sort of concrete from an idea he got seeing the foundations of a Nash house he once inspected in Regent's Park in the late 1960s when he worked for the GLC. He used crushed bricks and other lumps of builder's rubble stirred into the concrete mix which when ground down produced a multi-coloured effect which was then polished. Outram nicknamed the concrete 'Blitz-crete' because when he asked the Concrete Association if they knew anything about this sort of cement they said something similar had been used to make air-raid shelters out of the rubble of blitzed houses in the Second World War.

Clive Aslet wrote: 'There is a ... sense of completeness to which the harmony of the colours greatly contributes.' John Outram says that 'the Rausings encouraged me to develop a new pallette of external materials. The colours and patterns that I use are generated by deciphering the meanings in traditional architectures. Of course, as a modernist, who does not do "period style", I do not restrict my access to these. One of the most useful traditions is that of India where I was brought up and which we have in Britain, via Gothic.' The huge windows bring the garden and park right into the house yet, unlike some modern houses, when the weather gets rough the solidity and great comfort of the interior renders it an inordinately cosy house. The oval entrance hall is one of the best modern rooms in Britain. The walls are of polished stucco with bands of burr elm veneer edged with aluminium, and two circular lanterns light it from above shining directly on to two circular geometric patterns inlaid into the stone floor like a cross-section of a Corinthian column. Each banded section at the edge reflects the number of months in the year, days in a month and hours in the day.

Dr Rausing took a great interest in the way the house was built and Mrs Rausing planned the layout of the rooms. The disciplined forms and industrialized qualities of the structure pleased the one and the rich composition of materials and colours pleased the other. This is a house that stands outside fashion, being neither modern nor post-modern. It is personal to its three creators.

IGHTHAM MOTE

Kent

Kent is one of the cosiest counties in England. Its soil is fertile and, as a result, its gardens are sumptuous. It has chalk downs, tile-hung and clapboarded houses and cottages, Kentish ragstone churches with hunched wooden bell towers, steep deep lanes dipping down into shaded dells and place names that often end with 'den' – Horsmonden, Tenterden, Smarden – meaning a wooded glade or a forest retreat. The village of Ightham between Sevenoaks and Tonbridge is full of comforting half-timbered houses with over-sailing upper storeys, exemplified in the sixteenth-century George and Dragon Inn. On a knoll a little away from the middle of the village the medieval church contains some beautifully carved monuments to the Selby family of Ightham Mote. Dorothy Selby, who died in 1641, was famous for her needlework and her memorial is inscribed with some heroic couplets which begin:

> *She was a Dorcas*
> *Whose curious needle turned th' abused stage*
> *Of this lewd world into a Golden Age.*

On the way to the Selby family home, the road leads past rose-filled gardens nestling behind high laurel hedges. There are sudden glimpses of orchards and beyond them blue wooded horizons and as the road narrows into a lane, cobnut groves darken the way which becomes tunnelled by trees. Here deep in this wooded cleft of the Kentish Weald lies Ightham Mote, one of the loveliest medieval and Tudor manor houses in all England. This is E Nesbit country where, as a child, she had come to live for three happy years. Her children's books from *Five Children and It* to *The Railway Children* are laced with descriptions of Kent, and Ightham Mote recalls Albert's uncle's house in the '*Wouldbegoods*'.

'The Moat House was the one we went to stay at. There has been a house there since Saxon times. It is a manor, and a manor goes on having a house on it whatever happens. The Moat House was burnt down once or twice in ancient centuries – I don't remember which – but they always built a new one, and Cromwell's soldiers smashed it about, but it was patched again . . . The room we had breakfast in was exactly like in a story – black oak panels and china in corner cupboards with glass doors. These doors were locked. There were green curtains, and honeycomb for breakfast. After brekker my father went back to town. . .'

Nothing changes. There are ducks on the moat, pink valerian hanging on to the brick and stonework, silvery box-framed walls, leaded lights and contented parties from local Women's Institute groups sitting in shaded corners of the garden wearing white cotton hats. The cobbled inner court of the house is the sort of place you would like to linger in indefinitely – the quietude and peace are tangible. Inside there are seventy-three higgledy-piggledy rooms of different dates and heights and on different levels encircling the courtyard, including an oriel room, a solar, chapels, a crypt, an apple store, halls, boys' rooms, drawing-room, billiard-room and butler's pantry.

From the fourteenth century onwards Cawnes, Hauts, Clements, Allens and Selbys have lived here until, being an archetypal English idyll, it appealed to the first of its rich American incumbents, General William Jackson Palmer, the founder of Colorado Springs, who rented it in 1880. When Henry James visited for Christmas in 1887 he wrote: 'Seventy people were accommodated in the great high-roofed dining hall, with our backs to the Yule log, we carved dozens of roast beefs, turkeys and plum puddings. There was a band in the court, a Christmas tree and afterwards, a dance, in costume, by the children of the house . . . The affair was organized, perfectly, by the village inn-keeper, in that competent, immediate way in which you can get everything of that kind done in England . . .'

At the end of the nineteenth century Ightham was bought by Sir Thomas Colyer-Fergusson who, despite his legendary meanness, carried out much repair and restoration. His grandson, Sir James, put it on the market in 1951. An American stationery millionaire, Charles Henry Robinson, who had fallen for the house as a young man, happened upon the advertisement in *Country Life* and recognized his dream. He bought it on a romantic whim and made it his summer home, having made necessary urgent repairs. Robinson bequeathed it to the National Trust, who took possession in 1985 on his death at the age of ninety-three.

Through the garden runs a stream so there is a continuous sound of rushing water which falls into the moat. According to the *Gardeners' Chronicle* of 2 February 1889, 'lazy young gentlemen have been known to lay on their couches and fish out of the window . . . Ferns revel in the shady nooks, and the whole has a beautiful gardenesque, but at the same time quaint old-world look, which is perfectly delightful.' The present gardener has done the National Trust proud and his cut flowers which adorn the house in jugs and glass vases make the place so welcoming that you want to move in.

KNOLE

Kent

Virginia Woolf's novel *Orlando* is dedicated to the love of her life Vita Sackville-West who was brought up at Knole. It is described by Vita's son, Nigel Nicolson, as 'the longest and most charming love letter in literature'. Vita is the eponymous hero/heroine who changes sex over the four centuries in which the novel is set with Knole as its background. On her retirement in 1928, Orlando drives in a motor car '. . . up the curving drive between the elms and oaks through the falling turf of the park whose fall was so gentle that had it been water it would have spread the beach with a smooth green tide. Planted here and in solemn groups were beech trees and oak trees . . . All this, the trees, deer and turf, she observed with the greatest satisfaction as if her mind had become fluid that flowed around things and enclosed them completely. Next time she drew up in the courtyard where, for so many hundred years, she had come, on horseback or in coach and six, with men riding before or coming after . . .'

There across the 1,000-acre park where the world and his wife may wander stands Knole, not like a house but a small town with its legendary 365 rooms – legendary because in fact no one has ever counted them. Each front is dramatically different and within their boundaries seven courtyards – like the grandest of Oxford colleges – unfold. First the green court with its huge arched doorway and secondly the stone court until the more intimate heart of the house is reached. Although the house is bigger than almost any other in England, at no stage does it feel daunting, only friendly. Vita Sackville-West wrote that Knole '. . . has a deep inward gaiety of some very old woman who has always been beautiful, who has had many lovers, and seen many generations come and go . . . It is above all an English home. It has the tone of England, it melts into the green of the garden turf, into the tawnier green of the park beyond, into the blue of the pale English sky.' When Vita's father died in 1928 she did not inherit the house she loved so with an 'atavistic passion' – instead the title and the house went through the male line to her father's younger brother. This technical fault – her gender – caused her much sadness and she hardly ever visited the house again but when Knole was damaged by a bomb in 1944 she wrote: 'I always persuade myself that I have finally torn Knole out of my heart . . . and then the moment anything touches it every nerve is *à vif* again. I cannot bear to think of Knole wounded, and me not there to look after it and be worried about it.'

Knole is the creation of two men: first Thomas Bourchier who became Archbishop of Canterbury in 1454 and a Cardinal in 1473 and who was here for forty years from 1446 onwards and secondly Thomas Sackville, between 1602 and 1608. There may have been a modest manor house on the site when Bouchier bought it for £266 13s 4d and was later followed by four successive Archbishops of Canterbury ending with Cranmer. Henry VIII acquired Knole in 1538 as a royal palace and Queen Elizabeth then gave it to her cousin, Thomas Sackville. After becoming Lord Treasurer he was made the first Earl of Dorset in 1604. He enlarged the house considerably and rendered it swoopingly Jacobean with its whirling Dutch gables and sentinel leopards. He made a Tuscan colonnade in the stone court and lowered the high roof of the hall with a plaster ceiling. He replaced the plainer screen with a wild and sumptuous one and remodelled nearly all the ceilings. In short he pulled the whole house together. Towards the end of the seventeenth century the first Earl's grandson Edward Sackville bought Knole's collection of furniture and textiles when he was Lord Chamberlain, including the famous 'Knole settee' with its adjustable side panels. The third duke was a keen cricketer and employed a small squad of professional cricketers including the bowler 'Lumpy' Stevens, whose prowess was partly responsible for the introduction of the third stump.

In the 1890s by the time Vita's mother Victoria was the châtelaine, funds were beginning to run out. Despite this she set about making Knole into one of the most comfortable houses in the land installing a telephone in 1891, central heating and bathrooms with hot running water. By 1902 the house was fully electrified. Lavish weekend house parties ensued. She began to accept money and gifts from the immensely rich John Murray Scott who, when he died, left her £150,000 and the contents his house in Paris which comprised a substantial part of the famous Wallace collection. She immediately sold it for £270,000 to a French art dealer and spent the proceeds. By the 1920s Knole was up for rent like so many great houses such as Blickling and Corsham Court. Nobody took it and in the end after Lionel's death it passed to his brother Charles.

In 1940 Charles wrote to his son Eddy, 'At this moment, we are all under the influence of the budget . . . it is the end definitely for such houses as Knole . . .' In 1946 the family handed over the house to the National Trust with an endownment towards its maintenance. Ten years later, Eddy, the fifth Lord Sackville, told the *Daily Mail* from his Irish home, 'Ireland suits my temperament, I prefer it to that big place in Kent.'

OPPOSITE

Green Court, looking towards the entrance front of the house built for Archbishop Bourchier in the 1460s.

PORT LYMPNE

Kent

Sir Philip Sassoon was a fabulously rich politician, with strong artistic leanings. He was a Trustee of the National Gallery, the Wallace Collection and the Tate. He was private secretary to Field Marshal Haig and to Lloyd George; he was Under Secretary of State for Air and MP for Hythe from 1912 onwards. Soon after he became the latter he commissioned the architect Sir Herbert Baker, who was born in Kent but had been practising in South Africa, to build him a house on the dramatic escarpment above Romney Marsh.

The Roman fort of Lemanis hangs on a clay slope below, its ruined walls once twelve feet thick and twenty feet high enclosed a semi-rectangular fort of about ten acres. It stood on what was once the cliff directly above the Channel whose waves beat below. The great 'sixth continent' which constitutes the hundred square miles of Romney Marsh is relatively new reclaimed land. Here on the heights above, with the widest view imaginable the quarter of a million-pound Port Lympne rose – a cross between a Cape Dutch farm and an East Anglian manor house. Over the next twenty years Sir Philip added and embellished it in wildly opulent style. As Mark Girouard describes, 'Sir Philip Sassoon, was torn between the standards of *Country Life* and Metro Goldwyn Meyer'. In an effort to reflect the spirit of the Romans he asked the architect Philip Tilden to add what Pevsner describes as 'an overdose of magnificence' which constituted a large 'bachelor wing' probably the last to be built in England and a gigantic Roman swimming pool with a fountain jetting up from it into the Kentish sky. Sassoon would look out at it while he was having breakfast and encourage the footmen who worked in the house to bathe at that time. From the pool the grandest possible marble steps, as though they had come straight from Hollywood, scaled the great height from the swimming pool down the cliff to ever more spectacular gardens. Posh society folk and political friends flocked to Port Lympne including Charlie Chaplin, T E Lawrence, Bernard Shaw, Stanley Baldwin, Winston Churchill and Lord Mountbatten. Chips Channon's wife likened Tilden's Moorish bachelor's wing around the courtyard to a Spanish brothel. Young airmen visited from the nearby flying field at Lympne to mingle among Sassoon's grand house parties. Informality prevailed and formal introductions were dispensed with, perhaps because there was no hostess.

Despite his lavish style of entertaining Sir Philip was in fact one of the most important patrons of the arts of his generation. He had been deeply affected by the arrival of Diaghilev's 'Ballets Russe' in 1911 which had displayed such bright and clashing colours with their Leon Bakst's sets. Port Lympne blazed with colour. The dining-room was decorated with lapis lazuli. Above the cornice was a frieze of African men and animals painted by the artist Glyn Philpot. The drawing-room walls were covered with an allegory of France being attacked by Germany with the former eventually victorious. It was painted by the Catalan artist Jose-Marie Sert in complicated symbolism ending with triumphantly trumpeting elephants over the chimneypiece. Here in this private exotic world Lloyd George conferred with Marshal Foch before the Treaty of Versailles. Port Lympne pleased the French so much, with five of Sir Philip's Rolls-Royces to carry them about, superb food and wine and Sir Philip himself speaking perfect French and organizing everything that they returned again and again.

The 'Tent' room at Port Lympne was painted by the young, precocious Rex Whistler who had become a darling of the twenties' high society gay fraternity. Whistler transformed the room into a blue-and-white striped tent and the *trompe-l'oeil* effect blended in with the real blue-and-white striped curtains draping the windows. Through gaps in the tent he painted vistas of far away countryside and in one depicted the beautiful Faringdon House with a little boy waiting for a paddle steamer and a coroneted 'B' painted on the trunk beside him. This was a reference to Lord Berners who lived at Faringdon and whom Rex Whistler had recently befriended.

The Port Lympne 'Season' when 'everyone' came down to Kent and to Rye was an extremely short one in early August. Sassoon brought armies of extra gardeners from his main residence who filled the beds with thousands of bedding plants in the 'chequered' garden, the 'striped' garden and the 'clock' garden. In 1929 Sir Philip died suddenly in his house in Park Lane, London, at the age of fifty-two with nearly £2 million in the bank.

In the 1960s no more flamboyant character could have bought Port Lympne than John Aspinall, the saviour of 44 Berkeley Square, which contains one of London's greatest interiors. Curator of London's most famous gaming establishment, the Clermont, he retired to Kent, set up a zoo and has kept this extraordinary artistic and social document of the early twentieth century in apple-pie order, as well as creating a further painted room of jungle, mountains and portraits of his wild animals in his zoo at Howletts. He has also restored much of the garden which is meticulously maintained.

OPPOSITE

A flamboyant touch of imperial Rome is given to Port Lympne by the great bathing pool which lies on the axis of the garden front.

13 LINCOLN'S INN FIELDS

London

'Architecture is the queen of the Fine Arts,' wrote Sir John Soane, 'Painting and sculpture are her handmaids, assisted by whom ... she combines and displays all the mighty powers of Music, Poetry and Allegory.' He believed that it was necessary to have a visual training in all the arts in order to achieve 'perfection in architecture' and his house in Lincoln's Inn Fields became a museum of works of art in his lifetime. He arranged it as a series of studies for his own mind, but left it to the nation in the hope that architectural students would use his collection for reference.

There was considerable uproar in legal circles when a developer named William Newton threatened to build thirty-two houses in the fields beside Lincoln's Inn. He won the day in the late 1630s and more development followed. Today the square abounds with lawyers' offices, but still retains an air of quietude away from the river of traffic in Holborn. An air of strict legality hovers above the plane trees in the central gardens. The houses are reserved, until that is you notice the south-facing number '13 Lincoln's Inn Fields' which breaks all the rules. It is flooded with sun when there is any to be had. It would never get planning permission today. It belonged to Sir John Soane, the architect of the Bank of England and the Dulwich Art Gallery. The strange façade was originally designed by Soane as a loggia which he later filled in with windows to give extra space in the house.

Soane was a genius. His architecture was wild and original and annoyed the purists. He was miles ahead of his time, combining elegance with amazingly modern details such as recycling the wasted heat from chimneys through the passages of a house. The son of an Essex bricklayer, he was born in Goring-on-Thames and started his working life as an errand boy. He entered the office of the architect George Dance the Younger and later of Henry Holland. His talent at drawing was soon recognized and he won the Royal Academy Gold Medal for a design of a Triumphal Bridge. Sir William Chambers saw it and introduced him to George III and his career began to soar. His house in Lincoln's Inn Fields, in which he combined a home, a studio and a gallery, encapsulates his genius and his brilliance.

Soane first moved to 12 Lincoln's Inn Fields in 1792 and over the next forty-five years added numbers 13 and 14 and fiddled with them and filled them to the brim, incorporating every architectural trick he knew. As soon as you venture through the front door you lose all sense of orientation. Nothing is normal. The use of space is quite extraordinary. The dining-room which is combined with the library, has mirrored arches, shutters and circles above the books. The reflections are endless and, by candlelight, dazzling. Even on a dull day at lunch time the fire irons and fenders, the furniture and worn leather seats glisten with their weekly polishings. It's a man's room, painted Pompeiian red and bronzed green,

as is the little study and dressing-room directly off it. It is like the captain's cabin on a ship with not an inch wasted and a tomb-like doorway just wide enough for a body. The breakfast room is fantastic, with its domed ceiling and inset mirrors which give it a sparkling brilliance, and it is so satisfactorily practical as well. The picture-room which houses Hogarth's *Rake's Progress* has huge and surprising swinging doors showing more pictures than you would think possible in so small a space.

Soane was an obsessive collector. He scanned the sales catalogues and haunted the sales rooms. He did not always go to the auctions, but Mrs Soane, a considerable heiress, often did and it was she who bid for Hogarth's *Rake's Progress* at Christies in 1802 and secured the eight canvasses for £570. The house is crammed with *objets d'art*, architectural models, drawings and paintings (including Turners), and all arranged in an inimitable and intimate way.

There are optically elusive corridors of Corinthian style and crypts beneath which were once the back yards of the houses. The custodians refer to them as the Valley of Death since they house so many remnants of Greek tombs and a gigantic Egyptian sarcophagus. If Soane was purported to be a depressive then the upstairs drawing-rooms could not be merrier. They are painted in the most wonderful 'patent' yellow with stiff silk curtains to match and when the sun shines through the stained glass on the sides of the glazed-in loggia you might as well be in the south of France.

OPPOSITE
A bust of Sir John Soane presides over the view from under the dome at the heart of the house. The collection of plaster casts and antique fragments was assembled partly for the instruction of his pupils.

LEFT
The façade of No. 13, seen from Lincoln's Inn Fields. The first-floor windows were originally an open balcony.

SPENCER HOUSE

London

On 20 December 1755 Lord Spencer secretly married his childhood sweetheart, the eighteen-year-old beauty, Georgiana Poyntz during a ball for his coming of age at his ancestral home of Althorp. He was good-looking, impulsive and prone to lavish gestures (the diamond buckles on his honeymoon shoes were valued at £30,000). When the young Spencers began socializing in earnest they decided that their London house in Grosvenor Street was too small by half. In May 1756 John Spencer bought a ninety-nine-

ABOVE

Gilded palm trees form a screen in the Palm Room, the best-preserved of Vardy's interiors. The room was used by men after dinner.

year lease on a site near St James's Palace looking on to Green Park. A house had already been designed by John Vardy for the unfortunate Lord Montfort who had committed suicide a year before. Lord Spencer took the architect and his plans on as part of the package.

Perhaps because he never boasted, nor put himself about in society as did so many of the eighteenth-century architects, Vardy was unsung. He was born within sight of Durham Cathedral – no mean childhood inspirer – and during the 1740s became an assistant to the already famous and popular William Kent. On Kent's death in 1748, he worked from the Office of Works for the Government, taking on private work as well. Spencer House with its unusual, brilliant and exceptionally long pediment, filled with relaxed and sumptuous carving, was wild and brave. It was perhaps not strictly in keeping however with the aims of the purist Greek revivalists who were beginning to hold sway. At the time of its building Lord Spencer, unable to depend on his own judgement where taste was concerned, fell under the guidance of

General George Gray who was at the time secretary of the Dilettanti Society. The club, still in existence today, had been founded in 1734 by a group of cultivated gentlemen who had been on the Grand Tour of Europe looking at architecture and who wanted to encourage classical styles and objects in England. Gray determined to make Spencer House an essay of Greek revival perfection. He employed the darling of the Dilettanti, James 'Athenian' Stuart, to decorate the main rooms on the first floor to reflect his love of Rome and Greece – and the 'Painted Room' remains perhaps England's most celebrated neoclassical room. Luckily Vardy's great triumph, the palm room, survived General Gray's strict overriding hand in the décor. It is a series of niches and arches, domes and half-domes intersected with voluptuous and realistic palm trees – he designed a mirror and teak furniture which echoes the palm leaf motif. Also, the shallow cantilevered stone staircase with its balustrade of extraordinarily beautiful painted *trompe-l'œil* drapery is another of Vardy's lingering rococo touches.

When Spencer House was finished Arthur Young wrote in 1768: 'I do not apprehend there is a house in England of its size better worth the view of the curious in architecture, and the fitting up and furnishing great houses, than Lord Spencer's in St James's Place. Nothing can be more pleasing than the park front, which is ornamented to a high degree and yet not without profusion; I know not a more beautiful piece of architecture . . .' Today the view of Spencer House from the park is every bit as fresh and fine as when it was built. It is a brilliant house.

During the agricultural slump of the late-nineteenth century Spencer House was let, but the sixth Lord Spencer moved back in 1910 as he was by then Lord Chamberlain to Edward VII and afterwards George V, and needed to be near the palace. His son, the seventh Earl, redecorated the whole of Spencer House in 1926 but from the 1930s onwards its fabric deteriorated. It was let to The Ladies' Army and Navy Club and in 1942, at the height of the Blitz, all its original doors and chimney-pieces, skirtings and mouldings were removed to Althorp. In 1985 the lease of Spencer House was acquired by RIT Capital Partners plc under the chairmanship of Lord Rothschild who proceeded to carry out one of the great restorations of this century. As Lord Spencer and Horace Walpole had done before him, Lord Rothschild sought the advice of a 'committee of taste' including David Mlinaric, the chief decorator, Christopher Gibbs, the antiquary, Colin Amery, the architectural historian and Dan Cruikshank and John Martin Robinson as architectural advisers. Some of the greatest British craftsmen were employed – Hare and Humphreys as painters, Dick Reid as the master carver – and the house today stands as a tribute to their art and craft, to their patron and to the unusual Mr Vardy.

ABOVE
*The west front,
overlooking St James's
Park, was designed by
Vardy in 1756.*

ABOVE
*The garden front.
Walpole's house
consisted of the round
tower and the
wing to the right; the
wing on the left was
added by Lady
Waldegrave in
1860–62 to her
own design.*

RIGHT
*Walpole's library,
designed in 1754. The
chimneypiece is
modelled on
Aymer de Valence's
tomb at Westminster
Abbey.*

STRAWBERRY HILL

Middlesex

'It is a little plaything-house that I got out of Mrs Chenevix's shop and is the prettiest bauble you ever saw', wrote Horace Walpole in June 1747 to his friend and cousin, Henry Conway, having just found the house of his dreams by the Thames at Twickenham. 'Two delightful roads, that you would call dusty, supply me continually with coaches and chaises: barges as solemn as Barons of the Exchequer move under my window; Richmond Hill and Ham Walks bound my prospect ... Dowagers as plenty as flounders inhabit all around, and Pope's ghost is just now skimming under the window by a most poetical moonlight.' Alexander Pope, the poet, had died a few years before and his famous grotto sparkling with clinker and coloured stones lies hidden to this day beneath a boys' school just up the road.

The little house that Pope had found, known locally as Chopp'd Straw Hall, was built by Lord Bradford's coachman who was thought to have paid for it by selling his employers hay and feeding his horses on chopped straw instead. Walpole only discovered the name Strawberry Hill when he was inspecting the lease before he bought the house and its five acres for £776 10s 0d in 1749. It was his dream because it was in such a brilliant position, in a highly fashionable area and, due to the improved roads, was only two hours from the centre of London. Strawberry Hill could obviously be a centre and even a hub of the social life which Walpole envisaged and which became a reality. Already by the age of thirty he had become a social catch. The younger son of the Prime Minister, Sir Robert, he was to become one of the most notable figures of the century, not least because of his extraordinary chronicling of the times through his prolific letters which today make up forty-eight volumes in the Yale edition of his correspondence. They provide an extraordinary social document of the eighteenth century and display Walpole's energy, sensitivity and wit. He was also a great antiquary, the creator of a private printing press and the author of *The Castle of Otranto,* the first ever Gothic novel. He enjoyed being the social leader that he was and although he admired classical architecture, he obviously wanted to be 'different' and so created the Gothic fantasy around Chopp'd Straw Hill. It was deliberately irregular and assymmetrical. Walpole had many words for his own invention one of which was Sharrawaggi which expressed a want of symmetry. So the house grew higgledy-piggledy with battlements and quatrefoil windows, pinnacled finials and the Gothic ogee everywhere. Walpole employed an informal 'committee of taste' which included the illustrator Richard Bentley, Mr Robinson at the Board of Works who dealt with overseeing structural matters and John Chute who lived at The Vyne in Hampshire.

Strawberry Hill's fame grew. People flocked from London to see it for not only did it contain wonderful paintings and furniture, but also myriad eccentric oddities. Walpole had collected such pieces as Queen Mary's combs, the pipe smoked by Van Tromp during his last sea battle and King William's spur which he dug into the flank of Sorrel at the Battle of the Boyne. A gallery was built with an elaborate fan-vaulted ceiling to house his ever-increasing collection and Walpole began to entertain on a lavish scale. He described to his friend George Montagu on 11 May 1769: 'Strawberry has been in great glory – I have given a festino there that will almost mortgage it. Last Tuesday all France dined there. Monsieur and Madam du Châtelet, the Duc de Liancour, three more French ladies whose names you will find in the enclosed paper, eight other Frenchmen, the Spanish and Portuguese ministers, the Holdernesses, Fitzroys, in short we were four and twenty. They arrived at two. At the gates of the castle I received them dressed in the cravat of Gibbon's carving, and a pair of gloves embroidered up to the elbows that had belonged to James I. The French servants stared and firmly believed that this was the dress of English country gentlemen.' Walpole clearly loved to show off and was the life and soul of every party, ever inquisitive, ever amusing. Laetitia Hawkins wrote about him at the time that 'his figure was . . . not merely tall, but more properly *long* and slender to excess; his complexion and particularly his hands, of a most unhealthy paleness . . . His eyes were remarkably bright and penetrating, very dark and lively: – his voice was not strong, but his tones were extremely pleasant, and if I may say so, highly gentlemanly . . . he always entered a room in that style of affected delicacy, which fashion had made then almost natural; *chapeau bas* between his hands as if he wished to compress it, or under his arm – knees bent, and feet on tip-toe, as if afraid of a wet floor.'

Walpole died in 1797 and left Strawberry Hill to his niece, Anne Seymour Damer, who found the house too expensive to keep up and passed it on to its eventual heir, Lady Waldegrave. In 1856, a decade after Lord Waldegrave had died and sold the extraordinary contents of the house in a thirty-one-day sale which made a record £33,450, she decided to restore and expand the now derelict Strawberry Hill. By that time she was married to George Granville Harcourt but he died soon afterwards, so still only in her thirties she set about expanding Strawberry Hill. She added ever more elaborate Victorian Gothic to the original 'Strawberry Hill Gothic' – the style that Horace Walpole had created and which became part of English architectural language.

CHISWICK HOUSE

Middlesex

Chiswick House was designed in 1726 by the brilliant, avant-garde and rich young architect Lord Burlington. At the time of its building it was a pioneer work in neoclassical architecture, and still looks as though it belongs on the outskirts of ancient Rome, rather than in the midst of London's modern suburbs. Approaching the villa through the southern gates off Great Chertsey Road, it presents its dazzlingly elegant façade head on, gleaming white beneath dark cedars. A yew hedge with busts on tall plinths set in its arches around the forecourt. Two urn-ed and ballustraded stone stairways lead up to the *piano nobile* and under the perfect portico copied from the Temple of Jupiter Stator in Rome. Inside the layout is geometrically symmetrical. The central saloon of such a villa was designed for 'feasts, entertainment and decorations, for comedies, weddings and suchlike recreations', wrote the Venetian architect Andrea Palladio whose designs Lord Burlington had studied during his Grand Tour.

William Kent is purported to have decorated the richly gilded interior with its domed ceilings, voluptuous swags and grand overdoors. Although there is no documentary evidence, it seems almost certain that he was heavily involved, for Burlington had admired and supported Kent, since meeting him in Italy, helping him get commissions; indeed Kent ended up by living at Burlington House. They became close friends, and Burlington began his letters to Kent: 'Dearest Gusto'. Lord Burlington, heir to one of the richest Anglo-Irish dynasties, already had a town house in Piccadilly (the present Royal Academy of Arts), which he had had altered and partly reconstructed in 1716. He is supposed to have built this Palladian dream at Chiswick for contemplation, conversation and entertainment and also as a private gallery, library and club. Here he could entertain his friends, many of whom were artistic celebrities and came from all walks of life. The poet John Gay wrote, here at Chiswick:

Pope unloads the boughs within his reach,
The purple vine, blue plum, and blushing peach

Lord Burlington was one of the greatest patrons of the arts of his century. He supported writers such as Pope, Swift, Gay and Thomson, and brought Handel to England and to live at Burlington House. He was extraordinarily generous and Walpole described him as having 'every quality of a genius and artist except envy'. He was bound to provoke criticism in some circles: his contemporary Lord Hervey described Chiswick as being 'too small to live in and too large to hang a watch'. Burlington was a modest man despite the exuberant architecture he designed. He was buried at his beloved childhood home of Londesborough in Yorkshire. He specifically asked that there should be no monument and to this day there is just a small plaque.

Having only one surviving daughter when he died in 1753, Chiswick passed through her to her son, the future Duke of Devonshire. His family continued to enjoy Chiswick and a press cutting of the early 1800s describes a 'breakfast' given by the Duchess of Devonshire: 'The day being beautiful rendered the delightful villa and grounds another Paradise. Around the house pots of the finest flowers were placed, and similar attentions were paid to the internal decoration. Two tables, forming a triangle, were laid out for forty, in an elegant saloon adjoining the library. The breakfast consisted of lamb, veal, hams, fowls, chickens, with prawns, etc; the dessert pines, strawberries, cherries, etc. Much taste and elegance appeared in the arrangement of the tables, and her Grace's good spirits and affability greatly enlivened the repast. It was three o'clock before the company began to assemble, and four before the principal part arrived in different carriages, principally drawn with four horses. A few minutes after four, the Duke of York came in a post-chariot and four, with three outriders . . . The company sat down to table, the Duke of York's band, in full uniform, playing several favourite pieces of music. Soon after five the company returned to the lawn, and several little parties went on the serpentine lake, where they were rowed by gentlemen adept in that healthful exercise. After perambulating through the walks till seven o'clock, the illustrious and distinguished visitors departed.'

The 'serpentine lake' still winds its shady stretch to the west of the villa and a wide cascade crashes down from an elaborate rusticated cavern into its southern end. English Heritage now looks after the house.

KNEBWORTH

Hertfordshire

High on its well-wooded hill commanding the Great North Road, Knebworth stands supreme in its pocket of ancient rurality – out of the swing of this Hertfordshire urban hinterland. The house is the wildest, wackiest, most fantastic miniature fairy-tale palace complete with turrets, castellations, cupolas, huge griffins on stone gate piers, gigantic gargoyles and as many high Gothic details as can be packed on to one building. Its appearance is almost entirely due to the extraordinary legend of his time, Sir Edward Bulwer Lytton. Novelist, poet, dramatist, orator, occultist, statesman and patron of the arts, he was one of the brightest stars of his age. He was a wit, a fantastic dandy and his house is redolent of his character.

The original house was built by Sir Robert Lytton in around 1500 near the parish church and the then 'village on the hill', but by the middle of the eighteenth century it had been abandoned with the death of the last male heir. By the early 1800s it had become a fashionably romantic site and a passer-by of the time wrote: 'After Haddon Hall in Derbyshire I think Knebworth the most perfect specimen of the hospitable habitations of our ancestors which I have seen in the country.' By the time Elizabeth Lytton inherited it she was already married to General Bulwer (whom she disliked) and lived at Heydon Hall in Norfolk (see page 86) (which she disliked even more) with their three sons – William, who succeeded to the Norfolk estate; Henry, who became a politician, diplomat and Palmerston's biographer; and her favourite and youngest son Edward who was eventually to inherit Knebworth. When her husband died in 1807 she abandoned Heydon Hall and came to what was then the large fairly dilapidated house at Knebworth. She was by all accounts a formidable woman and in 1811 thought nothing of pulling down three of the four sides of the red-brick Tudor quadrangle and of covering the remaining section with stucco. She quarrelled with everyone around her including the rector and, as a result, conducted her own daily prayers in the drawing-room. She planted trees around the church so that she could not see it from her house and built a mausoleum in the park so she would not have to be buried in the churchyard. When her son Edward married a beautiful and wild-eyed girl from County Limerick called Rosina Wheeler she was furious and stopped her son's allowance, refusing to receive Rosina at Knebworth. The marriage was tempestuous from the start and, even though they eventually separated, their acrimonious battles continued until his death. By the 1830s Edward was becoming a well-known and successful novelist and his historical novel *The Last Days of Pompeii* solved all his financial problems. He became a Whig MP for Lincoln and St Ives but switched to the Tory party later in life having been persuaded by his great friend and literary colleague, Benjamin Disraeli.

On his mother's death in 1843 Edward, by now the toast of literary and fashionable London, went to town on Knebworth. He smothered it with Gothic embellishments. He employed John Crace, one of Pugin's closest collaborators, to decorate the interior with rich and exotic curtains and wallpapers with a central theme of dedication to Henry VII and his Tudor ancestry. Crace's work has survived in the first-floor State drawing-room where Elizabeth I was entertained in 1588. In the rest of the interior, including the magnificent Jacobean panelled banqueting hall, the Gothic overlay was removed in Edwardian times by Sir Edwin Lutyens, who married into the Lytton family. Nineteenth-century

Knebworth bristled with artists, poets and politicians, and for a time Edward employed a resident medium. Charles Dickens, a close friend, took part in amateur theatricals at Knebworth. By the 1850s Edward had written over three dozen novels and plays he had made a few enemies as well, not least in Sir Alfred Tennyson whom he attacked as 'School-miss Alfred'. Tennyson was forced into a bitter response in verse and mocked Lytton as a 'rouged and padded fop'. However he put Knebworth on the map in no uncertain manner and although today his fame has faded, he lives on in the house. His descendants and present incumbents the Lytton-Cobbolds have made Knebworth one of the most famous rock concert venues in England.

AUDLEY END

Essex

Thomas, Lord Audley who died in 1544 is buried in Saffron Walden church beneath a black marble tomb – '. . . no blacker than the soul and no harder than the heart of the man who lies buried there' wrote Thomas Fuller in his *Worthies of England*. Audley sailed whichever way the wind most favoured and, at his own admission, didn't believe in God 'or any sects of religion'. In 1533 he became Henry VIII's Lord Chancellor and immediately conferred the legal authority on Henry's divorce from Catherine of Aragon. In 1535 he passed the death sentence on Sir Thomas More, the great humanist who had dared to oppose Henry's religious reforms. In 1536 he presided over the trial of Anne Boleyn who was convicted on fraudulent charges of treason and executed in the Tower, brokered the annulment of Henry's marriage with Anne of Cleves and played the key role in the trial and execution of Catherine Howard. He complained that he only had £800 a year which was not enough to pay his housekeeper and was not only given the priories of Aldgate and Colchester, but also Walden Abbey, where he built 'Audley Inn' on the site of the present house.

From Abbey Lane in Saffron Walden a footpath leads through fields and into the sweeping park of Audley End. The majestic house rises in its midst – still confident, still imperious, a vestige of what was once the biggest and grandest of all. It was Thomas Audley's grandson (also Thomas) whose mother had married into the Howard family who built it after being made Lord Chamberlain and the Earl of Suffolk, by James I. Carried away by *folie de grandeur*, he flattened his grandfather's house and proceeded to create that which had, Celia Fiennes remembers, 'a noble appearance like a town'. When James I visited it he remarked that it was too great a house for a king but might very well suit a Lord Treasurer. By this time it had cost £200,000 and enclosed two enormous courtyards, one containing State apartments, the other for the royal entourage. In 1619 he was found guilty of embezzlement, extortion and bribery. He was committed to the Tower with his rapacious wife, Catherine. In the end he was released having agreed to pay a £30,000 fine (later reduced to £7,000) but died a disgraced man with gargantuan debts.

From that day onwards Audley End became a white elephant. Charles II decided to buy it at a knock-down price of £50,000 from the ruined Howards, but only used it occasionally on his way to Newmarket races. By the end of the seventeenth century the house had returned to the Howards.

Few people in England could afford to keep up such an enormous house. The formal garden stretched as far as the eye could see, the River Cam had been straightened into a canal in front of the house, miles of red brick wall surrounded the park and the huge Tudor stables were as big as a mansion in themselves. The Countess of Portsmouth (the Howard heiress), demolished the great outer court and part of the inner one in the eighteenth century, and when Sir John Griffin took it on in the 1760s through a co-heir he revolutionized its Jacobean spirit, swamping it in the trappings of the day. Robert Adam was engaged to design glamorous gilded and delicately painted new reception rooms, John Hobcraft was commissioned to give the chapel a face-lift in Strawberry Hill Gothic style. Capability Brown was charged with sweeping through the grounds. Classical temples, bridges and columns sprang up, cascades and rockwork, while the formalized Cam was transformed into a casual serpentine. In the nineteenth century, Griffin's heirs the Nevilles had reverted to the Jacobean taste and moved the reception rooms back up to the first floor. At no stage however did either 'improver' touch the miraculous great hall, Audley End's glory with its fantastic richly carved screen, a memorial to the embezzling earl, at one end, and a magnificent Vanburgh double stone stair with two-storeyed arches at the other. Today Audley End belongs to the nation under the auspices of English Heritage.

RIGHT

Biagio Rebecca's portrait of Sir John Griffin, Lord Howard de Walden, which is set into the panelling of the saloon.

OPPOSITE

The garden front. The ground-floor gallery, between the projecting wings was originally an open arcade. The nineteenth-century parterre garden, which had been grassed over during the Second World War, was replanted by English Heritage in the 1980s.

ELTON HALL

Cambridgeshire

On 31 August 1937 Lord Spencer wrote to the owner of Elton Hall from Althrop in Northamptonshire about an impending visit by Queen Mary: 'As the visit is a private one, it would be best not to have the flags out, but it would be nice if the villagers could welcome Her Majesty. The best way would be to let them know an hour or so before the time, so that no one will have time to tell outsiders of it. Please wear an ordinary country suit. It would be very nice if your niece was there to help you receive the Queen and also your brother. Queen Mary will of course understand that you are only living in part of the house and that your carpets and curtains are not perfect, but she is greatly looking forward to coming and seeing all your interesting and lovely things . . .' Perhaps as late as 1937 families were still breaking the bank by redecorating their houses in order to impress a king or queen whose arrival was imminent. The Probys of Elton Hall, however, were unlikely to have put themselves out, for their house was already in good order and their ancestry gave them the confidence not to want to show off.

On its south side, Elton presents almost every style of house building there is. It is a riotous and happy mixture incorporating a fifteenth-century tower and chapel built by the original Sapcote owners, undulating on to a mixture of Gothic and classical styles, all pulled together to make a ravishing ensemble with crenellations topping every available roofline and gable. 'The trouble is my family never pulled anything down,' says the present Proby incumbent. 'They just went on and on adding.' In consequence the house spread-eagles in different directions and at its entrance presents a charming muddle of a Victorian addition to a late-seventeenth-century front which in turn is joined at right angles in a series of zigzags to the Tudor core.

The River Nene, which winds past Fotheringhay where Mary Queen of Scots was so shamefully beheaded, continues its journey through Elton's park. In the eighteenth and nineteenth centuries the drive meandered through it and passed the small clump of trees to the east of the house where the ghost of Robert Sapcote was often seen to appear. Apparently he got so angry if he lost

money at cards that he would retire early from the card table, hide in the undergrowth and rob his guests on their way home. Today the short straight drive leads from the village street down a wide avenue of the tallest limes imaginable and Robert Sapcote's ghost is seen no more.

The Proby family were connected with Elton in the sixteenth century when Sir Peter Proby, who was comptroller of the Household of Elizabeth I, was granted a Crown lease of the Elton Water Mill. When his grandson, Sir Thomas married the daughter of a local landowner who possessed the site of the present hall, he decided to build a family home here in 1666. By this time the original Sapcote house was in a run-down state. Rather than pulling it down and starting afresh, Thomas began the family tradition of adding on. From that point onwards the house continued to increase in size and in its display of various architectural styles. The interiors were filled with more and more beautiful things. The library remains one of the finest private collections in the country. It is contained in the oldest part of the house in immensely satisfactory Victorian bookcases. Although a famous Gutenberg Bible was sold in 1909 to pay death duties, it still possesses Henry VIII's prayer book, containing his own writings, as well as Catherine Parr's, her third husband Thomas Seymour's and

Princess Mary's (afterwards Queen Mary). More than anything the library demonstrates the Probys' consistent scholarship, knowledge and love of books from Sir Peter's time until today.

Although Elton was shut up during the middle of the twentieth century, the present Probys have brought it back to life by making it into a loved and lived-in family home and they have done much to the surroundings. Kempt gardens have sprung up as if by magic from long-abandoned rabbit-ridden lawns around the house. Avenues have risen up in the park or been cut through the woods in this flat, ancient Cambridgeshire backwater. Mrs Proby has built a pretty Gothic orangery with an octagonal pool in front of it.

In the cellars the Probys found a portrait of Kitty Fisher by Joshua Reynolds where it had been put by a prudish forebear who thought it inappropriate to hang a portrait of a King's mistress. She has now been reinstated where her beauty can be admired – but too late for the 1937 Royal visit. After this, Lord Spencer wrote to Proby on the 11 September 1937 to say '. . . how greatly Queen Mary enjoyed her visit to you at Elton and to thank you for all the trouble you took to make it such a great success. She was so greatly interested in all your lovely things . . .'

HELMINGHAM HALL

Suffolk

Deep into a rare pocket of unadulterated Suffolk countryside where hedgerow oaks abound and roads twist like rivers, Helmingham Hall stands in the midst of one of the most beautiful parks in eastern England. At the western edge stands the silvery flint Church of St Mary with its sixteenth-century tower and beyond it, 400 acres of ancient oak trees. Some are nearly 1,000 years old: they lean this way and that, each one more majestic than the last with their immense girths and sudden stag branches. John Constable, whose brother was steward at Helmingham, lived for some time at Helmingham rectory and in 1801 painted a number of versions of *A Dell in Helmingham Park* (the oak depicted is still here). Two large herds of red and fallow deer which have been here for centuries roam the park, as well as Highland cattle and Soay sheep. Towards Pettaugh a high brick obelisk pierces the sky above the oaks, built in 1860 from the bricks of a collapsed walled garden. It stands on the Mound (hills in Suffolk are few and far between) which was used by the Helmingham volunteers to practise their musketry during the Napoleonic Wars.

This is the stronghold of the Tollemache family who have lived in Suffolk since the eleventh century. The hall, at the end of a straight avenue of 400-year-old oaks, is surrounded by a wide and defensive pike-filled moat whose two drawbridges have been raised every night since 1510. The Tollemaches came from Avranches on the Normandy coast with William the Conqueror and lived at Bentley near Ipswich for the first 400 years. In 1487 John Tollemache married Elizabeth Joyce who was heiress to Helmingham. Together they set about rebuilding the old hall and completed the present house in 1510, retaining the basic shape of the original manor house with its internal cobbled courtyard. This has never changed although successive members of the family made their marks. During the Civil War Helmingham was one of the headquarters of the Secret Society of the Sealed Knot which was instrumental in bringing Charles II back to the throne. While in exile in Paris, he wrote several letters to Elizabeth Tollemache – a Scottish fickle woman who simultaneously was enjoying a close friendship with Oliver Cromwell. The Georgian Tollemaches removed most of the gables and covered the half-timbering with brick and tile-hanging, the Regency Tollemaches asked John Nash to turn the house into a castle and he covered it in grey cement and castellations (the cement was fairly rapidly removed), then the Victorian Tollemaches decorated the hall with diamond brick patterns.

If nineteen generations of Tollemaches have loved and looked after the house, which over the centuries had fallen into complete disrepair, the present generation love the place no less. The house glows with the pride of being well cared for, but it is the garden which is their gift to the place. It is inspired. On the west side of the house there is a large walled garden which is surrounded by its own deep moat on the sloping banks of which are a profusion of wild flowers from orchids, cowslips and fritillaries in the spring to corncockle, moondaisies and columbines in the summer. Old maps and drawings show that the original shape of the main walled garden pre-dates the house by many years, and was most probably a Saxon enclosure built to protect stock from marauders.

Once inside the wrought-iron gates of the walled garden your eye is led straight to the brick piers at the other end by long lengths of herbaceous borders spilling by late summer over a grass path whose perfect edges are like freshly cut cake. The garden is divided into eight large vegetable plots just as it has been since Elizabethan times. Each year iron arches form tunnels of sweet peas, runner beans and ornamental gourds. Beyond the safe enclosing comfort of the walls and out across the moat on another grass causeway you reach the wild flowered orchard. On the east side of the house is a new rose garden containing one of the greatest collections of old species mixed with lavender and foxgloves and enclosed in a yew room on three sides. With it is a box parterre echoing the brickwork diamonds on the house and incorporating the Tollemaches' initials before it. The house forms one backdrop and the park the other.

OPPOSITE

In the twentieth century Helmingham Hall has become celebrated above all for its garden, which now so beautifully sets off the Tudor brickwork of the house's façades. It is made yet more picturesque by the battlements, casements and pinnacles added by Nash and John Adey Repton at the beginning of the nineteenth century.

MELTON CONSTABLE

Norfolk

Melton Constable is in the middle of nowhere. The wind blows in fiercely from the North Sea and whips the woods into landward-leaning wedges. There always seems to be a pale and silvery light across this huge park with its reed-edged lake and partridge covey-d cornfields beyond. The red-brick, stone-dressed house with its hipped roof is one of the most hauntingly romantic houses in the country. Perhaps this has a little to do with it being the major star in the film *The Go Between* where one of English literature's great tragic love-affairs was enacted but much more to do with its startling, tall beauty rising majestically from this flat wide-skied corner of north-west Norfolk.

Melton Constable is an ancient place – Houghton, Holkham and Raynham are modern in comparison. In 1245 the last of the male Constables died young leaving Editha, his sister, as the sole heiress. She married Sir Thomas Astley in 1236. Her redoubtable descendant was Sir Jacob Astley, one of the bravest of all Royalists during the Civil War. His prayer before the Battle of Edgehill in 1642, during which he was hurt, lives on:

'Oh Lord thou knowest how busy I must be this day: If I forget thee, do not thou forget me.'

His gallant defence of Bosworth Bridge against Essex is well recorded and at Naseby on 14 June 1645 he led the main body of foot soldiers. The Civil Wars dealt harshly with Melton's Royalist owners and it was young Jacob, the only surviving child of two first cousins, who succeeded to the family home in 1659. In 1664 he began to build the present house (sometimes referred to as a 'Wren house') to his own design. There were other homes being built on these lines in other parts of England – Coleshill (which burned down in 1952), Ramsbury Manor and Thorpe – and although their owners will have looked through the same books and known the work of Inigo Jones, none the less each house belongs to its own landscape, through its materials, its builders' idiosyncratic ways and its owners' whims and preferences. Sir Jacob was a highly intelligent and determined young man who inherited Melton Constable when he was eighteen and at twenty-three had begun building. The old Tudor quadrangular courtyard house had been badly damaged by Parliament troops and it was around its ruins that the present house rose up. Already showered in honours by the recently reinstated Charles I, in recognition of his family's late brave allegiance to the Royalist cause, young Sir Jacob was to become a faithful public servant in his own right – he sat for forty-four years in Parliament and lived until he was ninety, thus spending sixty years in the house he had built. He filled it with fine things and lavish decoration including the staircase with beautiful plasterwork on the ceiling above, laced with sumptuous swags of fruit. The ceiling in the red room too is rich with plaster fruits and game birds set in frames.

In 1700 he had added stable buildings and a clock tower to a vestige of the Tudor demesne, set apart from the main house, but as his descendent, Lord Hastings, wrote two centuries later: 'It is perhaps a pity that this old wing was not demolished, for it has acted as a magnet to successive generations and has caused the house to become somewhat unwieldy and shapeless.' In 1810 Sir Jacob Henry Astley added corridors to the east side of the wing and put on a new roof. He also built a two-storey gallery connecting with the 1670 house. In 1845 the sixth Baronet who had become the sixteenth Lord Hastings by claiming the ancient barony turned the house around and built on a *porte-cochère* on the north side. In 1887 George, Lord Hastings added to the south end with the Tudor room and tried to make all in keeping with the 1670 house. The next Lord Hastings added again. Thus there is a veritable village which has grown up which none of the recent owners has been brave enough to sweep away. But still Sir Jacob's seventeenth-century house somehow retains its grace and dignity.

OPPOSITE
A view from the south-west, across the parterre laid out in the 1850s.

HEYDON HALL

Norfolk

The demesne of Heydon, with the Elizabethan house at its heart, is an East Anglian idyll in a mildly undulating and secret corner of north Norfolk. The family, who have farmed the estate for the last thirty years, hung on to their hedges when all about were losing theirs. Today the oasis of Heydon shines out, anchored by woods and secret dells, with rich and varied hedgerows. The Hall, the village, the outlying farms and cottages are all built of the same rose-red local brick which still more anchors the whole ensemble to Norfolk. Beyond Newhall Wood, which is carpeted in bluebells in the spring, is the dead-end turning for the village. There is a working smithy, brick-pedimented rows of estate cottages, a bow-windowed post office, a gabled grange down a short chestnut avenue and a wide green with a pump in its midst. A row of tiny seventeenth-century cottages called 'Widows' Row' is dwarfed by the great flint perpendicular church and, beyond, two little brick lodges stand sentinel to the winding drive through the sylvan park where horses graze under huge spreading oak trees.

Heydon Hall, with its clustered chimneys soaring above the three pinnacled gables, is built of the palest rose-red brick with pale gold stone dressings. It is framed by a wide flank of high woodland and faces out down a chestnut avenue stretching away to a view three miles away of the spire of Cawston's church – one of 659 in the county. The house was commissioned in the 1580s by Henry Dynne, who was Auditor of the Exchequer, and who had owned the estate since the fifteenth century. On his death it was sold and was eventually bought in 1650 by the locally born and infamous Erasmus Earle, who first made his name as the unflinching Recorder of Norwich. On Christmas Day 1648 he passed sentence of death on several Royalist sympathizers who were rioting in the streets of the city. Not unnaturally Oliver Cromwell admired him and made him a member of the Council of the State. With the small fortune he accrued in consequence he bought Heydon and established himself as the head of a county family. On the death of a later Erasmus Earle, Heydon passed to his sister Mary, a pasty-faced lady who married William Wiggett Bulwer who inherited the ravishing Elizabethan house, Wood Dalling Hall. They plumped to live at the grander Heydon.

Their descendant, William Earle Bulwer who inherited Heydon in 1793, had been at school with Nelson in North Walsham and, like his friend, was a true romantic. He had abducted a girl of his own age from her boarding school and although they never married, he refused to marry anyone else and he lived with her until she died tragically as a result of being kicked by a horse. William's improvements to the estate, including installing the first agricultural steam engine in England, set him back £50,000. Later his marriage to Barbara Lytton, the heiress of Knebworth was unhappy from the outset. Despite her husband's protestations of love, she always disliked being at Heydon. He would write to her in London about the drifts of snowdrops in the garden but it was like water off a duck's back. As soon as he died in 1807 she raced back to her high-flying life together with their youngest and her favourite son, Edward Bulwer Lytton who was to become a famous figure. Their eldest son, William Lytton Bulwer was conscientious in his stewardship of Heydon. He entertained 2,000 farm workers to dinner in the park on his coming of age and proceeded over the years to build on to the hall in true mid-Victorian style, rendering it treble its original size. He was described by his brother Edward, who eventually inherited Knebworth, as a man 'whose moral dignity and austerity of character . . . would be hard to equal'.

By the twentieth century the Bulwer coffers were low; the family had retreated to a house in the village and let the unwieldy white elephant the hall had become to whoever would take it, while its fabric steadily declined. It was not until William Bulwer Long inherited it in 1970 with the 'sound' advice that he should demolish the entire building and sell all the land, that Heydon saw the happiest of endings. William had married Sarah Rawlinson, whose father had been a tenant of the Hall. They determined to return the place to what was his inheritance and her childhood home. Through sheer determination, hard work and astute and exemplary management of the farmland they set about reducing and restoring the Hall (with the help of the architect Stuart Taylor, the interior designer David Mlinaric and a grant from the Historic Buildings Council) to its original Elizabethan glory. Today it stands as a paragon of successful adaptation, lived in without staff by the energetic family who love it. The old walled garden is brimming with vegetables again and herbaceous borders and a rose garden bloom under its walls. The harmony of Heydon is complete.

BELOW

The entrance front, built in 1580. It was for many years
engulfed by later additions, which were mostly demolished
in the 1970s.

BLICKLING HALL

Norfolk

Robert Lyminge was a genius at creating theatrical stage sets and Blickling is no exception; its startling and formal grandeur rises from a dim, flat, lane-laced corner of north Norfolk and the first sight of it knocks you for six. Mountainously undulating yew hedges wave gently down to meet the service wings which flank the house, with their lyrical Dutch gables. Lyminge had finished Hatfield House a year before and was by now well into his stride. His employer at Blickling, Sir Henry Hobart, a rich London lawyer, was brave enough to give his architect a free rein. He had bought the estate in 1616, for £5,500. It was legendary in the locality for being the birthplace of poor Anne Boleyn: much of her Tudor house was left standing and was incorporated in the new swanky mansion begun in 1619. It is hardly surprising that Anne Boleyn's ghost haunts Blickling by returning on every anniversary of her execution riding in a black hearse-like carriage drawn by four headless horses and driven by a headless coachman. She is dressed all in white and her hands support her severed head which rests upon her knees. 'Just before midnight this startling apparition appears and advances slowly up the avenue which leads to the hall. At the door it vanishes but within the old Jacobean mansion there are corridors along which a headless spectre glides. No one heeds it for the occupants of Blickling Hall have grown accustomed to its visits – even the servants hear without a tremor the rustling of its ghostly garments,' wrote William A Dutt in the early 1900s in *Highways and Byways in East Anglia*.

Sir Henry spent £10,000 on the rebuilding of Blickling and oversaw one of the finishing touches on the rainwater hoppers – the casting of his initial 'H' together with a 'D' for his wife, 'J' for his son John and 'P' for his daughter-in-law Philippa. Blickling is like a pocket-size version of Hatfield House and infinitely desirable as a result. Rather than being overwhelmed at its entrance court, you marvel at it. The house is light, elegant and happy-looking to this day and its Jacobean exterior remains untouched. Inside, however, the Georgian Hobarts could not resist re-creating the Adam style, though one room, the long gallery which stretches almost the whole length of the east front for 123 feet, escaped. The Hobarts' relationship with Blickling ended when the eleventh Marquess of Lothian, its ultimate inheritor, left it to the National Trust on his death in 1940. He was an idealist and an eccentric. Blickling had become gloomy and had long been let when he decided to move there in

1932. He employed thirty-three workmen to bring the house back to life.

The garden to the east of the house has undergone all the fashionable changes that owners were wont to make because they were so fashion-conscious. The Jacobean garden was formal with geometrical layouts of walks, hedges, beds and rectangles. The entire scheme was swept away in the early eighteenth century and the garden made to appear more expansive and natural-looking. The eighteenth century saw various additions of temples, statues and a beautiful orangery. In the 1820s the Norfolk-born John Adey Repton, Humphry Repton's son, was employed and all the latest trellises, pedestals, alcove seats and even Repton's Hardenburg basket were introduced. In the 1870s a complicated new form of flower garden was executed and extraordinarily elaborate flowerbeds abounded, much to the consternation of Christopher Hussey who, in the 1930s wrote in *Country Life*: 'To the modern eye the pattern area is too small in scale. The lines of the design are lost in a multiplicity of dotted beds, beautifully filled but without perceptible relation to each other or to the house.' Today the garden remains as its last designer, Norah Lindsay, left it – a tribute to its Jacobean past.

'The situation is highly pleasing' wrote Hannah More in 1777. 'More so to me than any I have seen in the east. You admire Houghton, but you wish for Blickling; you look at Houghton with astonishment, at Blickling with desire . . . the park, wood and water of this place are superior to those of any of the neighbouring estates.'

HOUGHTON HALL

Norfolk

Norfolk is never as flat as in the imagination. Beyond Houghton's verdant park, huge cornfields of bright brown earth roll gently out of the sound of the sea and the narrow ribbons of road cut between wide grass verges which once were drove roads. The ancient, dead-straight Peddar's Way track crosses over and over the winding ways to Houghton from Sedgeford and Snettisham, Amner and Hillington, Flitcham and Grimston. Families on their summer

holidays sit restlessly in hot, full cars, crowding the main roads to Hunstanton and Cromer, longing for the sea, little knowing what they are passing by just a village or two away. Small plantations of woodland begin to abound at Bunkers Hill two miles away and there are thick dark woods at Blackground. Then the house is suddenly before you, beyond the great iron gates – the herd of white deer grazing in the distance across the park – a paragon of beauty, Houghton's haunting quality has much to do with its loneliness, its being away from the world and this is perhaps why that social butterfly Horace Walpole, whose father had built the house, eschewed it: 'In the days when all my soul was tuned to pleasure and vivacity, I hated Houghton and all its solitude; Houghton I know not what to call it, a monument or ruin!'

The Walpoles had been living at Houghton for nearly 600 years when Sir Robert Walpole, the first prime minister of England, was born. It was he who built this discreetly beautiful, pale-faced Palladian palace which was, and still is, the largest house in Norfolk. The original

designs were prepared by Colen Campbell in 1721, but Sir Robert then employed the Yorkshireman Thomas Ripley who was said to have walked to London to seek his fortune. He started work as a carpenter and ended by succeeding Grinling Gibbons as 'chief carpenter to the King's works'. Houghton was his first architectural job (he built The Admiralty two years later). Campbell had designed towers for the corners of the house but Walpole, who wanted to out-do his contemporaries, asked for cupolas. He certainly did not wish to have his house built of brick – the only material available in Norfolk. Ripley suggested the extravagant measure of using stone from Yorkshire to face the house. It was quarried near Whitby and brought down by boat to King's Lynn. The result was spectacular; Houghton became a star.

If Walpole's heart was hard, his eye was faultless. As well as spotting the talents of the untried and untested Ripley, he also gave William Kent his first big architectural job. Most of Houghton's ceilings, mouldings, floors, state beds, tables and chairs were designed by the great man and remain in the house. Walpole's collection of pictures was legendary but, after his death, it was sold to Catherine of Russia in order to pay the debt of his grandson, the third Earl of Oxford, who had let the estate run to rack and ruin. (A Holbein was recently sold by the present marquess which should maintain Houghton for posterity.)

After Sir Robert's demise, Houghton was seldom so loved again. It has never changed hands but it has often lain empty, for when male heirs ran out and the Cholmondeleys came into Houghton through the female line, they favoured their estate in Cheshire. Houghton was hardly used in the nineteenth century. It was offered to the Duke of Wellington, who preferred Strathfield Saye, and later to Edward VII, who bought Sandringham instead. Without Sir Robert's magic hand, Houghton became a melancholy place. However in 1913 it was revitalized by the fifth Marquess of Cholmondeley and his wife, the fabled Sybil Sassoon – heiress to her brother Sir Philip – who lived there for over fifty years and lavished it with pictures and love. Today, their grandson follows in their footsteps and never tires of improving it, most lately by restoring the huge walled garden: 'My grandmother always talked of Houghton as Sir Robert's house, and this has guided me in all the changes I have made . . . Houghton today is a synthesis of Walpole, Cholmondeley and Sassoon elements, reflecting the ups and downs of nearly 300 years of history, while still dominated by the ebullient personality, energy and taste of Sir Robert.' Houghton will always have a faint air of melancholy when the rooks caw in the evenings. The small church in the park, with its tower built by Sir Robert, houses no monument to the creator of the acres of beauty outside it.

*A view of the astonishing
front entrance through the
scarcely less astonishing
forecourt screen. The
flanking piers are capped
by consoles bearing
sarcophagi.*

Harlaxton is so extraordinary and so dreamlike that it is almost unreal. It spreads its splendour gigantically at the end of a short avenue and entering the main body of the house is possibly like entering heaven. Above the cedar staircase is a swirling mass of clouds and swags and shells and tassels and putti and baskets of fruit topped by a pale blue clouded sky. The house is one man's wild and extraordinary vision – Gregory Gregory's – and its first designs were carried out by an up-and-coming architect of the day, the thirty-two-year-old Anthony Salvin. Mr Gregory was not, as might be expected, one of the new rich who were building sizeable houses through the nineteenth century but instead was a cultivated bachelor who had inherited a modest amount of money through local property. Harlaxton was his personal fantasy which probably cost him around £200,000 and to which he devoted all his time and energy. He never married and had few staff by Victorian standards (only fourteen). It is somehow sad that the house seems to have been built for many more servants, children and guests – even the attic bedrooms have decorated ceilings. The plaster work and stucco work are perhaps a statement of Mr Gregory's unrequited love and fantasy family life.

When Charles Greville, a guest of the Duke of Rutland, was staying at Belvoir Castle nearby, he visited Harlaxton on 4 January 1838 with various members of his house party: 'To-day we went to see the house Mr Gregory is building, five miles from here. He is a gentleman of about £12,000 a year, who has a fancy to build a magnificent house in the Elizabethan style, and he is now in the middle of his work, all the shell being finished except one wing. Nothing can be more perfect than it is, both as to the architecture and the ornaments; but it stands on the slope of a hill upon a deep clay soil, with no park around it, very little wood, and scarcely any fine trees. Many years ago, when he first conceived his design, he began to amass money and lived for no other object. He travelled into all parts of Europe collecting objects of curiosity, useful or ornamental, for his projected palace, and he did not begin to build until he had accumulated money enough to complete his design. The grandeur of it is such, and such the tardiness of its progress, that it is about as much as he will do to live till its completion; and as he is not married, has no children, and dislikes the heir on whom his property is entailed, it is the means and not the end to which he looks for gratification. He said that it is his amusement, as hunting or shooting or feasting may be the objects of other people; and as the pursuit leads him into all parts of the world, and to mix with every variety of nation and character, besides engendering tastes pregnant with instruction and curious research, it is not irrational, although he should never inhabit his house, and may be toiling and saving for the benefit of persons he cares nothing about.'

HARLAXTON MANOR

Lincolnshire

The Gregory family, through a succession of widowers and bachelors, held on to Harlaxton until the 1930s by which time it was nothing more than a shell with one bathroom, and no electricity or telephone. In 1937 an advertisement ran in *The Times*: 'To save from demolition, a purchaser required for Harlaxton Manor near Grantham. The labour of an age in piled stones, it ranks definitely as one of the stately homes of England. Ample suites of reception rooms, eighty bedrooms . . .' Mrs Violet van der Elst, a dedicated campaigner against capital punishment and a spiritualist, came forward and saved it, and in consequence Henry Thorold, the great Lincolnshire historian, believes she should be canonized. She spent over £250,000 on Harlaxton, which was made through the first brushless shaving cream 'Shavex', the manufacture of which she had pioneered in her kitchen. She also produced other beauty preparations and the door to her sitting-room used to be covered in a thickly padded material which, when pressed, exuded scent. Today what Alec Clifton-Taylor describes as 'this unforgettable and amazing house' is used and looked after by the University of Evansville and has 160 students in residence during its academic year.

LEFT
The cedar staircase, an extraordinary baroque composition animated by theatrical plasterwork.

BELTON HOUSE
Lincolnshire

Belton House is sublime. It was built like so many of Britain's great houses on the spoils of the great Elizabethan legal bonanza. Richard Brownlow entered the Inner Temple in 1583 and after only eight years he was earning £6,000 a year. He spent at least two-thirds of his income on buying land for investment, some of which was in Lincolnshire, but preferred to live with his wife Catherine in Enfield nearer London. On his death the estates he had accrued were divided between his two surviving sons and 'Old' John was left Belton as well as surrounding estates. Having no children the latter passed Belton to one of his nephews, 'Young' John on the condition that he should marry his cousin Alice Sherard. They appeared to have fallen in love by natural causes and were married in Henry VII's chapel in Westminster Abbey when they were both just sixteen years old.

The young couple threw themselves full tilt into London society, bought a substantial house where Bloomsbury Square now stands and decided to build a house on their estate in Lincolnshire which befitted their rank. Discussion will always continue regarding who was the author of Belton House. It certainly resembled almost to a 'T' the demolished Clarendon House in London which had been built by the genius of his age Sir Roger Pratt. All through the nineteenth century it was assumed that Sir Christopher Wren had been the architect, but rich men of that Carolean period could order a house on the very latest lines quite easily – lines which were in fact English reinterpretations of Italian architecture – and Sir John Brownlow would certainly have got the best the doctor could order. The latest theory is that William Winde, who was a fellow member of the Royal Society with Sir Christopher Wren, was its possible architect. Whoever designed the house, it was the builders who applied the final magic; they were the ones who fitted the house into its sweeping Lincolnshire landscape. Belton feels inexplicably right. This has something to do with a perfection of scale which is inimitable and indefinable. When you first see Belton, perhaps from a lane high on the hill above, it simply takes your breath away.

Successive Brownlows tried to imprint their tastes upon the house and various members of the Wyatt family were employed to override the perfection of the original Carolean house. A Wyatt doorway still spoils the entrance front but otherwise it was the enlightened late Victorian Brownlows who took away all the Wyatt trickery and brought the house back to its virtual virgin state. They even commissioned neo-Carolean interiors and in this were forerunners of a new attitude to architecture which began at the start of the twentieth century. Addy (Arthur) and Adelaide Brownlow Cust were a good and worthy couple who played a large part in local life, he as Lord Lieutenant to Lincolnshire, she as the perfect hostess at Belton. They also moved in a *risqué* circle known as the Souls, a group of high-minded and intellectual aristocrats whose band included Arthur Balfour, Margot Tennant, George Curzon and the childless Addy and Adelaide's cousin and heir, the notorious Harry Cust. The group of Souls began after a dinner party given by the Brownlows in the late 1880s when Lord Charles Beresford, who was present, ridiculed the intensity of the conversations the rest of the dinner party were having and said, 'You all sit and talk about each other's souls – I shall call you the Souls.'

Harry Cust, who was to inherit Belton, died four years before Addy. He was one of the greatest womanizers of his age and having seduced half of London society, he married Nina, the daughter of Sir William Welby-Gregory who lived not far from Belton. In true Byronic style he wrote poetry and his best-known work 'Non Nobis' is in the *Oxford Book of English Verse*. The Brownlow family eventually relinquished Belton to the National Trust in the late 1970s – it having already been the centre of great romantic intrigue and speculation during the 1930s. Peregrine Cust and his wife Kitty were close friends of the Prince of Wales, who often came to stay at Belton in the company of Wallis Simpson. When Edward succeeded to the throne in 1936, 'Perry' Brownlow was made Lord in Waiting to the King and was his most valued adviser. He tried in vain to get Mrs Simpson to stay at Belton for he feared that if she went abroad the King would follow her. Mrs Simpson eventually went to Cannes and Perry Brownlow pressured her to renounce the King and advised her on the wording of an announcement saying that she had given him up. In the end it was up to the King himself and it was he who decided to abdicate. Perry was always connected with the abdication although he had done his utmost to make things, 'right'.

BELOW

Dorney from the north, with the late fifteenth-century parlour
wing on the left. On the far right is the Tudor brick tower of
the parish church.

DORNEY COURT

Buckinghamshire

Dorney Court is as English as could be. It has never been got at by over-zealous restorers. It has quietly changed and adapted to suit its owners' needs over the last 600 years and its waving roofs and barge-boarded gables are woven together like tapestry. It really does not matter where the medieval starts or the Victorian begins because it has a completely homogenous feel and demonstrates that as long as a family loves a house it will go on living and adapting on a relative shoestring. The Palmers, who have owned it since the 1500s, have never had any money to speak of. They have simply patched up the house as and when it was necessary as their forebears had always done. If a wall looks as though it might collapse because the original timber is rotting, the wood is simply replaced with seasoned oak by the local building firm who understand the quirks of Dorney Court. The house's survival has depended on this foresight and good stewardship.

A drive through laurel-floored woods leads to this perfect pocket of timelessness among a sea of modern progression. The M4 motorway whirs half a mile away, and the far off fields which fifty years ago were hay, are under houses now, a garden centre spreads its glass houses and sundries through the old kitchen garden. But there stands the manor house, an unperturbed survivor, across a little meadow and backed by the ravishing Tudor church tower, all rose-red brick and half-timbering, straggling, oversailing, and looking as though it were growing out of the ground like the fat sculpted yew hedges which guard it.

Inside, the layout of the house has changed little from the fifteenth century. A protective and cocooning feeling pervades – each room feels like a safe haven, panelled to the hilt. In the cosy parlour several Turkey carpets are laid on top of each other and a huge open fire keeps the room snug and the watery Thames dampness at bay. All around there is an eccentric mix of family treasures, from early portraits of *Seven Eminent Turks* brought back from Constantinople by Sir Roger Palmer, an ambassador to Charles II, to leopard-skin rugs and rocking horses. In the spectacular great hall with its original roof and the linen-fold panelling, there is a large carved stone pineapple standing in the corner which commemorates the first pineapple ever to be grown in Britain – here at Dorney. There is a haunted bedroom which none of the Palmers will sleep in and a pink bathroom suite from the 1930s in an oversailing bathroom. One or two Palmers have protested against the Elizabethan scale in the past. A Victorian family member got fed up with the low-ceilinged dining-room and made himself a mock William and Mary one, and an eighteenth-century Palmer tacked on a flimsy classical front which was later taken off. There was never enough money for a radical and irrecoverable overhaul.

The church, which rambles on to almost touch the court, is calm and happily not Victorianized and still has a family box pew albeit half the height it was originally. The nave and chancel were ceiled for the sake of warmth and comfort. In the little north chapel is the splendid Garrard tomb (sometimes spelt Gerrard, they were grocers who owned the court and gave their name to Gerrards Cross), the family into which the Palmers married in the sixteenth century.

Dorney village, on the west of the huge common, feels half feudal and half commuter-belt. It lies on the west side of the great wide common in this absolutely flat Thames valley country, beyond the willows at Eton Wick. The common is speckled with tethered ponies, sheep and

BELOW
One of a series of seven portraits of sultans brought back from Constantinople in 1663 which are hung in the hall.

cattle, and occasional joggers. It belongs to the lords of the manor of Dorney and its upkeep is settled by the villagers at the manor court each year, a satisfactory system which has been going on for centuries.

MILTON ERNEST HALL

Bedfordshire

Through flattish country north of Bedford, the A6, littered with huge road signs, winds past disused airfields and acres of oil seed rape stretching between young woods and spinneys. Just south of the village of Milton Ernest, there is a view looking down on to the wide level meadows and cornfields of the Great Ouse valley, where cattle graze beside dark grey arches of the railway viaduct, and the Hall suddenly rises gold, cream, brown and red beyond the willows beside the deep-cut river. It is lofty, compact, precise and brilliant.

Milton Ernest Hall is William Butterfield's only country house. He designed it for Benjamin Helps Starey who was married to his sister Anne, to whom Butterfield was very close. They were born a year apart and although Butterfield had six brothers and a sister Jane, he treated the Starey family as his own, always coming to Milton Ernest for Christmas and at other times. His father had been a chemist in the Strand and Butterfield began his career at sixteen, as an apprentice to a builder and then to E L Blackburne, a little-known architect. Butterfield's evangelical upbringing and strong moral convictions led him to move in serious religious circles. He became a member of the Ecclesiological Society in May 1844 which resulted in a series of major church commissions. As Mark Girouard describes in *The Victorian Country House*, 'Butterfield built his life round the Church of England and Gothic architecture and he did not keep them in separate compartments; building was his way of serving the Church, and Gothic architecture an expression of the traditions and values he found in Christianity.' Throughout his life he continued to build churches, rectories, convents, hospitals, colleges (including Oxford's Keeble) and steered clear of the profitable private sector. Milton Ernest was a labour of love for the Stareys.

Benjamin Starey was in the linen-bleaching business and later became a director of Price's Patent Candle Co. He is purported to have invented a plaited wick that did not need snuffing. By the middle of the nineteenth century he had made a lot of money and as a hedge against the inflation he was expecting from the Gold Rush, decided to invest in land. He bought the Milton Ernest estate in 1853 and recorded in his diary on 28 September the same year, 'I took Mr Butterfield to see the house and garden which was desolate. The house thoroughly bad irreparable: and it was decided to build a good family residence which the plans for were then put in hand and in February 1854 we began to take down the old house and stack away the materials.' By July 1858 the Starey family were settled in the new Hall.

Butterfield was highly professional and efficient, an innovator and a perfectionist. He believed in the traditional methods of house building, not with a single firm, but with separate builders and craftsmen, each skilled at their own particular trade. He, or the Clerk of the Works, would then orchestrate the programme. A boat was bought to carry the stone two miles down the Ouse from the stone quarry at Pavenham, and the sand and gravel was dug from the park.

The house rose, with a Gothic castle-cum-convent on its entrace front ('I always thought the fairy princess lived here,' said John Starey who stayed here as a small child in the early 1930s and still lives in the neighbouring Home Farm), and a happy biscuit-coloured stone and polychromatic riot of colours and materials on the garden front. He was the 'good family residence' the Stareys wanted and was as gay as Butterfield could make it. Tall, thin, striped chimneys straddle the precipitously steep tiled roof with its pencil-thin dormer windows, and brick eyebrows rise above the stone-dressed windows. Inside, the rooms are tall and neat with solid and elaborate chimneypieces of different coloured marbles and everywhere there is light. As Butterfield's biographer, Paul Thompson, points out, 'The advantage of Gothic romanticism is that windows could be put in exactly where light was needed'. The library has a high bay window shaped like an apse which looks out across the sunken lawn towards the vestiges of a lime avenue.

Once there was a long avenue of elms which lined the front drive and led from the main road straight-as-a-dye to the Hall. Today the entrance gates are closed, but the church of All Saints, which crowns the rise above the straggling village, still forms the perfectly aligned *point de vue*. The church was restored by Butterfield at the Stareys' expense between 1864 and 1865. After a number of set-backs on the Stock Exchange Benjamin Starey was forced to sell Milton Ernest in 1872 which saddened Butterfield who considered it his home. Lord Ampthill lived here for ten years from 1909, but in 1919 Benjamin's son John Helps, having spent thirty years in Ceylon making money as a tea planter and as an investor in Malaysian rubber plantations, bought the Hall back again. During the Second World War it was requisitioned by the Americans who built Nissen huts all over the park. Glen Miller was billeted here, as is well remembered in the village (he once played at their weekly hop) and it was from the Hall that he left on December 15 in 1944 to take the small plane to Paris which was never seen again.

The Hall is now a nursing home, for which it is admirably suited, but its surroundings have never recovered. The wide lawns are lumpy and rabbit-ridden, beech and laurel hedges have overgrown into small trees, the banks of the Ouse near the house are waist-high with nettles, and the walled garden is choked with weeds.

100 FAVOURITE HOUSES

KELMSCOTT MANOR

Oxfordshire

Kelmscott Manor is well hidden. Its peaceful village lies across willowy meadowland on the Oxfordshire side of the upper Thames where narrow roads wind among low, unhedged fields past barns and dovecotes. Kelmscott's houses and cottages are built of the local pale golden limestone, as is the 'manor', an unassuming sixteenth-century farmhouse built by the Turner family, who farmed the surrounding land for three centuries. They added a wing in the 1670s. In 1871 the Turners let the house to William Morris and Dante Gabriel Rossetti. Down the narrow lane, past the Plough Inn, the glorious gabled manor is glimpsed first above the secretive garden wall. It is its honest ordinariness which appealed so to Morris. 'How I love the earth, and the seasons and the weather, and all things that deal with it, and that grows out of it, as this has done', he wrote.

The inside of the house is much as it was in the 1870s when Morris, the craftsman, poet, manufacturer and socialist, was designing the 'Willow Bough' wallpaper, writing *The Haystack in the Floods*, and watching his wife Jane fall in love with Rossetti. The atmosphere is still redolent of these three pre-Raphaelites, their friends, and generations of Turners before them. The furnishings are hand-woven, the furniture hand-hewn. The sixteenth-century part of the house is rambling and small roomed; the seventeenth-century addition is more open and elegant with Renaissance fireplaces and Jacobean panelling.

Everywhere you look there are paintings by Rossetti, embroidered curtains by Jane, wall hangings by Morris and richly decorated Kelmscott Press books. When you look from a bedroom window to the River Thames meandering slow and wide down from Lechlade towards Oxford, it isn't hard to imagine William Morris coming upon Kelmscott for the first time, having arrived by boat. 'Over the meadow I could see the mingled gables of a building where I knew the lock must be, and which now seemed to combine a mill with it,' he described in *News from Nowhere*. 'A low wooded ridge bounded the river-plain to the south and south-east, whence we had come, and a few low houses lay about its feet and up its slope. I turned a little to my right, and through the hawthorn sprays and long shoots of the wild roses I could see the flat country spreading out far away under the sun of the calm evening, till something that might be called hills with a look of sheep-pastures about them bounded it with a soft blue line. Before me, the elm-boughs still hid most of what houses there might be in this river-side dwelling of men; but to the right of the cart-road a few grey buildings of the simplest kind showed here and there . . . We crossed the road, and again, almost without my will, my hand raised to the latch of a door, and we stood presently on a stone path which led up to the old house.'

Kelmscott is a hard place to leave. It has a strong sense of peace. On the way back along the village street you can see the Ernest Gimson-designed cottage, built for May Morris, William's daughter, in 1915, and the Memorial Cottages designed by Morris' friend and partner, Philip Webb for Mrs Morris in 1902. There is a stone relief on the front carved by George Jack from a sketch by Webb. Last of all, in the cemetery, beside the Church of St George, hidden behind a large bay tree, is the grave of William Morris who died in the early autumn of 1896 and was carried through the village in a yellow farm wagon with red wheels wreathed with vine and willow boughs. Jane, Jenny and May Morris lie beside him, marked by a coped stone which was also designed by his dear friend, Webb. The border encircling the top of the four-poster bed at Kelmscott is hung with Morris' words embroidered by May Morris:

> *The wind's on the wold and*
> *the night is a-cold,*
> *And Thames runs chill*
> *twixt mead and hill*
> *But kind and dear is the*
> *old house here*
> *And my heart is warm*
> *midst winter's harm.*

OPPOSITE
The main entrance, from the gateway to the road.

BELOW
Morris' bedroom. The bed hangings were designed by his daughter, May, in 1891 and the coverlet, embroidered with flowers, was made by his wife.

ROUSHAM HOUSE

Oxfordshire

A single-track tree-shaded road leads through this dim corner of golden-stoned Oxfordshire towards Rousham where, on the village street, a Victorian gate lodge of lichen-covered stone with tall ornamental chimneys and box parterre heralds the house. Huge limes line the curving drive through the park where strawberry roan Longhorn cattle graze and the stern façade of the hall looks haughtily down its short avenue. There are Mille-feuille booted bantams, with feathers like tortoiseshell butterflies, strutting about the utterly beautiful stable block.

Rousham is ravishing in every way. It is William Kent's masterpiece. Horace Walpole eulogized it – in essence he said it was 'Kentissimo'. Kent was a true artist,

OPPOSITE

A prominent feature of the gardens is the Praeneste Terrace, an arcade of seven pedimented arches, overlooking the river.

character and soon made a lot of influential friends, among whom was the future Earl of Leicester for whom he was to later build Holkham Hall in Norfolk and also the Earl of Burlington to whom he became very close. It was the latter who introduced Kent to the owner of Rousham, General James Dormer, an old soldier who had served with the Duke of Marlborough and had been Britain's minister in Lisbon. He was fond of the fashionable artistic clique who included such figures as Swift and Pope, and often had them to stay at Rousham. Dormer was already quite old and ill by the time he thought of asking Kent to make alterations to his house and redesign his garden. 'If Kent can be persuaded to come I shall take it very kindly', he said.

Pope's *Genius of the Place* was duly consulted and Kent created the magic that Rousham now possesses. He dressed up the Jacobean house which had been built by Sir Robert Dormer in a straight battlemented parapet and he glazed the windows with octagonal panes. He made low wings on the garden side with little Gothic ogee niches and inside he embellished one small room with every trick in his book from over-doors to over-mantels to swirly scrolls and swags so that it remains a homage to his genius.

The garden, lovingly maintained by the present owners, the Cottrell-Dormers, remains almost exactly as he planned it although grown now to matured perfection. A mile away on the near horizon stands a sham ruin to act as an eye catcher and below it a mill, rendered romantically picturesque by Kent. Across the park to the west there is a Palladian gateway and beside it Cow Castle with a stable on one side and a garden seat on the other. Kent dictated the way he wanted his visitors to walk so that everywhere there were surprises and vistas and, as Walpole wrote in a letter, '. . . the garden is Daphne in little, the sweetest little groves, streams, glades, porticos, cascades and river imaginable; all the scenes are perfectly classic'. The River Cherwell winds at the bottom of the gardens, and paths wander this way and that, giving sudden and unexpected views of sculptures, temples and pools.

Nearer the house is a huge walled garden with one of the best herbaceous borders possible. A small pond in its midst is stuffed full of great crested newts, there is an ancient and perfect orchard, and rising beyond is the church tower with its beautiful-sounding bells. The best of England is rolled into one here at Rousham.

ABOVE

The north front, facing the garden. The central block, designed in 1635, was given new bay windows in the nineteenth century. It is linked to the small wings added by William Kent in 1738–40.

miles ahead of his time, and was the forerunner of the whole Romantic movement of the seventeenth century. His garden designs were a snub to the rigid formality of what had gone before. He did away with flowerbeds within sight of the house to give the impression that the surrounding lawns merged seamlessly into the park beyond. Animals were kept at bay by an invisible ha-ha and everywhere was verdant glory.

William Kent was born at Bridlington in Yorkshire in 1685 and began his apprenticeship as a coach painter in Hull. A member of the local gentry noticed his talent for painting and a group of Yorkshire squires raised the money to send him to Italy where he accompanied the collector John Tellman. He was obviously an engaging

STANTON HARCOURT MANOR

Oxfordshire

The Harcourts are the only surviving Norman Conquest family in Oxfordshire. The tattered remains of the standard carried for Henry VII at the Battle of Bosworth Field still hangs over Robert Harcourt's tomb in the village church. They abandoned Stanton in 1688 and built another house nearby at Cokethorpe, and then another at Nuneham Courtney in the 1750s. Meanwhile Stanton decayed but the gatehouse, curving long and low down a little lane to the church, was used at various times as a dower house. The Harcourts finally came back here after the Second World War.

Where the River Windrush splits in two and winds through marshy meadows to a slow bend in the Thames, Stanton Harcourt lies low among pools, ditched pastureland and willows. Pylons strut across the middle distance, and all around are huge lakes in old gravel workings. House-high elders and guelder roses fill the verges along the watery, yellow-flagged way to the village. You feel you have reached a magical island – thatched cottages, the stuff of calendars, line the street and gradually the vestiges of one of the earliest unfortified manor houses in England begin to unfurl. There is no pomp and ceremony: the entrance curls in past the Manor Farm – once part of the great house – to a jumble of farm buildings.

You walk through a stone arch in the wall into Arcadia. The gatehouse, half in the shade of a walnut tree and half covered with *Magnolia grandiflora* and wisteria, encloses one side of the garden and ancient battlemented walls the others. Across the lawn at the end of a little avenue of Irish yews shaped like large green bottles is 'Pope's Tower' whose low doorway set among ferns reveals the original manor chapel complete with fan vaulting, red brocade kneelers, jugs of roses, a John Piper pen and ink of Saints and an air of recent worship. During two secluded summers, when the manor had already been deserted for thirty odd years, Alexander Pope translated the fifth volume of Homer's *Iliad* in the little panelled room at the top of the tower. The romance of the ruin had captured his imagination.

Against the garden walls whose crevices are filled with self-seeded snapdragons and ornamental thistles, there are headily scented mock orange bushes, Buff Beauty roses, giant mulleins and comforting lashings of goose grass among the columbines. Arched doorways lead from one garden to another. Past lavender and geraniums to where a *Hydrangea petiolaris* climbs sky high up the old kitchen which even Pevsner, not given to superlatives, describes as, 'one of the most completely medieval kitchens in England, and certainly the most spectacular'. This dizzy seventy-foot-high room with conical ceiling and vents for the escaping smoke was fancifully likened by Pope to the Forge of Vulcan, the Cave of Plyphems and the Temple of Moloch. It now houses a number of dusty marble busts.

Through another door in the wall there is yet another world of wide walks, high apple trees, old roses, urns in the middle distance, Boar's Hill on the near horizon, and way beyond the line of poplars a Bronze Age stone circle stands firm against encroaching gravel workings. A swan with cygnets on her back sails along an inlet, and there are moorhens and water lilies on the great fish pond and everywhere reflected in the water and at the turn of every path is the beautiful Church of St Michael, stuffed full of Harcourt memorials.

OPPOSITE

Pope's Tower, the chief surviving element of the medieval house, was built in 1460–71 to contain the chapel and priest's lodging. In the background is the church of St Michael.

DRAYTON HOUSE

Northamptonshire

Opposite the proud perpendicular church with its regal stone lantern a lane leads out between stone cottages from the village of Lowick across Harper's Brook and, once over a cattle grid, becomes the ancient drive towards Drayton House. There on a rise above in this wide and undulating park, the house rises in the distance looking like a huddled medieval village with a muddle of chimneys, curling smoke and towers rising up from within a protective wall. As you get nearer, elaborate battlements and cupolas focus on the skyline and you realize that you are nearing a noble pile. Drayton is incomparable. In 1,000 years it has never been let or sold. It has passed from the de Drayton family through marriages or some other family connection to the present owners, the Stopford Sackvilles. The house, with a pure thirteenth-century Gothic undercroft, has grown organically in the pale grey limestone of the region to become one of the most glorious houses in the land.

As the drive turns in towards the entrance front you realize that the house is surrounded by a series of formal enclosures containing gardens, a huge fish pond and the entrance court, all walled in the same gentle grey stone. The walls are pierced with arched entrances or grand gate piers from which flows the most beautiful iron work of any country house. From the entrance court flanked on its southern side by the stables you walk through a great crenellated wall, to an inner court which stops you in your tracks. Ahead a façade, like a stage set screening the old house behind, rises up golden and swaggering, a real work of art – baroque to the hilt with long differently

pedimented windows and classical busts above and urns standing on top of the dramatic parapet. Shallow steps lead up to the central windowed doorway above which a huge carved military trophy spills. On either side are classical colonnades. Drayton's beauty is transcendent. This formal approach and startlingly grand entrance feels decidedly un-English. Perhaps this is because there is no other house like it: it is rare in having retained its seventeenth-century formality around it, unlike most other grand houses whose owners swept it away in the rush for eighteenth-century improvements.

Although there are large sections of the house built by Simon de Drayton in the thirteenth century, and many subsequent enlargements, it was in fact Sir John Germain who gave Drayton its crowning glories. He was a shadowy figure and is suggested by some to be an illegitimate brother of William of Orange. He married Mary, Lord Peterborough's daughter, who was formerly married to the Duke of Norfolk. She died in 1705 and, much to her family's fury, left Drayton to her Dutch husband.

It was Germain's connection with the Royal family which perhaps enabled him to employ all the top craftsmen of the day who were working on various royal palaces. First there was the great architect William Talman who was Wren's contemporary, then there was the ironsmith Jean Tijou and the cabinet maker Gerrit Jensen. It was the combination of these virtuosos of their day, adding to the already great additions by the third Lord Mordaunt in the 1580s and Lord Peterborough from the 1650s onwards, which has made Drayton so exceptional.

Inside there is the same harmony which flows through the whole and yet the house contains every grand element of every period that you would expect. The vaulted undercroft leads easily into the medieval great hall, which in turn was transformed at the end of the seventeenth century by the insertion of panelling and a barrel ceiling. The dining-room is smothered in fine late eighteenth-century plaster work by William Rhodes set with oval mirrors from which candelabras reflect their glow. The walnut staircase at one end of the house, to compliment the oak staircase at the other, is one of the wonders of its period. It is a timber spiralled cantilever stair built about 1680 of oak with a winding walnut balustrade and is even earlier than Wren's famous cantilever stone stair in St Paul's Cathedral.

From every window distant views of Northamptonshire are framed by the formal walled gardens. Perhaps the saving of Drayton from the fashion gurus of the eighteenth and nineteenth centuries was through Lord Germain's second wife, Lady Betty, who on being widowed preferred to stay with her cousins, the Sackvilles of Knole (see page 65). Having no children she left Drayton to a Sackville and thus it remained a secondary house until the 1840s when it was carefully redecorated.

CANONS ASHBY
Northamptonshire

In this mild, unnoticed corner of Northamptonshire the village of Canons Ashby is now nothing more than a few cottages with a strange truncated church full of Dryden memorials but once, before the Black Death, it had been much bigger. That was when the Augustinian canons had their priory here and their great fish ponds were well stocked. By the middle of the sixteenth century, the priory had gone and this house had evolved – always quiet, always unassuming. 'Everything appears to be a natural growth of the circumstances', wrote the architect J A Gotch in 1921, 'not calling for admiration, as in many modern fine houses, but quietly compelling it. Quiet it is, indeed, the keynote of the place, a quietude conducive to study and to the maintenance of old-fashioned peaceful ways.'

The Copes, a prominent Puritan family from Banbury, had acquired the priory lands after the dissolution of the monasteries and soon afterwards John Dryden, a member of an old Cumbrian family, married a daughter of Sir John Cope and it was they who built the core of the present house – a great hall range with a kitchen at one end and a tower at the other in red brick. The house was then extended by Sir Erasmus Dryden at the end of the sixteenth century who enclosed the courtyard and decorated the 'Spenser Room' and the Winter Parlour. He was a friend of the poet Spenser who is supposed to have stayed at Canons Ashby. The Drydens were Parliamentarians during the Civil War and used to leave food on the wall beside the road for the soldiers. This so annoyed the Cavaliers that they quite often came in the middle of the night and stole it. The last major changes to Canons Ashby were in 1710 when Edward Dryden succeeded (a nephew of the poet laureate, John). He put on a modern front with sash windows and terraced the gardens with walls and beautiful gateways, flights of steps and vases. He also planted the yew trees.

Canons Ashby's unhurried air has much to do with its Victorian incumbent, Sir Henry Dryden, who lived here for sixty years and was an antiquary. Unlike nearly every Victorian house owner he was not an 'improver'; he merely relished what was already around him. He had his clothes made for him in the village, and as they never changed in style, by the end of the 1880s he was still wearing nankeen trousers, a striped waistcoat and a loose cravat which were the fashion in the Regency period. He wrote articles on diverse subjects and produced a folio volume on St Magnus' Cathedral, Kirkwall, in the Orkneys. He stored thousands of measured drawings that he had made of Canons Ashby and other churches and buildings in the country in his book room and he gave a lecture to the Northamptonshire Archaeological Society entitled 'On Mistakes Concerning Architecture Committed By Myself'. In fact he was rather a good architect and designed many of the cottages in and around the village and the estate. Church Cottage, on the roadside between the house and the church, is a typical example of his quiet style. He was an indefatigable walker and sometimes used to dress up as a tramp and make friends with wayfarers along the road. He would then tell them where they could expect a good meal and, taking a short cut across the fields back to Canons Ashby he would be there in time to entertain his astonished comrades plying them with ale he had made. It contained a lot of bicarbonate of soda and was brewed in the brew house across the pebbled court. He had only one daughter who was an accomplished historian herself, a photographer and the author of several books on such diverse subjects as the art of hunting and church embroidery.

After Henry's death the house passed to his younger brother, Alfred, who lived in Putney and practised as a barrister. However five years after inheriting Canons Ashby he decided to move here permanently. His son, Sir Arthur, continued to live here until his death in 1938 and from then on Canons Ashby was let and fell into bad repair. The National Trust has now restored the house and gardens to a state the anonymous author of the 1904 article on Canons Ashby in *Country Life* would have approved of. 'Alterations and additions were made to the house in the times of Queen Elizabeth, James I and Queen Anne; but from the latter date onward the successive owners have been wise enough to preserve the house, both outside and inside, from the vandalism which has disfigured so many of the medieval mansions of "merrie England", and Canons Ashby and its surroundings are now much what they were in the Queen Anne period, when the men, in all the bravery of embroidered coats, and the ladies in their dainty brocades and laces, may have paced the terraced garden or wandered beneath the spreading trees which surround the mansion.'

OPPOSITE

On the edge of what is still a quiet country road, Canons Ashby has scarcely changed in outward appearance since the early eighteenth century, when the doorcase visible in this photograph was added; it leads into the hall. The sixteenth-century entrance tower is visible rising above the roofs on the right.

EASTON NESTON

Northamptonshire

Easton Neston is not so much grand as perfect. It does not flaunt itself, it does not stand high on a hill commanding the countryside all around but instead retains a rare and settled dignity. It remains noble as the day it was born at the turn of the seventeenth century. Its proportions are so right that the first sight of the house takes your breath away, its stone from nearby Helmsdon is as fine as England can produce and the giant columns and pilasters with their Corinthian capitals retain all their virgin crispness.

On the southern boundary of this placid county of 'spires, squires and mires', Easton Neston's park slopes towards Towcester where inns abound along the original Watling Street and the racecourse crowns the hill. Down Mill Lane in a small cottage the sieve-maker Peter Empson had lived with his son Richard in the fifteenth century. The boy grew up to become Henry VII's chief financier and, with his pockets well lined, came home to buy the estate of Easton Neston, 'the Elysian fields' he had looked on as a child. He got a licence to empark and to crenellate his house in 1599. However he did not enjoy the high life for long – six years later he was beheaded by Henry VIII, and the estate was eventually bought in 1535 by the Fermor family, whose fortune accrued as their social status ascended over the following century.

In 1692, Sir William Fermor was made Lord Lempster and being a cousin of Sir Christopher Wren asked the great man to design his new country house. Wren almost certainly built the brick-and-stone-dressed wing originally, one of two and designed to flank the main house, but it was his pupil Nicholas Hawksmoor who took over the building and made the central block his own. It was built in the mid-1690s and its grand front, which differed from the original model, was put on a little later and finished in 1702. This was the age of powerful and cultivated architecture and on its completion the house was manifoldly praised. 'It cannot be easily surpassed by any seat in Europe,' wrote John Morton later in the eighteenth century in his *History of Northamptonshire*.

The windows are as tall as the cedar trees on the lawn; the hall, though shortened with a new ceiling from its original height, is lofty, majestic, and dwarfs the gumboots which litter its entrance. The cantilevered stone staircase, as simple and elegant a piece of engineering as any modern technology could produce,

RIGHT

A view across the entrance forecourt to the west front. On the left is the surviving wing of the late seventeenth-century house which Hawksmoor remodelled.

LEFT
Although much of the
interior has been
altered, Hawksmoor's
staircase remains as he
designed it, with its
magnificent wrought-
iron balustrade. The
monochrome wall
paintings were
executed by Thornhill
in 1709–11.

has the shallowest of steps, which give the climber or descender the effect of gliding upwards or downwards. Whereas the principal rooms are of double-height, on each side of the house is a small, wooden staircase off which spring four floors whose rooms are low, cosy and panelled. The former dining-room, now the drawing-room, sports the most elaborate plasterwork of the 1730s which swirls round huge and rather intimidating hunting pictures, inducing Mr Pevsner to describe the effect as 'gay, but curiously restless'. The house has a predominantly eighteenth-century feel, with its light, elegant rooms and lack of passages, although there have been changes: besides the hall renovation, Christian, Lady Hesketh commissioned Roderick Gradidge and David Hicks to make a small second library, with exaggerated cornice and projecting piers.

Hawksmoor planned grand formal gardens around his new house, in the manner of Le Nôtre, and the eastern view was punctuated by a great canal. The latter remains a vestige of Hawksmoor's vanished vision. If you stand on the stone stairway which leads from the house to the garden the canal shimmers in the distance across the park, drawing the eye to far-off new woods created by the present Lord Hesketh who has done much planting throughout the estate. In the 1920s Sir Thomas Fermor Hesketh brought back much of the garden's formality which the Georgian landscapers had swept away. He made a formal forecourt at the front of the house and elaborate parterres on the garden side with squiggles of yew among brick patios and a spectacular circular basin with a fountain in its midst. In the tall trees beyond, the present Lady Hesketh cleared large tracts of tangled undergrowth in which she discovered a lake and small island – part of a lost landscaping scheme. It is now restored.

The long, languorous drive which leads to the London road and the grandest Coade stone gatescreen ever seen, passes through Towcester Racecourse with its inspired stand designed by Frank Roberts in 1997.

BELOW

*From the west, the house nestles into the landscape, perhaps
explaining why it was once known as 'Compton-in-the-Hole'.
The porch is one of the later Tudor embellishments to a much
plainer house of about 1500.*

COMPTON WYNYATES

Warwickshire

Lost among wide-verged lanes where oaks tower above the hedgerows and small golden-stone villages huddle around greens, Compton Wynyates lies low in its secret bowl of steep, tree-girt hills. To the north-west the great bowl opens out on to a gentle downward slope towards the wide Warwickshire vale below – its small woods and copses shaped by centuries of hunting. 'When I came out in front of the house from a short and steep but stately avenue,' wrote Henry James in *English Houses*, 'I said to myself that here surely we had arrived at the farthest limits of what ivy-smothered brick-work and weather-beaten gables, conscious old windows and clustered mossy roofs can accomplish for the eye. It is impossible to imagine a more finished picture. And its air of solitude and delicate decay – of having been dropped into its grassy hollow as an ancient jewel is deposited upon a cushion, and being shut in from the world and back into the past by its circling woods – all this drives the impression well home. The house is not large, as great houses go, and it sits, as I have said, upon the grass, without even a flagging or a footpath to conduct you from the point where the avenue stops to the beautiful sculptured doorway which admits you into the small, quaint inner court. From this court you are at liberty to pass through the crookedest series of oaken halls and chambers, adorned with treasures of old wainscotting and elaborate doors and chimneypieces.'

Compton Wynyates stands as a proud reminder of just how beautifully the English could build in their own inimitable style. It is the last blast of an unassuming and innocent art without any fanciful foreign trappings – architecture without architects. The bricks change colour from rose to red to orange to umber. The stone dressings are of golden limestone, now lichen encrusted, the roofs' tiny stone slates are like scales of a fish. Each façade ebbs and flows, its windows vary in size, its chimneys rise above at undulating heights. It is a symphony of asymmetry which as a whole is more beautiful and homogenous than any rigid symmetry could ever be. Nikolaus Pevsner describes it as England's most perfect picturesque house. Perhaps the perfection of its indefinably appealing scale has something to do with the house having been once enclosed by a moat so that any additions and changes had to be confined in the compact, allotted space. Perhaps the calm of the place has to do with the security of its encompassing and descending parkland and terraced lawns.

Some say Wynyates was derived from the name 'wind-gates' which alludes to the wind that blows from the north through the north-west entrance to the bowl in which the house sits. Others say it is derived from a vineyard which used to thrive on the southern terraced slope of the park above the now vanished medieval village that stood near the Comptons' fortified manor house within its moat. The Comptons have been at Compton Wynyates since the 1100s. The house that stands today was built at the hand of Edmund Compton and more predominantly his son William who built the entrance porch with its beautiful carved animals around the arch, the towers and the chapel. Close friend and Keeper of the Privy Purse to Henry VIII, William was knighted and given the privilege of adding the Royal Lion of England to his coat of arms. He was also given the dilapidated Fulbrook Castle near Warwick, which he then proceeded to use as a quarry with which to enhance Compton Wynyates. Legend has it that the chimneys which now tower above the house were brought in their entirety from Fulbrook, so strong was their mortar. The Great Hall's timbers and oriel window are certainly from Fulbrook.

Sir William's descendants, who became earls of Northampton in 1618, remained close to the Royal family and until the onset of the Civil War had entertained every crowned head at their conveniently placed house in the very heart of England. They played a strategic part in fighting for Charles I against Cromwell: the second Earl and three of his loyal sons took part in the Battle of Edgehill (the latter were knighted on the field). The Earl was killed at the Battle of Hopton Heath in 1643. His sons continued defending the cause but Compton Wynyates was captured in 1644 after a two-day siege. The Roundheads tore down the church, and threw the Compton tombs and effigies into the moat. Despite a valiant last effort six months later, when the Comptons returned in the dead of night and recaptured the stables and outbuildings, they were ultimately unsuccessful. The Parliamentarians ordered that the moat be filled in to stop any further attempt at defence and the family finally repaired to their other home of Castle Ashby.

In 1774, the eighth Earl of Northampton lost vast amounts of money in an electioneering campaign which went wrong. From Switzerland where he had holed up, he directed his agent to pull down the redundant Compton Wynyates in an effort to cut costs. The latter took no heed and instead denuded the house of its furniture and ornament in order to pay off the debts. Towards the end of the nineteenth century, the Comptons finally came back to their beloved Compton Wynyates and from then on it has continued to be their family home.

HONINGTON HALL

Warwickshire

'There is no better way to plunge *in medias res*, for the stranger who wishes to know something of England, than to spend a fortnight in Warwickshire. It is the core and centre of the English world: midmost England, unmitigated England', wrote Henry James. Stratford-upon-Avon is no longer unmitigated England, but Honington most assuredly is.

Down the big bold Cotswold hills past the Whispering Knights and the Rollright Stones into less swaggering terrain, Warwickshire's countryside is unshowy and unassuming. No more are there thousands of enormous elms, known as 'Warwickshire weeds', along the hedgerows. At Long Compton the feeling of the Cotswolds fades fast – over the lich-gate to the church is a tiny thatched cottage of brick and half timbering.

Towards Stratford on the eastern banks of the Stour lies the village of Honington. Gate piers topped with stone pineapples stand on either side of the turning and herald the way down across a beautiful four-arched bridge with ball finials on the parapets. Between the leaning alders you can glimpse the hall itself in the half distance – 'unmitigated England'. A little further on, the road leads through the village green straddled by houses and cottages, some pale or dark gold stone, some brick like the satisfactory farmhouse with ivy neatly trimmed against it, one black and white and at the eastern end of the village the perfect, thatched 'Rose Cottage', pale blue paintwork against its white-washed walls and carpets of grape hyacinths lining the garden path to the trellis porch over the front door. It is as opposite as you could get to the grander-than-grand gate piers to the hall, which are red brick and vermiculated stone topped by newly restored stone balls ten times the size of a football. The mild park spreads out towards the far off and lofty spire of Tredington Church and then to the west there is a sudden and heart-stopping view of the front of the house.

Honington Hall has an utter, indefinable rightness of scale about it. It is built of brick the colour of mid-red wallflowers and just as rich, its stone dressings are golden, its elegance sublime. Over the ground floor windows are busts of Roman emperors let into stone arches, and under the hipped roof there is a deep white-painted cornice. It was built in 1682 by an inspired unknown, for Henry

RIGHT

All Saints, the parish church, was largely rebuilt in 1680–85. In the distance is the early-eighteenth-century monument to Sir Henry Parker and his son, Hugh.

OPPOSITE

Busts of emperors in oval recesses enliven the entrance front, which faces east.

Parker who was MP for Evesham, a merchant tailor and owned a coffee house near the Temple. In his monument in the church he looks very self-important, depicted standing life size in white veined marble talking to his son Hugh who predeceased him. They are both wearing high-heeled buckled shoes, long flamboyant curly wigs half-way down their backs and voluminous cloaks. By the 1740s the Hall had been sold to the son of a London brewer, Joseph Townsend, who married Judith Gore, a Yorkshire heiress. They went to town on the house in no uncertain manner, replacing the Carolean casement windows with sash, building on an octagonal saloon and swathing the inside of the house with the most rich and sumptuous plasterwork imaginable. Some say it is by Charles Stanley, the Anglo-Danish sculptor and plasterer who worked in

England at the time of the Townsend's aggrandisements but there is no documentary evidence. Certainly, it is astounding and as you enter the hall, the effect is overwhelmingly wonderful.

From the western windows you can see a porticoed temple and the river below the sloping lawn, and to the south, clipped yew hedges and cedars. The bothy, dovecote and archway of the stables are Elizabethan for there was an earlier house on the site, just as there are the vestiges of an earlier church where now a Carolean church stands, rebuilt by the Packers.

Honington is the best of England, it keeps quietly out of the limelight, and is well-loved and cared for. It is simply just right.

BELOW

*Externally, Arbury's richest effects are concentrated on the south
front, overlooking the garden and lake. The three large windows
in the centre light the dining-room.*

ARBURY HALL
Warwickshire

A few Forest of Arden oaks still survive in the bluebell woods and the beautiful park around Arbury Hall in this stranded pocket of rural Warwickshire, on the very edge of Nuneaton. In 1586, John Newdegate, a scholar and country gentleman, swopped his house of Harefield in Middlesex for the sergeant-at-arms Edmund Anderson's new house at Arbury – 'a very fair structure in a quadrangle form'. It had been built by Anderson on the site of an Augustinian priory beside the Hall Pond, but since his work necessitated him being in London most of the time he found Arbury inconvenient. John Newdegate died soon after moving to Arbury. His son, also John, who was knighted in 1603, was married to Ann Fitton, sister of the famous beauty Mary. She was free with her ways and said to be the 'dark lady' of Shakespeare's sonnets. Richard Newdigate (he spelt his name differently) who inherited Arbury in 1642 was made a judge by Oliver Cromwell, became Lord Chief Justice and on returning to the Bar at Charles ll's Restoration, made so much money that he was able to buy back the old family estate at Harefield as well as an adjoining estate to Arbury. He was knighted in 1677. His son Richard built the beautiful brick stable block with its curvaceously swooped central gable and stone windows. The grand doorway was designed by his friend Sir Christopher Wren (for which the latter was paid with a pair of £11 candlesticks).

Then came Sir Roger Newdigate who, in 1750, began his revolutionary remodelling of Arbury, rendering it the best eighteenth-century Gothic Revival house in England. It was ahead of its time, daring and finer than Sir Horace Walpole's house at Strawberry Hill, the building which lends this particular style its name. Although several advisers like Sanderson Miller, Henry Keene and Couchman of Warwick were involved in the plans, Sir Roger designed much of it himself. The interior of the house is richer and rarer than you could ever imagine – fan-vaulted ceilings covered in a lace of fine plasterwork spring above you; all is light, elegant, inventive and romantic. The lofty dining-room, which had been the Elizabethan great hall, is perhaps the most spectacular room of all.

Arbury is the only house in Britain with its own private canal system and though only the vestiges remain, they are enough to stir a sense of wonder and admiration for the remarkable, polished and intelligent Sir Roger, who created it as well as the house. He read theology at Oxford, became a distinguished antiquary, was MP for Oxford for thirty years, had avant-garde architectural tastes, wrote a dissertation on Hannibal's march across the Alps and founded the prestigious Newdigate Prize for poetry at Oxford. Sir Roger's father, Richard, had begun a 'boatways' system at Arbury in the early 1700s, by making use of the existing stream which flowed across the estate, so that he could transport timber from his woods to be used in his coal mines at Collycroft. Sir Roger elaborated on this, creating a system comprising five short canals – some now nettle-filled – which cut through his collieries and parks, single, double and triple locks, pools galore, and an underground boat house. Sir Roger was a romantic – he named one of his boats the *Hester Barge*, after his second wife, and loved to take her and parties of friends on long canal trips, returning to graceful Gothic Arbury in the setting sun.

'If only some English Watteau had been there to paint it; the castellated house of grey-tinted stone, with the flickering sunbeams sending dashes of golden light across the many-shaped panes . . .' wrote George Eliot, who used Arbury as her model for Cheverel Manor in her collection of stories, *Scenes from Clerical Life*. She was born here on the estate to which her father was agent, but later quarrelled with her family, never to return. Her novels tell of remembered places: 'These things make the gamut of joy in landscape to Midland-bred souls – the things they toddled among, or learned by heart . . .' she wrote in *Middlemarch*.

STANFORD HALL

Leicestershire

The Civil War diverted men's thoughts from house building but after the Restoration fresh starts were made all over England, and Stanford Hall was one such house. It is set in a flattish stretch of middle England – battleground country between Naseby and Stanford – where the M1 now whirs a dull and distant note on windless days.

There is a serenity about the place which is all pervading. The River Avon flows gently by and the level park stretches all around out into well-hedged hunting country. The Hall was designed by William Smith of Warwick in the late 1690s. He was commissioned by Sir Roger Cave who wanted an elegant modern house instead of the ancient pile beside the church on the other side of the river where his family had lived since the early 1400s. Roger's father and grandfather (both Thomases), had put up a spirited defence when a group of Parliamentarians had visited both the manor house and

manor house for safety and it was not until the 1930s that the glass was discovered packed in wooden chests. It has now been restored to the church. As a result of his brave stand for the Crown, Sir Thomas was imprisoned in Northampton Castle for two years. After the Restoration, as the first Cave Baronet, he became High Sheriff of Leicestershire and Deputy Lieutenant for Northamptonshire and had the satisfaction of imprisoning the man who arrested him.

Sir Roger died in 1703 before the interior of his new Hall was completed, but his son Verney finished the house and commissioned Francis Smith of Warwick, William's brother, to build the east front of the house and the stately brick stable block in the 1730s. He had planned a balancing wing on the west side of the house to incorporate offices but it was never built. The Smith family's renown had spread well beyond Warwick by the time Stanford's saloon was remodelled by William Smith the Younger in 1745.

By the nineteenth century the house had passed through the female line and while Thomas Adrian Verney-Cave – known as TA – was living with his parents in the house in the 1890s, he decided to electrify it himself. He installed a turbine machine powered by damming a stretch of the Avon and in order to give minimum disturbance to his parents he took up just two floor boards in each room. Down one hole a piece of meat was dangled while a ferret with a flex round its neck was despatched down the other. The ferret took the shortest possible course to the meat and the wiring was in place. Stanford was thus electrically lit in 1898.

One of TA's best friends was England's great pioneer aviator, Percy Pilcher, who was tragically killed in the park at Stanford in 1899. There is a museum in the stable block celebrating early aviation, whose principal exhibit is a replica of the 'Hawk', the flying machine in which Pilcher was killed. There is a monument to his memory erected by the Royal Aeronautical Society on the other side of the river from the house on the spot where he crashed.

Hidden in the trees, the church is one of the wonders of central England, being stuffed full of monuments and hatchments. There is a particularly beautiful tomb commemorating Sir Thomas Cave who died in 1558, effigies of him and his wife lie on top, their fourteen children kneel below. The house and church are inextricably linked through the Cave family and it is impossible to visit one without also seeing the other.

ABOVE
A detail of the mid-sixteenth-century monument to Sir Thomas Cave and his wife in St Nicholas, Stanford.

the church after the Battle of Naseby. They stood on the roof of the house brandishing a firing piece and surrounded by men armed with muskets and villagers armed with forks and spades. The bells rang wildly in both house and church. Before he went to prison he had the forethought to store much of the extraordinarily beautiful medieval stained glass from the church in the

ABOVE
Stanford from the
south. To the right are
the stables.

MIDDLE ENGLAND 119

NEWSTEAD ABBEY

Nottinghamshire

Never an abbey, but called such for romantic reasons, the Byron family bought what was a priory for £810 in 1540 from Henry VIII. The body of the church was destroyed and leaving the exquisite late-thirteenth-century west façade and much of the priory including the refectory, the great chamber and the dorter were made into rooms. The fifth 'Wicked' Lord Byron built a Gothic castle having already built two little castellated forts in the garden. He kept a twenty-gun ship afloat on the lake and entertained friends with mock battles. He wantonly neglected the house, cut down most of the trees in the park to sell and sold off the deer. When he died this haunting half-ruined Gothic 'Abbey' became the property of the sixth Lord Byron, his great nephew, who was to become the greatest idol and sexual icon England had ever known. The future poet was ten when he inherited Newstead and was living in modest lodgings in Aberdeen where his mother had fled to to escape from mounting debts. Byron's father, 'Mad Jack', had first eloped and married Lady Carnarvon and with her had a daughter, Augusta, and secondly married Catherine Gordon of Gight, an impetuous Scot who became Byron's mother. Newstead was by then dilapidated:

> Newstead! fast-falling, once-resplendent dome!
> Religion's shrine! repentant Henry's pride!
> Of warriors, monks, and dames the
> cloister'd tomb
> Whose pensive shades around thy ruins glide,
> Hail to thy pile! more honour'd in thy fall
> Than modern mansions in their pillar'd state;
> Proudly majestic frowns thy vaulted hall,
> Scowling defiance on the blasts of fate.

Thus wrote the poet in his long 'Elegy on Newstead Abbey'. Byron restored some of the rooms in the north-west corner of the house for his own use and some in the south-east part for his guests and, although he only lived here intermittently – spending much time abroad or in London – it none the less had a profound effect on him and as his biographer, Fiona McCarthy, describes: 'It was here that the sense of dynasty and history, always a strong theme with Byron, impressed itself on him, as he was thrown into surroundings of aristocratic grandeur after a glum, restricted life in lodgings with his mother in Aberdeen.'

In 1802 he made his precocious 'first dash' into poetry and the following year fell 'distractedly in love' with his next-door neighbour, Mary Chaworth from Annesley Hall. Byron was desperately good-looking and although his first public foray into poetry had been a resounding failure, his publication of 'Childe Harold' was a resounding success. He began to be lionized by the literary set and his love life was the talk of the town; not least through his long affair with his half-sister Augusta who bore him a daughter. In January 1814 he was snowed up at Newstead together with Augusta at the height of their incestuous affair. She was to write later about Newstead: 'I tried to banish it from my *thoughts*, but I cannot banish it from *my dreams*, where it haunts me eternally.' Although Byron was to have a much publicized affair with Lady Caroline Lamb his love for Augusta was constant and his desire to keep hold of Newstead, the home of his ancestors, genuine. When Boatswain, his Newfoundland dog died, Byron built him a marble monument, sacrilegiously near the high altar of the old church, which bears the inscription 'Near this Spot are deposited the Remains of one who possessed Beauty without Vanity, Strength without Insolence, Courage without Ferocity, and all the Virtues of Man without his Vices.' By 1816 with scandal and pressing debts in his wake Byron retreated abroad, never to return and in 1817 Newstead was sold for the enormous sum of £94,000. Byron's poem 'On Leaving Newstead Abbey' kept the dream of this place he was never to see again alive in his memory.

> Thro' thy battlements,
> Newstead, the hollow winds whistle
> Thou, the hall of my fathers, art gone to decay;
> In thy once smiling garden, the hemlock
> and thistle
> Have choak'd up the rose, which late bloomed
> in the way.

By the 1820s it seemed that half the women of Europe were in love with Byron and a few of them became his mistresses. His last and longest serving was Teresa Guiccioli who visited Newstead in 1832, eight years after Byron's death. As souvenirs to take back to Italy, she took a branch from the beech tree on which Byron and his sister Augusta had carved their names and also a scrap of silk from his bed curtains. Newstead now belongs to Nottingham Council having been presented to them by Sir Julien Cahn, a Nottingham businessman, in 1931. Byron would be pleased for his maiden speech in the House of Lords was about the plight of local hosiers and glove-makers in Nottingham whose trade had been ruined by the mechanization of industry.

OPPOSITE

The entrance front. From left to right are the façade of the late thirteenth-century church, the bay windows of the prior's lodging, and tower designed by John Shaw for Colonel Wildman, who bought the house from the Byron family.

THRUMPTON HALL

Nottinghamshire

Apart from its revered place in the hearts of cricketers and the romantic escapades of Robin Hood in Sherwood Forest, Nottinghamshire was never famous for much: for long centuries it was bypassed, and according to the county history, completely 'undistinguished by dramatic episodes'. It is only in the last two centuries that its face has changed dramatically

The handsome staircase inserted in about 1662 for the second Gervase Pigot.

and industry has sprinkled itself among the countryside in an altogether haphazard fashion. Factories and pit heads, power stations and pylons have sprung up between and beside farms and villages, mild manors and ducal estates. The county's famous son D H Lawrence, in *Nottingham and the Mining Country*, accused the Victorian promoters of industry of condemning workers to '. . . ugliness, ugliness, ugliness: meanness and formless and ugly surroundings, ugly ideals, ugly religion, ugly hope, ugly love, ugly furniture, ugly houses . . . The human soul needs actual beauty even more than bread . . .' Even in grim, stalwart unnoticed, unselfconscious Nottinghamshire, there is beauty.

A mile off the M1 behind the eight giant, smoke-belching cooling towers at Ratcliffe-on-Soar where the sky is laced with rows of pylons and the ribbon of river is dwarfed, there is a lane to Thrumpton. Just over the hill and down through an ash copse the village lies in a dead end. At the lane's bend is the original village and the church of

All Saints with a squat fourteenth-century tower and the chancel rebuilt by G E Street in the 1870s. Beside the entrance is a moving monument of a recumbent soldier in uniform under a canopy, built in memory of three young villagers lost in the First World War and inside a particularly elaborate monument to Gervase Pigot who died in 1669, which he commissioned for himself during his lifetime. He had also glorified the great house of Thrumpton Hall, just down the village street which his father, also Gervase, had built at the beginning of the century.

The estate had been confiscated from the Powdrills in 1605, together with the Babbington's of Kingston-on-Soar because they were the principal local families involved in the Gunpowder Plot. The Powdrills concealed Father Garnett, one of the leading conspirators, in the priest's hole here which lies at the foot of a secret staircase built in the thickness of a chimney breast. This hiding place was constructed, it is believed, by Owen, a Jesuit lay brother who was responsible for the construction of many famous hides including that at Boscobel and one at Sawston Hall in Cambridgeshire. Thrumpton was then conveyed by the Crown to Gervase Pigot who, followed by his son, rebuilt their new house on an H-shaped plan around the Powdrills' old one. The second Gervase married a local heiress and was able to lavish money on it. He built the saloon, and the magnificent staircase which rises to the top floor of the house, all rich with panelling and carving. He gave the house its swooping Dutch gables and spent so much money that when he died his mother was forced to mortgage the Thrumpton estate. The mortgage was taken up by John Emerton as a business proposition; he improved the village but never lived here and left it to his Wescomb relatives. John Wescomb, widowed and childless, was miserable here through the latter half of the eighteenth century: 'I live here alone and am melancholy, I see company and am ill', he wrote to his brother in 1797. Thrumpton then passed down the female line to Lord Byron, the poet's cousin, who built picturesque cottages and turreted brick entrance arches to the Hall in true Isfahan style. The present Seymour owners are Byron descendants.

Winding on down past low meadows the lane ends beside the banks of the mighty and immemorial River Trent, full of currents, weirs, locks and floodbanks. On the near horizon is Nottingham, the 'Queen of the Midlands', and another world again.

BELOW
*A view of the south front
across the formal garden.*

WIGHTWICK MANOR

Staffordshire

Wolverhampton is the chief town of the Black Country, and Wightwick Manor, in its way, one of the wonders of the world. It is a comforting house which lifts the heart, perhaps because the man who built it was good, stalwart and true. You feel that everywhere.

Hidden on a high-hedged and laurel-y hill in the lush western outskirts of town, Wightwick's bedrooms look out towards Shropshire. Because it is a cosy house, and is shown to the visitor by warm-hearted National Trust ladies who tell funny stories and love the place, it still feels like the Manders' family home. (They have a flat here.)

Samuel Theodore Mander, who built the house, was director of the well-established Wolverhampton firm of Mander Brothers, one of the oldest manufacturers of varnishes and paints in the country. He was brought up as a strict Congregationalist and teetotaller, and ran the family business both efficiently and with a strong social conscience. He married Flora St Clair Paint, who came

from Nova Scotia, and in 1888 the couple moved from a large semi-detached house in the town to their brand new ideal home a little out into the country. From here Theodore could go to work at the factory every day and to the Town Hall where he was a councillor.

Before he commissioned the house Theodore, who had always been interested in the arts, attended a lecture given by Oscar Wilde called 'The House Beautiful'. He recorded in his notebook what Wilde had taken straight from the ideas of Morris and Ruskin: 'Have nothing in your houses which you do not know to be useful or believe to be beautiful', and 'Do not use anything which you do not know to be a pleasure to yourself and which you do not believe was a pleasure to the workman who made it.'

Mander chose the Cheshire architect Edward Ould

who had designed many of the cottages at Port Sunlight for Lord Leverhulme and who was a practitioner of the 'Old English' style. His half timbering was not just decorative cladding, but proper box framing and what he built for the Manders was an elaborate medley of merry old England. It comprised every picturesque feature in the book – from tall clustered chimneys covered in zigzagging ribbing soaring above many gabled and hipped roofs to an owl and a bat carved on the corners of the porch – and everywhere there are echoes of old Cheshire houses like Little Moreton Hall, or tile-hung town houses in Chester.

Wightwick was the dream middle-class home for the time. Inside, the house is stuffed with decorations by Morris & Co. There is walnut panelling, De Morgan ruby lustre ware, glorious stained glass by Kempe let into leaded lights in casement windows, furniture fabrics and wallpapers designed by Morris, all flamboyant and voluptuous – 'Pimpernel', 'Tulip and Rose', 'Peacock and Dragon', 'Bird and Vine' and so on. There are light fittings by W A S Benson, *Love among the Ruins* by Burne-Jones and panelled inglenooks with medieval-style plasterwork ceilings and comfortable settles where you'd like to sit for ever by the fire. Everything is polished and buffed up and shining and extremely well made.

Around the walls abound later adornments in the form of literary inscriptions which served as inspirers to Theodore's son; calming lines from Robert Herrick, Joseph Addison, Walter Scott, William Morris, Ruskin, Shakespeare, and Robert Browning's line from *A Wall* on the Visitors' Staircase reads:

> *Hold on, hope hard in the subtle thing that's spirit:*
> *Though cloistered fast, soar free.*

Theodore junior also redecorated the nursery in the early 1930s; it is possibly one of the nicest rooms in Britain – light and happy with distempered green walls, yellowy cream woodwork and green linoleum. The curtain materials depict 'The House that Jack Built' and 'Alice in Wonderland' and are designed by Voysey. The smell of hot buttered toast is almost in the air.

OPPOSITE
The Oak Room. The fine Morris hand-knotted carpet and the bedroom furnishings made for Swinburne are part of the distinguished Pre-Raphaelite and aesthetic movement collections assembled by Lady Mander.

LEFT
A view of the house from the gardens, which were designed by the distinguished gardener Thomas Mawson in 1910.

HADDON HALL

Derbyshire

Haddon once belonged to Peverel, the bastard son of William the Conqueror, from whose descendants it passed to the powerful Derbyshire family of Vernons. The house's miraculous survival may have had something to do with its being unfortified, thus escaping siege and storm, and also with the fact that the Vernons shrewdly sat on the fence during the Wars of the Roses. The Manners family, who married into Haddon during the sixteenth century, kept a low profile during the Civil War. As a result Haddon was bypassed by the iconoclastic Sir John Gell, who destroyed so many fine houses in Derbyshire, while their main house at Belvoir was badly damaged by Cromwell.

Haddon's history of falling in and out of favour with its owners and visitors over the last 300 years displays better than any other house in England the swinging pendulum of fashionable taste. In the early 1700s, the Manners family, headed by the Duke of Rutland, found it too old-fashioned for words, particularly as their next door neighbours' new house at Chatsworth was rising by the day ever grander. They decided to move lock, stock and barrel taking their 100 servants with them to the more modern and comfortable Belvoir Castle in Lincolnshire. Fifty years later aesthetic critic Horace Walpole dismissed Haddon as an old castle 'which could never have composed a tolerable dwelling'. The artist Dayes was even ruder calling the rooms '. . . dark and uncomfortable. They convey but a low idea of the taste of our ancestors or of their domestic pleasures, yet was this place for ages considered as the very seat of magnificence'.

By the early nineteenth century the Picturesque Movement had rekindled a sense of the quaint in cultivated English hearts and the story of the beautiful young heiress, Dorothy Vernon who had eloped with John Manners, had been unearthed from Elizabethan hearsay and blown up into a legend. *The Tale of Dorothy Vernon* was published by the sugary novelist Elizabeth Meteyard in 1823, under the *nom de plume* of 'Silverpen'. This was followed by a three-volume novel by Lee

Gibbons called *The King of the Peak* the nickname for Dorothy's father, Sir Henry, the last of that line of male Vernons. It describes Dorothy's escape from the tower at Haddon to meet her lover, who was disguised as a forester, in every gushing detail. By the Edwardian era the romance of the abandoned Haddon was building up to fever pitch fired on by the pre-Raphaelite movement. There was even a rose 'Dorothy Vernon' which was described in a catalogue of 1900 as 'gallant pink in hue, of lovely form and with foliage that is practically evergreen'.

The ninth Duke of Rutland decided to make the restoration of Haddon his life's work and to convert it into a summer home for his family. In 1913 when he began his great task, its wood and stonework were perishing and the only running water came in one conduit to the kitchen and left by another. By the time the Duke moved in during the late 1920s Haddon was deemed to be the most picturesque house in the land and its cult was in full swing. At this time Mary Pickford had been chosen to star in the film *Dorothy Vernon of Haddon Hall*. A replica of the house was built in Hollywood. The Duke had performed a miracle of restoration, replaced timbers and stone from local sources rendering this great and ancient place into a seamless whole. As the historian Henry Thorold describes Haddon: 'It has no date: it is both very old and very young. But where exactly its magic lies you must determine for yourself.'

Today the romance of Haddon is complete. When you see it from across the wide valley on the lower slopes of the hill with the River Wye looping around it, it seems literally to grow grey among the trees as though it is and has always been part of the Derbyshire landscape. On first approaching it, it appears massive and even daunting but once the house and garden envelop you the atmosphere becomes welcoming and intimate. The entrance tower leads into the lower courtyard with its chapel full of silvery oak woodwork and with a three-decker pulpit. The archway under another tower leads into the upper court and the hall, parlour and solar but it is the long gallery which is the most sensational room of all. It is richly panelled in oak and carved walnut and built over the existing walls by John Manners who, after his famous love-affair, had married his beloved Dorothy and so brought Haddon to the Manners family. The gallery is flooded with light, lit by windows on both sides and at the end. These last look on to the gardens which clamber up and down the hillside linked by a flight of seventy-six steps and are as much part of the house as its chimneys and turrets.

The ninth duke's wife Kathleen, who was a great gardener, said 'I cannot describe what a joy it was . . . to make these old terraces come to life again with roses, honeysuckle, rock roses and lavender . . .'

OPPOSITE
A view from the terraced gardens. The prominent windows light the long gallery.

ABOVE
Roses and clematis in the garden, which is largely a creation of the twentieth century.

SUDBURY HALL

Derbyshire

Sudbury lies at the milder, friendlier edge of Derbyshire where the village of pretty brick cottages straddles the road between Uttoxeter and Derby. Suddenly, flaunting its front face to the passer-by, the startlingly beautiful Sudbury Hall stands proud across its green sward. It was largely built by George Vernon between 1659 and 1701. Vernon was worth £3,000 a year when he inherited from his father at about twenty-five. He married the heiress Margaret Onley from Catesby in Northamptonshire and led a worthy life being 'a prudent young man, sober and active . . . near allied to most of the gentry and nobility of Staffordshire, Derbyshire, Shropshire and Cheshire'. He was both High Sheriff and an MP for Derby and sided against Charles II no doubt to preserve his estates. During Sudbury's building he bought 1,200,000 bricks and kept careful account of everything he spent. He designed the house himself and presumably got exactly what he wanted. Architectural historians find Sudbury Hall a 'puzzling house': it did not conform to the style of the very latest houses of that period. The fact that Derbyshire was remote from London's social scene and the Vernons were confident needing others to condone it, resulted in this marvellous maverick – it displays all the most beautiful points of Jacobean house building which seem to be changing before your eyes into the perfect Renaissance house. George wanted a projecting two-storied porch and he wanted – what remains one of the greatest rooms in England – a long gallery as earlier houses always had, which stretches for 138 feet along the top floor of the house. The ceiling which was the most sumptuously decorated imaginable cost £101 2s 0d. The staircase too is possibly the most wonderful of its date in the whole of the British Isles. Its lavishness knows no bounds and it was probably designed by George Vernon

The gallery, 138 feet long, has wonderful late seventeenth-century plasterwork by Robert Bradbury and Edward Pettifer.

himself. At one stage he wanted pineapples on the banister posts but today there are the baskets of flowers he plumped for which can be taken off and replaced with candelabras when candles might be needed to light the stairs.

The locally renowned family of Vernons, from Haddon Hall, had married into Sudbury in the early sixteenth century. They were so desperate to hang on to their name after losing it to the Manners at Haddon (see page 126) that they married cousins and heiresses in steady succession. Family altercations were common. John Harestaffe who was steward to John Vernon at Sudbury from 1591 described a dispute when John's brother Henry married Dorothy Heveningham:

> *. . . Their house and name did formerlie intend,*
> *That all his lands should after him discend*
> *On Henry. But that marriage chang'd his mynd*
> *Soe much that afterwards he was unkynd*
> *Both to his brother's Infant, and his wyffe,*
> *Soe that amongst theim soon befell great styffe*
> *And suites in lawe.*

The feud ended with a Vernon marrying a Vernon and the good Mary Vernon, who had orchestrated it, built a house for the couple which formed the foundation of the present Sudbury Hall.

Later Vernons provoked poetry, for example an eighteenth-century owner of Sudbury, George Vernon. He was a brilliant horseman who, with the local pack of hounds, took part in a fifty-mile run:

> *. . . Come, gentlemen sportsmen, wherever you be,*
> *All you that love hunting come near unto me;*
> *The chase is now ended, you've heard Reynard's fall,*
> *So here's a health to Squire Vernon of Sudbury Hall.*

A nineteenth-century Lord Vernon was such a keen agriculturalist and an ardent admirer of the famous farmer Coke of Norfolk and of his contemporary William Cobbett, the radical essayist, that he proceeded to drain the large ornamental lake and grew maize along its bottom. He then bound Cobbett's works in handmade paper made from the maize. Sudbury was given to the Treasury in 1967 in part payment of death duty of the ninth Lord Vernon, and subsequently on to the National Trust.

BELOW
*The west front from
across the lake.*

HARDWICK HALL

Derbyshire

Bess of Hardwick built this, the best Elizabethan house in the land, when she was seventy years old. She was 'a woman of masculine understanding and conduct, proud, furious, selfish and unfeeling' wrote Edmund Lodge in *Illustrations of British History*. 'She was a builder, a buyer and seller of estates, a moneylender; a farmer and a merchant of lead, coals and timber; when disengaged from those employments, she intrigued alternately with Elizabeth and Mary, always to the prejudice and terror of her husband.'

Bess was born just to the west of the present house in 1527 into a family of the minor gentry. Her father died a year after her birth and left her £26 13s 4d. In her early twenties she went into service in a big household in Derbyshire before marrying her cousin, Robert Barlow. He died a few months after the marriage and left her a small income. Next she married Sir William Cavendish who was an elderly and extremely rich government servant with no male heir. He married her for her beauty and in order to please her he bought new property including the house and estate of Chatsworth. Bess bore William eight children of whom three daughters and three sons survived. Henry, the eldest, had no legitimate heirs although a contemporary described him as '. . . the common bull to all Derbyshire and Staffordshire'. Her second son's line produced the Dukes of Devonshire and her third, the Dukes of Newcastle and of Portland.

When her husband died in 1557, Bess married Sir William St Loe who again had no heir. He died five years later and left most of his property to his widow. In 1567 she married the Earl of Shrewsbury who, at forty, was head of one of the richest families in England. Within two years of the marriage Lord Shrewsbury was given custody of Mary, Queen of Scots who had fled to England and she continued to live in his many houses for the next sixteen years. Intrigues and complications multiplied and by 1584 the marriage had broken down and Bess and her sons were spreading rumours about Lord Shrewsbury and Mary having an affair.

Perhaps Hardwick would never have been built had Bess's marriage not collapsed. The year before she had bought the old Hardwick house and property from her brother who was nearly bankrupt. When Lord Shrewsbury died in 1590 Bess held all the reins and was one of the richest women in England. She came full circle and decided to build a brand new and extremely grand house a stone's throw from the old hall where she was brought up. It took about thirteen years to complete and to furnish. 'Hardwick Hall, more glass than wall' is 209 feet tall and remains timeless and modern. It stands in the heart of the Black Country, high on a sudden hill above the myriad disused coal mines, above Hucknall Wood and the great white ribbon of the M1 motorway. There are stag-headed oaks in the ancient park. Hardwick was almost certainly designed by Robert Smythson, a brave and original architect, and remains a monument to Derbyshire, being built from local materials and by local craftsmen who had worked for Bess for many years. The embroideries, which were mostly commissioned by Bess for the house or for Chatsworth, are unique.

Hardwick was a women-orientated household in Bess' day and the huge hall downstairs from which leads the wide shallow winding stone stair, was very much the centre of activity. All visitors, however important, had to make their way through this often crowded and noisy room which might be full of servants eating their meals or tradesmen delivering their wares. Life in Bess' time at Hardwick must have been quite cold, and the older she got the more tapestries she hung over the windows to keep out the wind which in winter whistled round this dramatically set and magical house. Mark Girouard described the redoubtable Bess, who has left her mark in no uncertain manner, as 'capricious, rash, emotional, fond of intrigue and gossip, easily moved to tears, the best of company when things were going her way and spitting with spite and fury when crossed. Her amazing vitality carried her unflaggingly through her four marriages and widowhood to her death in her eighties, immensely rich and still formidable. Her unrelenting acquisition of property and worldly goods, especially of property in the countryside of her birth, and if possible connected with her family and relatives, suggests the ambition of a local girl to demonstrate that the dim squire's daughter had made good in a sensational way.'

'When you enter the park,' wrote James Lees-Milne, 'you are overcome by the vast prospect of scale before you. Chatsworth is, you feel, a principality rather than a Country House, even measured by the noblest standards.'

CHATSWORTH
Derbyshire

Chatsworth lies in the Derbyshire of the High Peak which Byron likened to Switzerland or Greece and Henry Thorold feels to be a thousand miles from London. There are mountainous hills and moors, tors, caverns and waterfalls and in its midst a huge Elysian bowl opens out, sloping from the moors and woods on its rim, down into green pastures. When you cross the cattle grid into Chatsworth Park you are entering another country. It is a kingdom of its own. It is also the pride of Derbyshire and the feeling is so strong that if you are a southerner you feel almost an intruder; the place belongs to all the local people, who come to walk here from Buxton, Chesterfield and Derby, from Matlock, Baslow and Bakewell.

The wide River Derwent winds for almost two miles through the park, alders cling to the banks and a huge dark pool builds up above a great weir of white water. Just beyond, the park rises up past ancient oaks to the steep heights of Stand Wood where Bess of Hardwick's hunting tower commands an infinite prospect. Then, round the next river bend there is Chatsworth itself. The most majestic and perhaps the most loved house in England, dun-stoned and gilt-edged in the western sun, with its window surrounds decorated in real gold leaf.

'Not a palace, not a castle, not a museum, but a house – always called "the house". "I'll come across to the house", "See you at the house at 9.30", "I think he's somewhere in the house", "They're going round the house", a constant reminder of what the huge building is for: a place for people to live in,' writes the present Duchess of Devonshire. 'The house looks permanent; as permanent as if it had been there, not for a few hundred years, but for ever. It fits its landscape exactly. The river is the right distance away and the right width. The bridge is at a comfortable angle for leaning on and gazing from. The stone from which the house is built comes out of the ground nearby, and so it is the proper colour, on the bird's nest theory of building materials being at hand and of the place, and therefore right for the surroundings.'

It was here that Bess of Hardwick came in 1549 with her old husband, the rich Sir William Cavendish, whom she persuaded to buy land throughout her beloved Derbyshire. Chatsworth cost £600 and sported a fine house which Bess promptly pulled down. Fourteen years and £80,000 later she had built a huge pile, four, and in places five, storeys high, around a central courtyard. Not a trace of it shows on the outside today. In the late 1680s, a little over 100 years later, her descendant the first Duke of Devonshire commissioned William Talman to build the south front over Bess' already 'decaying and weake' structure. Talman then built the east front six years later and after a quarrel with the Duke, was sacked. The western and most famous façade was completed by 1707, almost certainly to the Duke's design, perhaps with the help of architect friends and acquaintances who came to stay, like Thomas Archer and Christopher Wren. Sadly the Duke died the year his front was finished.

The fourth duke, who had married the daughter of the celebrated amateur architect Lord Burlington, felt he must leave his mark on Chatsworth and commissioned James Paine to build a magnificent bridge and the most exquisite rusticated stable block to the north-east of the house. It is almost as grand as the house itself with its triumphant entrance arch topped by a clock tower and cupola. The sixth 'Bachelor' duke revolutionized things still more by building the north wing (designed by Wyatville) to incorporate the great dining-room and sculpture gallery. Inspired by Nash's village of Blaise Hamlet the Duke, together with his famous gardener Joseph Paxton, also built a new village in elaborately eclectic style and on a ducal scale, as well as greenhouses and garden spectacles in the grounds, the like of which had never been seen before.

The grounds of Chatsworth are what render it a cut above. Its miles and miles of different winding paths which climb the gradual slope and then the steep hill behind the house, past delicate glasshouses, brown hens, Elisabeth Frink statues, lupin gardens, waving beech hedges, grottoes, aqueducts, past trickling streams and waterfalls to the dark woods and lake on the skyline, seem infinite. The water works, which emanate from the reservoirs high on the hill, are matchless. The grand Cascade sweeping down shallow steps in endless falling curtains of water was constructed in 1696 by the first duke and has worked ever since and the 'emperor fountain', conceived by Paxton, which can shoot 290 feet into the air, are among the great sights of England.

The Duchess continues: 'It has taken more than 400 years to reach this apparently effortless state of perfection by a combination of luck and good management. The luck is that every generation of Cavendishes has loved and respected the house and its surroundings, and each has added something to it, and the good management is literally so in that no house has been better served by its stewards and housekeepers than has Chatsworth.' It is also her and her husband the eleventh duke's sheer determination that Chatsworth will carry on. They lead with a quiet, practical and democratic hand which has rendered the house the pride of Derbyshire.

ABOVE

Elizabeth Frink's horse in the foreground. The 'emperor fountain' beyond, conceived by Paxton, provides an astonishing spectacle in front of Chatsworth's south façade.

PLAS MAWR

Gwynedd

Conwy lies on the mouth of the river in that beautiful bit of north Wales described, quite rightly, by guidebook writers with an inordinate number of superlatives. For a start the little town is the *best* preserved fortified medieval town in Great Britain. To the north, around the great sweeps of Conwy Bay where the Great Orme head sticks out into the Irish Sea, is Britain's *longest*-reaching cable car which travels 5,320 feet to the cliff summit. In Conwy town itself is Britain's *smallest* house on the quayside, a tiny one-up-one-down built against the town wall which must have been cramped for the last occupants, one of whom was six foot three tall. Each of the two rooms is six foot by ten foot two inches. Then there is Plas Mawr, easily the best-preserved Elizabethan townhouse in the whole land.

The present town of Conwy was born in 1283 as part of the 'Iron King' Edward I's vision for Wales. The castle was completed soon afterwards and most of the circumventing walls are still here, some of them up to fifteen feet thick. An elegant suspension bridge designed by Telford crosses the great River Conwy and was designed to blend in with the medieval turrets and walls of the castle and the town. Conwy was divided into rectangular blocks by a grid of four major and several minor streets. The blocks were then further subdivided into individual house blocks which were rented to new immigrant settlers. By Elizabethan times when the substantial part of Plas Mawr was built, Conwy was definitely the place to live. The lawyers of north Wales by tradition lived in Caernarfon, the merchants in Beaumaris and the gentlemen in Conwy. Robert Wynn, the builder, was by then a gentleman.

His grandfather, Maredudd ab Ievan ap Robert, had the foresight to take on the lease on royal bond land in the remote uplands of Dolwyddelan, steadily increased his land holdings into the Conwy valley and ended his days in 1525 surrounded by many of his twenty-one children and a new house he had built at Gwydir. His eldest son inherited most of the estate, and his third son, Robert, having little prospect, worked in the household of Philip Hoby, a Protestant member of the Herefordshire gentry. Robert Wynn got a leg up through Hoby's rise in court circles, and. when Robert finally returned to his home in north Wales he began to play a worthy part in local affairs. He renewed his father's leases on the Dolwyddelan hills and it was with rent from these lands together with a little renegotiation and sharp practice, which no doubt he had learned around court circles, he became a man of considerable means.

At fifty Robert had married Dorothy Griffiths and wanted to establish a proper home for his new wife. He paid £200 for 'a mansion house . . . with appurtenances, one garden and three orchards' in Conwy. He then bought further plots of adjacent land until he had enough room to build, over the next twenty years, his wonderful house. Plas Mawr stands on a steep ascent and is an evocation of Robert's childhood home at Gwydir. It is a bold architectural statement of the Welsh Renaissance with its crow-stepped gables, pedimented windows and faceted pilasters. Inside, its plasterwork is a positive glory, and for rural grandeur and artistry unsurpassed. There are five rooms with decorated ceilings and overmantels, all brightly painted, all jolly and quirky and just as they would have been in Robert's day.

While the building went on, Robert's local status rocketed: he was a Justice of the Peace, he sat in Parliament for Caernarfonshire and was Sheriff of the County. Unfortunately Dorothy died without any children not long after Plas Mawr was begun, but in 1588 when he was sixty-eight he married Dorothy Dymock who was much younger and he proceeded to father seven children in six years. The old wound he had received beside Hoby in the Siege of Boulogne played up and 'some six years after his last marriage his body, being stirred in getting children at those years (untimely for that purpose), his wanted inflation took him in the leg extraordinary vehemence so that he supposed it would endanger his life.' A surgeon was called in and removed the remainder of the bullet lodged fifty years before. Following Robert's death in 1598 Dorothy continued to live at Plas Mawr with her family but through the next twenty or thirty years there were endless rows and wrangles over the will and bequests and the executor, Sir Roger Mostyn, was charged with mishandling the estate.

By 1637 Plas Mawr had been inherited by Robert's grandson and then passed through the female line to the Mostyn family who remain the freeholders to this day. Not lived in by the family since the late seventeenth century, the house has been restored and maintained by Cadw: Welsh Historic Monuments.

ABOVE

The richly decorated banqueting hall has retained its Elizabethan chimneypiece and plasterwork.

OPPOSITE

Plas Mawr stands on a narrow street in Conwy, an astonishingly rare and intact surviving Elizabethan town house.

PLAS NEWYDD

Anglesey

Plas Newydd on the island of Anglesey must have one of the most romantic settings in Britain. Across the wide water of the Menai Strait speckled with sailing boats and straddled a mile away by the elegant railway bridge of Robert Stephenson, it looks back to the gentle slopes on the opposite banks where emerald farmland stretches away into Snowdonia. Snowdon itself rises high above its surrounding hills. The light changes from hour to hour and the views from this well-windowed house are mesmerizing. There has been a dwelling on this site since the sixteenth century ending with the present-day plain Jane of a house which the Sixth Marquess of Anglesey brought about in the 1930s.

The original hall house of Plas Newydd and its estate passed from the Griffiths by various marriages to Henry Bayly who inherited the title of Lord Paget of Beaudesert. He was later made Earl of Uxbridge and his total territory together with properties in Ireland and England amounted to over 100,000 acres. At the end of the eighteenth century, on making some extra money from copper mining on Anglesey and from coal in his family's estates in Staffordshire, he had his house done over in the fashionable Gothic style and the interiors were given a neoclassical a make-over. The architect James Wyatt created a series of undulating apses and turrets and bay windows and pulled together what was then a jumble, in the Gothic fashion of the time. The park and garden were updated by Humphry Repton. The sixth Marquess found the Gothic style distasteful and blunted the points with Tudor window caps and cut off the house's pinnacles. Inside however the eighteenth-century feeling of lightness still pervades.

Lord Uxbridge's eldest son, Henry William, was the great hero of Plas Newydd. For a start he was considered '*le plus beau garçon d'Angleterre*', and to boot he became one of the most remarkable soldier-statesman Britain ever knew. He entered Parliament at the age of twenty-two and at twenty-five raised the 80th Regiment of Foot and later fought with it in Flanders under the Duke of York. He became second in command to Wellington, and his handling of the cavalry at the Battle of Waterloo on the 18 June 1815 won him a place in British history. When his right leg was smashed by grape shot while he was riding off the field with the Duke at the end of the day, he is supposed to have exclaimed: 'By God, sir, I've lost my leg!' to which the Duke replied glancing down: 'By God, sir, so you have!' and immediately went on watching the retreating French through his spyglass. On Henry's return the Prince Regent declared that 'he loved him . . . and that he was his best officer and his best subject . . .' and him a marquess. He chose the name of Anglesey where his beloved Plas Newydd awaited. A few years later he was given a recently invented articulated wooden leg which became known as 'the Anglesey Leg' and was still being commercially advertised in the 1900s.

With his first wife Lady Caroline Villiers he had eight children and then eloped with Lady Charlotte Wellesley, the Duke of Wellington's sister-in-law. He wrote to his brother Charles in the spring of 1809: 'An attachment is unfortunately formed between us. It is fought against for a long time. Alas, not long enough – passion gets the better of reason and finally we are driven to the necessity of the present step.' After expensive divorce proceedings he married Charlotte and had a further ten children. His eighteen children then presented him with seventy-three grandchildren, none of whom, according to the present Marquess and military historian, came to much: 'They were for the most part good examples of the "idle rich"'. The second Marquess' mistress was housekeeper in Buckingham Palace and when Queen Victoria came to the throne in 1837 there were thirteen members of the Paget family holding jobs at Court; they were later swept away by Prince Albert who described them as 'a plague of locusts'. The fourth Marquess was unadventurous and purported not to like the smell of foxhounds. He had the Anglesey pack sprayed with scent, and his yacht, moored off Plas Newydd, seldom left its moorings. The fifth and notorious 'dancing Marquess' may well have been the son of a French actor, and in 1901 he founded his own theatre company staging lavish productions at Plas Newydd. His passion for expensive jewellery and clothes considerably reduced the family fortunes. He died at the age of twenty-nine and was succeeded by his cousin the sixth Marquess who, obviously chastened by his immediate forebears' *risqué* behaviour, decided to straighten out the Gothic fantasy that had been Plas Newydd and present a sterner face to the world. However he proceeded to convert the interior into an exceedingly comfortable house on the principle that 'every bathroom should have a bedroom'. He commissioned Rex Whistler to paint the remodelled dining-room.

In 1976, the seventh Marquess gave the house to the National Trust. He and Lady Anglesey, daughter of the novelist Charles Morgan and one-time chairman of the National Federation of Womens' Institutes, continue to live in part of the house.

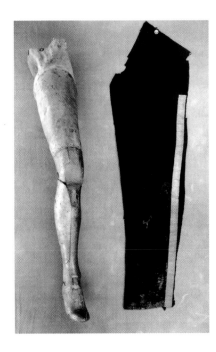

ABOVE

The wooden leg and trouser leg worn by the first Marquess of Anglesey, who lost his limb on the battlefield at Waterloo.

TREDEGAR HOUSE

Gwent

Evan Morgan, the last Viscount Tredegar whose family had lived here for 500 years, went out in typical 1930s style. He dabbled in black magic assisted by his old friend Aleister Crowley, the occultist, he wore a pet parrot on his shoulder and kept a menagerie of animals in the park including a kangaroo with whom he frequently boxed. He entertained on a lavish scale both on his large yacht *The Liberty* and at Tredegar, and his guests included such luminaries and socialites as H G Wells, Prince Paul of Greece and the fabulously rich Nancy Cunard. He died in 1949 leaving no direct heir and by 1951 the house was sold and became a girls' school. As Giles Worsley, the architectural historian, observed, the Morgans had come down 'the familiar slide from hard-nosed businessmen to titled philanthropists, idle playboys – and extinction'. Over the next twenty years Tredegar got battered about – its panelling was used as notice boards, its timbers became riddled with dry rot.

Llewellyn Morgan was living here in the early 1400s but was forced to forfeit his estate as punishment for supporting the rebellion of Owain Glyndwr. His descendants recovered the property and built a house towards the end of the fifteenth century. By the end of the Civil War in the late seventeenth century, the Morgan family's tastes were no longer parochial. They wanted to rebuild Tredegar as a fitting expression of their important position in society. William Morgan certainly had the means. In 1661 he had married Blanche the only daughter of Judge William Morgan of Therrew who was King's Attorney for South Wales and extremely rich. Tredegar became a symbol of the Morgan family's wealth and remains the most beautiful Restoration house in Wales. Its palest pink brick is unusual in this area of stone, and perhaps came as ballast from Holland. The first-floor windows are embellished beneath with stone swags of fruit, a rare form of ornament with its closest parallels only found in The Hague and on the town hall in Amsterdam. The ground-floor windows, like the doorways, have broken pediments surrounded by a lion and a griffin flanking a heraldic cartouche. The house was built between 1664 and 1672 and its unknown designer, who was probably a mason bricklayer or a carpenter, was brilliant. The gilt room sparkles with gold and is full to the brim with elaborate baroque plasterwork and carving. The chimneypiece is a mass of grotesque half-human figures clambering among vegetation. The carving in the brown room is lavish and finely worked.

By the time of the Industrial Revolution wealth had grown apace and the Morgans were quick to channel their income into commercial and industrial projects. Sir Charles Morgan exploited the mineral wealth of his land by promoting the establishment of coal mines and iron works together with the construction of canals and tramways by which the minerals could be transported. He

RIGHT

A view through the eighteenth-century wrought-iron gates to the entrance front.

was instrumental in the building of the Monmouthshire canal and encouraged the construction of a tram road from Sirhowy to Newport. A mile of this tram road passed through Tredegar Park and was locally known as the 'golden mile' owing to substantial profits made by the Morgans from the tolls that were levied on those vehicles using it. Two more generations of Morgans continued to jump on commercial bandwagons which the nineteenth century threw up, such as the development of Newport as an industrial and commercial town. Sir Charles who had inherited the estate in 1846 was raised to the peerage as Baron Tredegar and was succeeded by his son Godfrey who had survived the Charge of the Light Brigade. Godfrey was a generous public benefactor who helped to develop Newport's health, recreation and education and endowed much land. In Godfrey's day a servant at Tredegar wrote to her friend who was housekeeper at Erddig: '. . . Is it not ridiculous? Sometimes when he is alone we have twenty-three table cloths in the wash in a

week and when he has a lot of company we have anywhere from thirty-six to forty. His sister is Lady Hereford of Ludlow, and when she and her daughter come here there is plenty of work for everyone. The sideboard cloths are changed three or four times a week and My Lord has a clean cloth, on every tray taken up to him. I often say if cleanliness would keep any one alive, then Viscount Tredegar would never die.' He never married and from then on his successors' extravagant lifestyles and indolence saw the estate's decline. As Alan Pryce-Jones observed on the last Viscount's misfortune, he 'was born with far too much money, too little health and no practical sense at all'. In 1974 Newport Borough Council, in whose suburbs Tredegar now stands, bought the house with ninety acres and restored it to its true glory under the brilliant eyes of its successive curators, Christopher Hartley, David Beevers, David Freeman, Michael Hunter and Laura Beresford.

LITTLE MORETON HALL

Cheshire

Nearly every house with any pretension to a display of status was jeopardized in some shape or form during the Civil War. Royalist strongholds sometimes never recovered and Little Moreton Hall was one such. The Moretons had built it from the 1440s in four principal stages ending around 1580. The fact that the Moretons remained relatively impoverished due to their Royalist sympathies meant that the house remained virtually unchanged. By the 1720s it had been let as a farm and when the artist John Sell Cotman visited it in 1806 he found the house was a virtual barn, with chickens scratching for worms in the hall. He depicted it as a romantic reminder of a long-lost era, for the Moretons had lost their desire to keep it on as any sort of family home. In 1892 Elizabeth Moreton, an Anglican nun, inherited it and although she restored the chapel and kept the house propped up she had no use for it. At her death it passed on to her cousin Charles Abraham, the Bishop of Derby. The condition was that he never sold it. Charles Abraham hardly knew his cousin and had never heard of the house. 'I remember taking a day off at Lichfield in 1892,' he later recounted 'to run down and see what she said she had left me, and shall not forget the thrill as I topped the rise after Scholar Green, walking from Kidsgrove Station, and saw the front of the old black and white house in spring sunshine confronting me.'

That thrill, despite traffic and visitors and ticket office and the trappings that go with famous houses open to the public, still hits anyone who first visits this fairy-tale of a house.

The Victorians did not like Elizabethan architecture and it was only at the beginning of this century that houses such as Little Moreton Hall became symbols of homeliness. Although its quaint cosiness epitomized the idea of a romantic past the early Moretons who lived here appear to have been an argumentative and litigious lot and these panelled rooms must have echoed with their rows. In the mid-fifteenth century Sir Richard Moreton, who probably built surviving bits of the Hall, was bound over to keep the peace and his grandson William Moreton was involved in a quarrel with his neighbour Thomas Rode concerning which of them should sit in the highest place in church and who should go in front during processions. They called in an arbitrator to settle the matter called William Brereton who decided that the matter should rest on who owned the most land. This

turned out to be Moreton but Rode refused to accept the verdict and said that he was a relation of Moreton's anyway. A seventeenth-century William Moreton had a black sheep for a son called John, who, having been sent to Christ's College, Cambridge in 1614 when he was seventeen, was despaired of by all his tutors for being incessantly drunk and said he didn't mind if he never saw Moreton Hall again. He preferred London to Cheshire and only decided to return to Moreton towards the end of his life when his younger brother was well settled.

Bishop Abraham took on his task of caring for and undoubtedly loving the house, and was perhaps its ultimate saviour. In 1904 he employed the architect William Weir who was a devotee of William Morris and all his principles of invisible restoration – as though no hand but time had been near the building. When the architectural historian James Lees-Milne, who worked for the National Trust, first saw the house reflected in the waters of its small moat he recalled in *People and Places* the '... absurd half-timbered structure, crowned by an unbroken length of gallery window like some fantastic, elongated Chinese lantern, and toppling, if not positively bending over the tranquil water of a moat the whole an ancient pack of cards about to meet from the first puff of wind its own reflection, is something which once seen never can be forgotten.'

OPPOSITE

The gatehouse range, which almost seems to topple into the waters of the moat.

ABOVE

The decorative possibilities of half-timbering are exploited to the full in the courtyard: this view shows the south side.

WENLOCK ABBEY

Shropshire

Shropshire is the sixteenth largest county in England but the thirty-sixth in its number of inhabitants. In some places where the strangely shaped hill formations such as the Wrekin and the Long Mynd, the Clee Hills and the Clun Hills jut suddenly up into the sky like lumpy sandcastles on the beach, it feels empty and remote. Wenlock Edge is one of the strangest hills of all. Formed of Silurian shales it looks like a recumbent Saluki dog lying on a carpet of farmland; it is nearly 300 feet high, 18 miles long and never more than a mile wide. 'A lofty bank', as William Gilpin describes it in 1809 – 'We saw it at a distance running like a long, black ridge,

BELOW
These seemingly endless rows of windows light the prior's lodge, built in about 1500, on the east side of the courtyard.

OPPOSITE
The upper gallery, which connects the infirmary and the prior's lodge.

covered with wood, athwart the country . . . When we had attained the summit, we had no descent on the other side; this long ridge being the slope only of one of those grand, natural terraces, by which one tract of country sometimes descends into another.'

Much Wenlock lies below the Edge's north-eastern tip; it is an unassuming town of pale grey stone, half-timbering and brick. There is a half-timbered guildhall, a Norman and perpendicular church across from the handsome Georgian houses of Church Row, and close by in a side street the working Brook House Farm right in the centre of town with tractors, cattle and ducks. The quiet calm of the place owes much to the ruined Wenlock Priory with its delicate zigzagged interlacing arches on the wall of the chapter house. The ruins, set among topiary and tall trees, look on to mild park-like

surroundings, crossed with silvery stone walls where Hereford cattle graze. Undeveloped countryside comes right up to the old town's edges.

Wenlock Priory is the best-preserved of the few Cluniac houses in England and since the dissolution the priory has often been referred to as 'Wenlock Abbey'. Before the Cluniac monks arrived in 1070 there had been a nunnery here founded in 680 by St Milburga, daughter of the King of Mercia. It was destroyed by the Danes and 200 years later refounded by Earl Leofric and his wife Godiva as a college of secular priests dedicated to St Milburga. Today what survives are the great grand fragments of the early English Church, the remains of the Norman chapterhouse and the fifteenth-century prior's house. This has been continuously occupied since it was built by Prior Singer and it joins at right angles the Norman infirmary which in turn adjoins the chapter house. Richard Singer had already enhanced the priory's prestige during his thirty-five-year tenure (which saved considerable fees incurred through changes of prior). The church was embellished and repaired and the register records that during the reconstruction of the vaulting above the high altar several workmen and monks had serious falls and yet they all recovered miraculously which is thought to have been at the intervention of St Milburga who had already performed many miracles. The infirmary was also improved at this time which might have assisted in the injured men's recoveries.

At the priory's dissolution in 1639 the church gradually turned into a ruin and became a local stone quarry. However the infirmary and lodge were so new and comfortable that Thomas Lawley, who had bought the estate, decided to make them his home. For the next two centuries 'Wenlock Abbey' was never held in such high regard. In the seventeenth century the roof timbers of the great monastic tithe barn were sold to the Burgesses of Bridgenorth to repair their market house which had been burnt in the Civil War, and in 1698 Wenlock was bought by Viscount Gay, who sold it fifteen years later to Sir John Wynnstay and the house was let to a succession of tenant farmers. In 1857 Sir Watkin Williams-Wynn, who had inherited Wenlock, sold the property to his son-in-law, the Yorkshireman James Milnes-Gaskell, who had for some years been MP for Wenlock. He began repair work and made it into a home for his wife and son.

Wenlock Abbey's front is beautiful beyond compare. Its continuous runs of coupled windows divided by slender buttresses of pink and pale yellow sandstone, on which rest the eaves of the vast and unbroken expanse of old stone-tiled roof, creates an unsurpassed composition of building materials. It still remains one of Britain's most romantic homes.

PITCHFORD HALL

Shropshire

'That beautiful home of old Englishmen' wrote an anonymous *Country Life* correspondent in 1901, 'you may approach it, if you choose, by a delightful walk through the fields from Condover Station, passing as you go old Condover Hall . . . which, in its fine old frontage of stone presents a very suggested contrast to the more picturesque charms of ancient timber-framed Pitchford.' Dr Beeching axed the branch line which went to Condover. Instead you can approach Pitchford down tiny winding lanes which crisscross the Cound Brook and pass through remote hamlets until the wooded valley unfurls which hides Pitchford Hall hides. The small thirteenth-century church of pink sandstone with its tiled roof stands at Pitchford's gates, surrounded by yews beside a small tree-girt lake. It is beautiful – there are box pews, a Jacobean pulpit and the most wonderful wooden effigy of a recumbent knight in chainmail. This represents a thirteenth-century member of the De Pitchford family who were here from the time of King Stephen, who built the medieval open hall structure which still lies within the core of the house.

Pitchford Hall is by far the best half-timbered house in the country. In this region of half-timbering, Speke Hall in Cheshire may be more elaborate and Little Moreton Hall may be more crooked and quaint but Pitchford beats them into a cocked hat. It was Thomas Ottley, a rich Shrewsbury wool merchant who bought the property in 1473 and lived in what is now the west wing. His grandson added the two other wings enclosing the court. John Sandford, the leading Shrewsbury carpenter of the day, had taken up residence nearby in order to supervise the work. Above its red sandstone foundations the overwhelming motif is lozenges within lozenges producing the most exquisite design. This was a forest country, where materials for the building lay ready to hand and as *Country Life*'s turn-of-the-century correspondent continues, 'and many an oak bowed to the woodman's axe ere Pitchford Hall was raised. Go where you will, you will find few more beautiful examples than this of a style of architecture dear to the English mind . . .' Pitchford's roof is a work of art in itself with its pinkish sandstone slates – quarried locally – and its theatrical chimneys rising star-shaped at rhythmical intervals. The barge boards and the beam supporting the gables are all richly carved with trailing vines, the standard trademark of the famous Sandford family of carpenters.

The seventeenth century saw some minor additions such as the wonderful panelling in the drawing-room, the clock tower over the porch, the garderobe tower straddling the Row Brook and the famous half-timbered tree house built into the branches of an enormous lime tree on the hillside. By 1807 the male line of Ottleys died out, and the property went to Charles Jenkinson, a cousin, who became third Earl of Liverpool. He remodelled the great hall and the dining-room and built a conservatory in the old walled garden in the 'Tudor-bethan' style. By this time Pitchford's antiquity was beginning to be appreciated and when the future Queen Victoria visited it in 1832 she fell for its 'cottage-like' homeliness. When Lord Liverpool's grandson Colonel Charles James Cotes wanted to update the house in the 1880s he employed the architect George Devey who carefully removed all the Georgian features and restored some of the timberwork imperceptibly and quite beautifully. The most radical thing he did was to change the entrance to the north side of the house and to open

up the south-facing courtyard to create a garden. This is still every bit as wonderful as our correspondent continues to describe: '. . . On one side the land slopes down to the house, on the other it slopes away where grass terraces break the descent to the pleasant margin of the brook . . . and with most pleasant thoughts of the good old English house and fair domain do we forsake the lovely surroundings of Pitchford Hall.'

The nation forsook Pitchford when, due to the Lloyds crash and declining agricultural revenues in the 1980s, the house was offered for sale for the first time in over 500 years. So complete a family collection had built up over all that time and had been housed in the structure of the utmost rarity that it would have enriched the country for ever. The house may yet survive, though it is empty today and its family portraits, furniture, ceramics and silver are dispersed.

LOWER BROCKHAMPTON MANOR HOUSE

Herefordshire

Lower Brockhampton manor house stands today as a moving and romantic monument to the noble-spirited Herefordshire family who built it and lived in it for generations untouched by any *folie de grandeur*. It served the family well for 400 years until the eighteenth century when the young bride Betty Freeman of Gaines near Whitbourne married into the house and considered it too old-fashioned to live in. She and her husband built Brockhampton Court on the high ground of the park in the 1760s and employed a smart Shrewsbury architect called Thomas Farnolls Pritchard to design it. Meanwhile Lower Brockhampton was kept in reasonable condition and in the 1870s was restored sensitively by Mr J C Buckler, an antiquarian architect and famous topographical draughtsman. The Lutley family who had eventually come into the Brockhampton estate through marriage continued to live at the Court until 1946 when Colonel Lutley died with no heirs he left the estate and its beautiful manor house to the National Trust.

Timber was the cheapest and most popular building material until it became in short supply in the seventeenth century and the best timber was saved for building ships. Most of the early domestic architecture in Herefordshire is timber-framed and villages like Kingsland, Eardisley, Eardisland and Weobley are full of it. In the east of England, Kentish 'studding' or 'close studding' is the most common, in the west and the Midlands, square or 'box' panels are much more usual. They are then infilled with wattle and daub and were sometimes later infilled with brick or clad all over with an extra coat of another material thus disguising the timber framing.

There had always been a settlement at Lower Brockhampton. The remoteness and vulnerability of its site here beside the Paradise Stream with its ruined Norman chapel below the encircling woods and the heights of Bromyard Down necessitated a means of defence. So when John Domulton, a descendant of the old Brockhampton family, began to build the present house between 1380 and 1400, a moat was obviously a practical necessity. The stock could be herded within the moated area in times of trouble and the moat could also be used as a source of fresh fish. Originally the moat surrounded the house completely but was gradually filled in during more peaceable times. The building of Lower Brockhampton was highly superior to that of surrounding cottages which still survive. The massive timbers for the main structure would have been the pick of the woods in the surrounding Brockhampton estate and their decoration carved out by the best local craftsmen. The base cruxes are decorated by a shaft with a battlemented capital, and above the collar the raking struts are cut to form a quatrefoil. The great hall with its screens passage to divide off the service wings would have been the main living-room with a central open hearth and a louvre in the roof to allow smoke to escape. When he finished the house, John Domulton renovated the ruined chapel by putting in two new windows in the east and west walls, and he gave it an octagonal font cut from one piece of stone.

The gatehouse, a rare survival like Stokesay Castle's gatehouse in Shropshire, is what completes the picturesque ensemble of Lower Brockhampton. It was probably built to celebrate the marriage of Elizabeth Domulton and William Habington in the 1480s. It straddles the moat and has an oversailing upper floor, and the barge boards under its eaves have a beautiful trailing grapevine carved upon them.

One of William and Elizabeth's grandsons, John Habington, like a moth to the flame, couldn't resist the draw of the Court and eventually became cofferer to Queen Elizabeth I, well established and rich. His eldest son Edward, spending much time at Court, became a close friend of Anthony Babington, a Catholic courtier, who was concocting a plan for a general rising of the Catholics which would culminate in the murder of Queen Elizabeth and the liberation of Mary Stuart. Edward was tried for conspiracy on 15 September 1586 and five days later was hanged and quartered in St Giles' Field. In a speech from the scaffold he vehemently maintained his innocence. His younger brother Thomas, who had been in the same conspiracy, somehow escaped execution and remained in the Tower for six years. He was then permitted to retire to his father's estate of Hindley near Worcester, on condition that he did not leave Worcestershire. He proceeded to construct eleven secret chambers in which to hide priests in his house behind the wainscots of rooms built in the form of false chimneys and accessible only by trap doors.

OPPOSITE

On the left is the manor house, surrounded by its moat. It is approached by the picturesque Tudor gatehouse on the right.

BELOW
The varied ranges which surround the rose garden are
beautifully set off by the moat.
On the left is the chapel.

'My dearest William,' wrote Mary Lygon to her brother, the seventh Earl of Beauchamp, on 22 February 1899, 'I do hope you will be able to come with the Chamberlains . . . I rode with Eggie to Sukly; and then went to see the Elgars who are most pleasant. He has written some big orchestra theme on variations and each of the latter portrays a friend. I am one called "Incognita" but I only heard this today – as he was too shy to tell me and he would not play them . . . ' The Elgars lived in the Great Malvern Hills which act as a spectacular and theatrical backdrop to Madresfield. It is almost as though it is set down in Switzerland in its verdant park below the great hills. Mary's father the sixth Earl of Beauchamp had already transformed the ancient house where his family had lived uninterrupted since records began. It is first mentioned specifically in a charter of Henry I dating from the 1120s as being in the hands of a William de Bracy whose descendants, the Lygon family, have lived here ever since. William Lygon was created the first Earl of Beauchamp in 1815 and the family still live here to this day.

The earliest bit of the house was a great hall built in the twelfth century within the encircling moat which still surrounds Madresfield and was designed for the feudal and communal life of the Middle Ages. A manor house grew up around the hall which still remained as a dining-room through the Tudor period, and during the succeeding centuries this hall was added to, altered and renovated to suit the family of the time. In the nineteenth century an inheritance transformed the family fortunes. William Lygon, the first Earl, was an heir to one-third of the wealth of William Jennings, a godson of King William III and the interminable litigation following his death is said to have inspired Charles Dickens' firm of Jarndyce and Jarndyce in *Bleak House*. In consequence of this amazing wealth, the biggest changes of all were made to Madresfield. The architect P C Hardwick was employed by the fifth Earl of Beauchamp to make the house look Gothic and to do away with the classical elements of the last two centuries. This he did in no uncertain manner, bringing in many tricks of the Victorian trade together with barley-sugar chimneys and half-timbered gables redolent of the surrounding half-timbering of Worcestershire. It was carried out over a period of twenty-five years from 1865 ending with the final bell turret.

The sixth Earl played a large part in the Oxford Movement; he built several churches and helped to found Keeble College. He created the chapel at Madresfield from two rooms during the alterations of 1865 and in his day it was decorated purely functionally as a place of prayer. But it was the seventh Earl who was to bestow on Madresfield perhaps the greatest display of the Arts and Crafts Movement ever seen. (He was himself an artist and craftsman and there is a set of chairs covered in bargello – Florentine flame stitch needlework – which he embroidered in the house and also a small statuette he sculpted which shows a naked golfer in full swing modelled from a young Australian while he was Governor of New South Wales.)

The library is one of the greatest rooms in England and was decorated between 1902 and 1905. A wide bay window hangs over the moat where a window seat beckons. Everywhere around the 8,000 books, some vellum-bound by the Kelmscott Press and tied with olive green ribbon, is a sumptuous encompassing mass of carved, moulded and polished wood. Intricate tendrils of trees depicting the Tree of Life form the centre of a series of images – the monkish scholar, the farmer reaping, the doctor, the musician – which allude to the many different paths to learning and wisdom. The panels of the doors are carved with figures and the pewter door plates are decorated with stylized flowers and animals. Working from their Cotswold base in Chipping Camden were the master carvers Alec Miller and Will Hart all under the command of the great designer of his age, C R Ashbee.

From here a door leads into the chapel. '. . . there's the chapel, you must see that . . .' remarks Sebastian Flyte to his friend Charles Ryder in the novel *Brideshead Revisited* by Evelyn Waugh '. . . We entered it by the public porch (another door led direct to the house); Sebastian dipped his fingers in the water stoup, crossed himself, and genuflected; I copied him. "Why do you do that?" he asked crossly. "Just good manners." "Well, you needn't on my account. You wanted to do sight-seeing; how about this?" The whole interior had been gutted, elaborately refurnished and redecorated in the arts-and-crafts style of the last decade of the nineteenth century. Angels in printed cotton smocks, rambler-roses, flower-spangled meadows, frisking lambs, texts in Celtic script, saints in armour, covered the walls in an intricate pattern of clear, bright colours. There was a triptych of pale oak, carved so as to give it the peculiar property of seeming to have been moulded in Plasticine. The sanctuary lamp and all the metal furniture were of bronze, hand-beaten to the patina of a pock-marked skin; the altar steps had a carpet of grass-green, strewn with white and gold daisies. "Golly," I said.' Evelyn Waugh often stayed at Madresfield, being a great friend of the children of the seventh Earl, and he dedicated his novel *Black Mischief*, which he wrote at Madresfield, to two of the daughters.

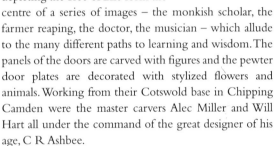

OWLPEN MANOR

Gloucestershire

Norman Jewson was out bicycling one summer's day in the early 1920s and stumbled upon the Cotswold idyll of Owlpen. Through this valley, one of the deepest in Gloucestershire, he had travelled to the lane's end where a small church stood on a high terrace on the wooded northern slopes and the Manor nestled below. The house was then half-strangled with ivy, and great yew trees as tall as the gables crowded in around it and stood sentinel along the short path which led to two beautiful ball-topped Queen Anne gate piers through which was a view to the fields and a wooded skyline on the other side of the valley. 'The house was rapidly falling into complete decay, but a caretaker lived in a kitchen wing and would show some of the rooms to visitors . . . The terraced gardens with a yew parlour and groups of neat, clipped yews remained just as they were in the time of Queen Anne, a gardener being kept to look after them. In spite of the dilapidation of the house,

which was so far advanced that one of the main roof trusses had given way, the great stone bay window had become almost detached from the wall and huge roots of ivy had grown right across some of the floors, it seemed to me that such an exceptionally beautiful and interesting old house might still be saved.'

Owlpen was Jewson's ultimate Sleeping Beauty and when in July 1925 it came up for sale he bought it together with its old garden and outbuildings for £2,200. Like Daneway, the ancient house near Sapperton which was an ideal of the local Arts and Crafts practitioners such as the Barnsleys and Ernest Gimson, so too was Owlpen a symbol of 'the accumulated experience of the past'. A host of talented local craftsmen were employed and Jewson supervised the gentle repair of Owlpen, not its restoration, which was the philosophy of the Society for the Protection of Ancient Buildings founded by William Morris of which Jewson was a dedicated member. All was subtly and carefully revived but because he could not afford to live there he sold it on at a personal loss the following year. His great friend the artist F L Griggs, who led a revival of etching in the tradition of Samuel Palmer and William Blake, made an etching of Owlpen Manor which showed a heavily romantic Arcadian England, with the house all hemmed in by yews. It became much sought after by collectors on both sides of the Atlantic as being a nostalgic symbol of Englishness. Griggs gave Jewson a proof of his etching inscribed 'To my friend NORMAN JEWSON, who, with one only purpose, & at his own cost & loss, possessed himself of the demesne of OWLPEN when, for the first time in seven hundred years, it passed into alien hands, & with great care & skill saved this ancient house from ruin'.

Today those tall yews have gone and having been such an introverted house for so long Owlpen Manor's southern façade now shows its face to the passer-by with its undulating roof and many different windows set all over the place in a jumbled and haphazard way. None the less, as perhaps only Cotswold stone can bring about, the whole looks utterly harmonious. The family of Olepenne were settled here in the eleventh century and in the middle of the fifteenth century John Daunt from nearby Wooton-under-Edge married into the line.

It was the Daunt family who made the romantic jumble which Norman Jewson found in such sad repair. They had built and improved on the house in slow stages over three centuries and they had created the garden with its terraces climbing up the hill behind, its layout of yew trees and its symmetrical paths. The Tudor Daunts built the middle section of the house which comprised a hall with a great chamber above it. Then Thomas Daunt II built the left-hand gabled section at the beginning of the seventeenth century and Thomas Daunt V remodelled some of the house by putting in sash windows and he created the garden between 1710 and 1720.

It is an utterly unassuming house with no pretensions to grandeur. There is Queen Anne panelling, there are bolection fireplaces, leaded lights in mullioned and transomed windows, early Georgian doorways, a panelled parlour and small winding stairs. From every window the garden can be seen huddling securely around this very special manor house.

BADMINTON HOUSE

Gloucestershire

When the last Dowager Duchess of Beaufort was taking some visitors around Badminton, she proudly informed them that the wallpaper in the dining-room was nearly 170 years old. One of the visitors was heard to murmur, 'You'd have thought they'd be sick of it by now', but they had completely missed the point. Badminton has been used and lived in brilliantly for the last 300 years, not in any fossilizing way but with change happening when it was thought necessary, either for comfort or to satisfy the eye or, as in the first Duke's case, for a bit of swank. It has the most relaxed air of almost any large country house in England. It seems to have missed out on the stuffiness and pomp of the nineteenth century as the great houses of Ireland did. There will always be hunting boots of every description in the hall, a motley lot of dogs and a gaggle of perplexed architectural historians who cannot make out who built what for certain. It is precisely this unworried and carefree attitude to the place that has maintained Badminton's special place in the English countryside: amidst its 22,000 acres and twelve-mile belt of fine trees, the enjoyment of sport and country pursuits has long been its *raison d'être*. The Horse Trials (begun in 1948 by the late Duke), are still the highlight of England's eventing year when 25,000 people swarm around the park with the house its ever-magical centre, just as the first Duke envisaged. When Queen Mary, who retreated here in the Second World War, came with a retinue of fifty-five servants and appeared to dinner each evening plastered in diamonds, it didn't suit the house at all. Likewise she hated it here. Perhaps you have to belong to the country to love the place.

Badminton's wide May tree-d village street with its yellow ochre-washed cottages and houses ends in a short drive to the great house and forms an integral part of the whole domain: it is not set haughtily apart. Blue wrought-iron gates open on to arch upon key-stoned arch, leading the eye through stone and colour-washed courtyards, giving glimpses of immaculate stables and farmyards and the Beaufort Hunt kennels, then through the last rusticated arch to the sudden sweeping urn-ed, Palladian-winged front of Badminton House.

The Somerset family first came into the estate when their castle at Raglan was destroyed in the Civil Wars. The Marquess of Worcester, who was then the head of the family, subsequently became the first Duke and decided to aggrandize what was then a modest gabled Elizabethan manor house. He built a majestic façade between 1664 and 1691 at a cost of £29,760 13s 2½d and from his new building radiated avenues in every direction across this flat-as-a-pancake stretch of Gloucestershire to the north and gently undulating stretch to the south, towards the very ends of his land like rays of the sun. Across these rides, twenty-four more intersected. The third Duke embellished and enlarged the house still further, giving it a more swaggering air, and the stable yards were developed and a new classical church sprung up in 1783, almost touching the house and flaunting voluptuously carved ducal memorials.

The north hall, one of the greatest rooms in Britain and remodelled under the auspices of the third Duke, is thought to have been designed by the great favourite of the Tories, James Gibbs. Laced with delicate plasterwork and double-height, its proportions are perfect; you want to dance across its floor the moment you enter and it is not surprising that the game Badminton was invented in its inspirational space. But walk out from the great front door and there at the end of a straight three-mile tree-lined avenue is another of Badminton's crowning glories, Worcester Lodge. It was designed by the great William Kent who, like Gibbs, was a fashionable and popular designer of the day. His Lodge contains a room above the great triumphal arch from which four tall windows look out on to infinite Gloucestershire. When Kent died in the middle of the eighteenth century, the third Duke then employed the genius Thomas Wright of Durham who had already been the astronomer at Wilton and created Gothic and wild fantasies for the third Duke including a castellated set of farm buildings and many of the rusticated cottages in and around the village. Successive Somersets have never ceased to enhance and maintain the house and park, and the present Duke's most recent creations have included beautiful formal gardens on the south and east sides of the house which have served to transform the atmosphere. He has also planted a massive wood in the shape of a star to commemorate his late wife.

SEZINCOTE

Gloucestershire

In the 1920s when Sezincote belonged to Colonel Arthur Dugdale and his idiosyncratic wife, Ethel, it resembled, in James Lees-Milne's words, '. . . an Irish country house, a trifle down at heel, a little chaotic, very dog-ridden, but cosy, the sort of house one reads about in a Mary Keane novel.' John Betjeman, as an undergraduate was a frequent visitor, and wrote:

> Oxford May mornings! When the prunus bloomed
> We'd drive to Sunday lunch at Sezincote:
> First steps in learning how to be a guest,
> First wood-smoke-scented luxury of life
> In the large ambience of a country house . . .
> Down the drive,
> Under the early yellow leaves of oaks;
> One lodge is Tudor, one in Indian style.
> The bridge, the waterfall, the Temple Pool –
> And there they burst on us, the onion domes,
> *Chajjahs* and *chattris* made of amber stone:
> 'Home of the Oaks,' exotic Sezincote!
> Stately and strange it stood, the Nabob's house,
> Indian without and coolest Greek within.
> Looking from Gloucestershire to Oxfordshire;
> And, by supremest landscape-gardener's art,
> The lake below the eastward slope of grass
> Was made to seem a mighty river-reach

> Curving along to Chipping Norton's hills.
> Crackle of gravel! in the entrance-hall
> Boot-jacks and mattocks, hunting mackintosh,
> And whips and sticks and barometric clock
> Were Colonel Dugdale's; but a sheaf of bast
> And gardening-basket told us of his wife . . .
> Dear Mrs. Dugdale, mother of us all,
> In trailing and Edwardian-looking dress,
> A Sargent portrait in your elegance,
> Sweet confidante in every tale of woe!
> She and her son and we were on the Left,
> But Colonel Dugdale was Conservative.
> From one end of the butler-tended board
> The Colonel's eyes looked out towards the hills,
> While at the other end our hostess heard
> Political and undergraduate chat . . .
> The onion-dome which listened all the time
> To water filling after-tennis baths,
> To water splashing over limestone rock
> Under the primulas and thin bamboo,
> The cottages and lanes and woods and paths
> Are all so full of voices from the past
> I do not dare return.

It is appropriate that Sezincote faces east. This Hindu and Mogul palace, glowing golden in the Cotswolds, displayed at the time of its building in the beginning of the nineteenth century an extraordinary daring and flew in the face of all those purist classical idealists and Members of the Dilettanti Society. The Cockerells who built Sezincote had actually been to India whereas the

majority of the grand tourers had only been as far as Greece. The Sezincote estate was bought in 1795 by John Cockerell, a colonel in the East India Company's service and a Quartermaster-General to Lord Cornwallis. He died three years later and left the new estate equally between his younger brothers Charles, who became a baronet and had also lived in India, and Samuel Pepys, an architect. They started on the garden immediately and as Samuel Pepys had never in fact been to India he leaned on the inspiration of Thomas Daniell and his nephew William whose famous series of drawings and aquatints were amongst the first images of India that the English had ever seen. The Daniells had spent three years in northern India and eighteen months in the south and recorded many famous monuments. Humphry Repton, the landscaper, was called in and translated the Daniells' shrines, bridges and ornaments. He made a snake pool

where a three-headed snake is coiled around a tree and spouts water from its mouth. Repton was so impressed by the Daniells' brilliance at creating views of India that he begged the Prince Regent to come and look. There is no doubt that the Brighton Pavilion, built a little later than Sezincote, was modelled upon it. The inside of the house is entirely classical. Perhaps Lady Cockerell had bargained with her husband: he could have his Indian exterior if she could have her classical interior. Certainly on entering you are unexpectedly in Greece. An extraordinarily elegant and light double-flight staircase curves upwards, and looking out from the bowed Venetian windows of the drawing-room on glorious Gloucestershire you forget completely that you had been in India. Sezincote will always be a happy house. It has a surprised and fresh look with its raised eyebrows above the windows, lacy verandahs and its perfect onion dome.

STANWAY HOUSE

Gloucestershire

Stanway lies on the lower slopes of a long steep hill, one of the last of the great Cotswold escarpment. Its beautiful buildings are scattered along a Pilgrim's or 'stony' way (hence its name) which wends its way southwards for a mile or so to the great ruined abbey of Hailes and then on up the wooded slopes to the isolated church at Farncote.

Stanway has changed hands only once in nearly 1,300 years. Its ancient and settled feel is absolute and although its buildings have evolved over 1,000 years, they form a glorious and golden whole. All, from the church to the fourteenth-century tithe barn to the dazzling Jacobean gatehouse to the Victorian stable block to the multi-gabled manor itself, are built of the same fine-grained limestone from the Jackdaw Quarry high on the hill, sometimes cut in huge five-foot blocks and sometimes delicately worked into intricately carved coats of arms.

The original Stanway Manor was granted to the abbots of Tewkesbury in AD 715 by two rich Mercian brothers called Odo and Dodo. Before this county was to house more abbeys than any other in England (provoking the saying 'As sure a God is in Gloucestershire'), four monks were already residing here in a cell and the monastic settlement grew over the next 700 years. By the sixteenth century the covetous Tracy family of nearby Toddington had seen the property development potential of Stanway. They ingratiated themselves with Thomas Cromwell, promoted the dissolution of Stanway by telling awful stories about it and attained a lease on it in 1533. It was one of the earliest monastic settlements to be dissolved by Henry VIII. Richard Tracy subsequently led the commission which dissolved Hailes, declared its sacred phial of the Holy Blood to be duck's blood tinted with saffron, and took part in the dismantling of the building. The Tracys were directly descended from one of the four knights who murdered Thomas à Becket and their infamy among the locals was legendary – 'The Tracys, the Tracys, the wind in their faces' they used to say as the Tracys fled the ghosts and curses of their past.

Stanway House itself was built between 1580 and 1640 on the site of the eighth-century manor. Sir Paul Tracy built the long gabled west front which faces out to the church and barn and is so much part of the whole cluster. He also built the Jacobean gatehouse, which mixes every style going and is perhaps the most beautiful building of all. Parts of earlier buildings were incorporated into the new house and there were further alterations in the eighteenth and nineteenth centuries, by which time the Charteris family, who still own Stanway, had married into the Tracy line. The feeling of the house remains predominantly Stuart. The oriel window of the hall with over 1,000 leaded lights floods the west side of the house with evening light. Cynthia Asquith, who was born here, referred to the window in her diaries as '. . . so mellowed by time that whenever the sun shines through their amber and green glass, the effect is of a vast honeycombe and indeed at all times and in all weathers of stored sunshine'.

Although the Charteris' main seat was at Gosford in Midlothian, the eldest sons often lived at Stanway and it was Mary, the wife of Hugo (Lord Elcho) who brought a kind of fame to Stanway in the late-nineteenth century when she made it a centre for the Souls (see Belton on page 94), the group of rich artistic intellectuals who discussed higher things. She reigned supreme if absent-mindedly at Stanway and condoned the local vicar's eccentric promotion of free love and whisky drinking, and even allowed him to create a home for sick horses and donkeys at the vicarage.

The grandest of chestnut avenues leads away to the north to the little village of Stanton, and directly behind the house is a series of terraces climbing dramatically higher and higher up the steep hill topped by a Vanburghian pyramid built in the 1750s. 'To the happy memory of John Tracy, gentleman', states the epitaph. Beneath it runs a culvert through which water is released by means of a sluice to run from the pond behind the pyramid, down a cascade and into a canal. It is a spectacular and ambitious garden adornment which had long since clogged up and ceased to work until it was restored and triumphantly opened in 1998 by the present incumbent's father with a fanfare and fireworks. From these heights you can see right across the Vale of Evesham, over the strange lumpy hills of Dumbleton and Bredon, to the Malverns and the Black Mountains of Wales.

OPPOSITE

The house's Elizabethan west front rises up behind the forecourt's north arch. In the background can be seen the inner side of the gatehouse.

ABOVE

There are no less than sixty lights in the great bay window of the hall.

FRAMPTON COURT

Gloucestershire

BELOW

A rich variety of superbly carved motifs gives a misleading impression of great size to the entrance front.

Frampton-on-Severn is one of the most beautiful villages in England, stranded between the M5 motorway and the mile-wide River Severn. It lies in unregarded flat, watery vale country with views westwards across the river to the Forest of Dean and the mountains of Wales in the blue distance beyond. Most of the village is tucked away in a cul-de-sac. A small road threads its way through the middle of the great wide Rosamund's Green, almost three-quarters of a mile long. A manor house, a brick farmhouse with a large duck pond before it, thatched cottages and barns are scattered along its edges. 'Fair Rosamund' Clifford was born at the ancient, rambling half-timbered Manor Farm on the west side of the green. Rosamund's Bower, a projecting first-floor window which looks out towards passers-by, is said to be where she sat when Henry II rode by and fell in love with her. She became his openly acknowledged mistress and her untimely death in 1176 was shrouded in mystery. One legend has it that Queen Eleanor picked up a silken thread dropped by Fair Rosamund from her embroidery and found their secret meeting place in the middle of the maze where the Queen offered her a choice of a dagger or poison. Another was that she was bled to death in a hot bath near Woodstock. The pink and white striped 'Rosamunda' rose is named after her. Descendants of the Clifford family still live at Manor Farm and opposite, half hidden by chestnut trees, ilexes and a long wall, is Frampton Court, also owned by the Cliffords. An elegant sweep of steps rises to the front door at the centre of the main

block and there are small wings either side with daringly high chimneys, similar to those of Vanburgh's design.

Frampton Court was built in 1731 by Richard Clutterbuck. He came from a Gloucestershire weaving family, and his grandfather, Nathaniel, had married Mary Clifford, the heiress to Frampton after the male line had ended. 'Clutterbucks' was a well-known type of strand cloth named after the weaver. During the first thirty years of the eighteenth century, amateur architects abounded and it is probable that Frampton was designed by Sir Edward Southwell, an enthusiastic amateur who revered Vanburgh, the architect of his own house at Kings Weston near Bristol or possibly by a British architect named Strahan.

'The craftsmanship within the house is of such wonder that it beggars belief' wrote Christopher Hussey. The panelling, doorways, cupboards, cornices and balusters are exquisitely worked and there is an eighteenth-century dog gate at the bottom of the stairs which concertinas out from the wall with perfect precision, in a series of curly crisscrosses. Looking from the drawing-room windows out over the park the sudden Cotswold escarpment rises from the flatness like a theatre backdrop behind a stage. You can imagine the five Clifford

daughters who lived here in the nineteenth century and loved it so. They never married. For years they catalogued the flora of the park and meadows around with exquisite watercolours and descriptions. Twenty years ago these were discovered in the attic at Frampton Court and produced as a book called *Frampton Flora*. In the garden and visible from the green, there is a 'Strawberry Hill Gothic' orangery which stands at the end of a rectangular canal in which it is reflected.

Beyond the green's end, the road bends and becomes an ordinary village street until, as the houses begin to peter out, it stops at the beautiful Church of St Mary, set alone and apart. A Judas tree hangs over the churchyard wall and there is a gravestone carved with a weeping willow by John Pearce. The church windows are mostly of clear glass and it feels airy and light as you enter. A track continues on to Splatt Bridge which spans the Gloucester to Sharpness canal and swings open to let the barges through. Beside it is the canal keeper's cottage, like a little Doric temple with a pediment and fluted columns in perfect Cheltenham-style Regency. Then there is marsh, merging with the muddy creeks and inlets of a swooping bend in the River Severn called the Noose.

TRAQUAIR HOUSE

Peebleshire

Down the wide straight avenue of limes, which leads from the Bear Gates, and across the wine-glass lawn stands Traquair, the archetypal romantic Scottish house. Great high hills rise behind it and what was once the Ettrick Forest is all around; now only a sprinkling of old yew trees remains. Here Scottish royalty stayed, as did Edward I and II of England, and took part in their favourite pastimes of hunting, hawking and fishing when wild cats, wolves, bears and wild boar roamed the woods. In 1460 James III of Scotland gave Traquair, then a simple defensive tower house of three storeys, with walls up to 6 feet 9 inches thick, to his master of music, William Rogers who nine years later sold it to the King's uncle, a Stuart and Earl of Buchan nicknamed 'Hearty James' for the sum of £3 15s 10d to be paid in two instalments. It is from him that the family who live here today are descended.

Before Hearty James could add to the tower as he had intended to do, he was killed beside King James IV on Flodden Field in 1513. Sir William Stuart extended and heightened the house in 1599 still rendering it a bastion of refuge with tiny windows and rooms. During the first half of the seventeenth century when his great nephew John Stuart became the first Earl of Traquair, the main block of the house was built and Traquair has been little altered since. His erratic and melodramatic career which had brought him enforced retirement when he had fallen from office in 1641 had brought the building about. He had been a favourite of Charles I and was made Treasurer Depute of Scotland and hence an earl. In 1646 he decided to rescue the King, was taken prisoner in England and when he eventually returned to Scotland years later he found that all his friends had abandoned him and his fortune was gone. He ended his days begging in the streets in Edinburgh with not enough money to cobble his boots.

After the death of 'the Beggar Earl' his son began the long Catholic tradition of the Earls of Traquair and the house remained a great bastion of the Catholic faith, surrounded by droves of Presbyterians who frequently ransacked Traquair trying to find objects of popery. Mass was celebrated in secret and a concealed staircase at the back of a cupboard was used as a priest's escape hole and to this day can be crawled through weaving in and out of secret passages down from the top of the house to the bottom. The fourth Earl of Traquair, suspected of being a Jacobite sympathizer which indeed he was, was imprisoned in Edinburgh Castle in 1715 shortly after his marriage to the beautiful Lady Mary Maxwell who had seventeen children by him. Mary's family were sympathizers too and during the 1715 rising her sister-in-law, Lady Nithsdale, set out from Traquair to London dressed as a man and bravely rescued her husband from the Tower where he had been sentenced to death for his part in the same rising.

One late autumn day in 1745 the fifth Earl, after wishing his guest Prince Charles Edward Stuart (Bonnie Prince Charlie) a safe journey, closed the most famous gates in all Scotland, the Bear Gates, behind him and promised that they would never be reopened until the Stuarts were restored to the throne. Traquair had become a living symbol of lost causes. In the seventeenth century the lands had extended through three counties but by 1800 the estate was greatly reduced. The eighth Earl however did much to patch up the reckless ventures of his forebears and modernized the farm buildings and estate. He was meticulous to a degree and particularly enjoyed sharpening razors, a service he readily undertook for all his tenants, free of charge. Being a confirmed bachelor he grew so tired of his family's efforts at matchmaking that he deterred any likely female suitors by putting stinging nettles in their beds when they came to stay. The earldom ran out the eighth time around and Traquair was inherited by the eighth Earl's sister, Lady Louisa Stuart who lived until her hundredth year when she decided to go to Edinburgh to buy a hat, caught a cold and died. Today Traquair feels calm, settled and happy. Its story is laced with stoicism, bravery and loyalty – still apparent today through the two ladies of Traquair – mother and daughter, keeping it very much alive and sharing it with the public through sheer hard work but ultimately as a labour of love.

OPPOSITE
A view of the forecourt, from the avenue.

BELOW
In a photograph taken early this century, the picturesquely tumbledown gate lodges flank the Bear Gates, which will never be opened until the Stuarts are restored to the throne.

DUFF HOUSE

Aberdeenshire

OPPOSITE

*From the south-east,
the powerfully
modelled forms of
William Adam's
design make a
dramatic impact.*

BELOW

*The view of
the Moray Firth from
the roof.*

Duff House stands high and proud near the rugged coastline of the Moray Firth where the cliffs are enormous and the sunsets brilliant. Next door is the grand little town of Banff, once a fashionable winter resort and still full of architectural surprises: a Venetian window here, a Greek column there, among the Scottish crow-stepped gables. Across the estuary of the River Deveron is the busy fishing port of Macduff which was expanded in the late eighteenth century when the harbour at Banff silted up. Behind Duff House a two-mile walk winds inland beside the wooded bank of the Deveron and up to the spectacular bridge of Alvah which crosses a forty-foot gorge.

The setting of Duff is as dramatic and beautiful as this, perhaps the best baroque house in Britain. It was designed by William Adam and although it was never finished and is missing its intended flanking colonnades which should have curved in a horseshoe shape to end in two wings, it seems to bowl you over all the more for its sudden rising from the land. It was commissioned by William Duff of Braco whose father was immensely rich, ruthless and sagacious and who owned many estates to which William later added. He had already employed the architect James Gibbs at his estate at Balvanie and after retiring as MP for Banff he resolved 'to settle at home and

his family pretty numerous and yearly growing he also Resolved for his Amusement and better Accomodation [sic] to make Considerable Alterations to his principall Mansion house near to the Town of Banff'. When a friend suggested that he should not add to the existing house but build a new one altogether and when he felt proud at being awarded an Irish peerage and becoming Lord Braco and rich enough with his income of £30,000 a year, he abandoned the plans for the old house and decided on a brand-new house by William Adam on a virgin site.

The foundation stone of the new mansion was laid on the 11 June 1735. From then on no expense was spared. The stone for the front façade was shipped from Queensferry along the Firth of Forth and the sides and back were built of Morayshire freestone. Timber was floated down the River Dee to Aberdeen and from thence to Banff from Lord Braco's new estate at Mar and more was brought from Norway. Lord Braco was a hard taskmaster and impatient as well as being tight with his money and litigious. He himself admitted, 'I am like all Scotsmen'. When, during the second year of operations the barrow men went on strike for a penny a day increase to sixpence, Lord Braco refused them and employed others. Later he tried to have two of the strikers put in prison for breaking their contract. He had rows with William Adam from the outset, first as to whether there should be an attic storey or not but mostly about the cost of everything. He wanted the best but he expected his architect to bargain for it. He was suspicious about everything and accused Adam of wanting 'to make a good Estate for himself out of this Single Jobb'. Lord Braco ended by calling Adam 'ane abandoned Rascal'. The whole episode caused Lord Braco such anguish that when he drove past the house he pulled down the coach blinds. He then proceeded to sue Adam unsuccessfully. The house cost £70,000 and remained unfinished; it was an empty shell inside.

In 1739 Lord Braco was made the first Earl of Fife and the house was to remain empty until his son, a Jacobite supporter with whom the first Earl had many rows, inherited it. He finished off the interior in the late 1750s, putting carved panelling and pilasters in the dining-room and by the 1780s had constructed the main staircase and completed the two big rooms on the second floor, planned originally as state rooms. The fourth Earl decorated the house still further but the last radical redecoration was in the mid-Victorian period by the wife of the fifth Earl who added much gilding. However in 1870 the fifth Earl decided that he preferred his remote property of Mar next to Balmoral. Duff House, gaunt and abandoned, became a white elephant until the enlightened Timothy Clifford of the Scottish National Gallery used it as his premier 'outpost' for paintings for which there was no room in the main gallery in Edinburgh.

ARDKINGLAS

Argyll

At seventy, though far from retired, Sir Andrew Noble, having earned a pile as chairman of his friend William Armstrong's armaments business, wanted to build the perfect holiday house. He was a practical man and deemed Robert Lorimer an efficient architect, as well as being one of Scotland's most inspired. Unlike his contemporary, Charles Rennie Mackintosh, who was busy stylizing his designs into elongated Art Nouveau shapes in Glasgow, Lorimer, from a solid scholastic family, took a more traditional and Baronial approach – based on his seventeenth-century Fifeshire home Kellie Castle. Sir Andrew Noble had said he wanted 'nothing but the best and hang the expense'. He had given Lorimer a virtual *carte blanche* but had asked that his bedroom be on the same floor as the dining-room. An immensely liveable plan emerged of saloon, drawing-room, dining-room and the main bedroom suite all encircling a small inner courtyard on the principal floor. A picturesque grouping was obtained to look as though the building had evolved over a few centuries. The crow-stepped gables, tiled roofs, battlements, turrets, rounded bays and dormer windows are all at different heights but all of the same local stone, described by a neighbour Charles Maclean as 'whisky coloured'. They all blend harmoniously in the extraordinarily beautiful site under huge hills and the house looks out across the glassy water of Loch Fyne.

Sir Andrew was not a brilliant businessman for nothing, and although his energetic bossy daughter, Lillias, had a lot to do with supervising the building works, it was Sir Andrew who had the final say and saw to it that the whole house was begun and finished in eighteen months at a cost of £55,000. Like his friend William Armstrong of Cragside, he naturally wanted all the very latest gadgets and mod cons. The electric light fittings which still adorn the house today are scintillatingly elegant and were at the time extremely advanced. The Arts and Crafts ideals of a merged practicality and romanticism are displayed at Ardkinglas to their optimum. The house was built to be rather like a hotel for all Sir Andrew's relations and friends to escape to during high days and holidays. All the rooms are either panelled or plastered and whitewashed. The layout of the guest quarters is highly efficient. Lorimer even designed the shower cages, which sit in turquoise-tiled niches, and the views from the bedrooms are dreamlike. The oak-panelled saloon where everyone gathered, with its silver electroliers hanging down like Art Nouveau jewellery, is dominated by a huge stone fireplace whose lintel is carved from a single slab of granite weighing more than five tons, and under which blazed an enormous log fire. Its windows look out in two directions, up and down the loch. The ceiling is rich in neo-Queen Anne plasterwork

garlanding itself round a central panel later painted by the Bloomsbury artist Roger Fry to depict Apollo in his chariot who, according to one member of the Noble family, appears to look distinctly car-sick.

Ardkinglas was completed in 1907 and for eight Edwardian summers was holidayed in to the full by the genial Sir Andrew and his Scottish-Canadian wife whose dream it had always been to return to the land of her forebears here on the west coast of Scotland. In 1915 Sir Andrew was 'called over' by the roaring of the stags in Glen Kinglas.

Today for Johnny Noble, Sir Andrew's great grandson, Ardkinglas is a family home. He still uses the high, white-tiled kitchen which remains exactly as it did in his great-grandfather's day and he still dines out on the balcony overlooking the loch on summer evenings. 'It may seem eccentric to some people, my living here as I do, but how many places can you go out and catch a salmon, or shoot a woodcock for dinner, or walk down to the shore

OPPOSITE
This photograph of the house from the north-east was taken in 1911, just four years after it was completed.

and gather your own oysters?' he says. The present laird's brilliance and innovative ideas have made Ardkinglas a self-sufficient estate. In the 1970s when he inherited it he determined to adapt it into a going concern. 'The days of seven gardeners toiling away to produce vegetables for the "big house" are long gone. Whether the sheep lived or died didn't make a ha'p'orth of difference to my great-grandfather. To me it does. But if you include all the tenanted enterprises being run from the estate, Ardkinglas provides as many if not more jobs than it did in Andrew Noble's time.' It was Johnny's idea to seed oysters on the shores of Loch Fyne and now twenty years later the fresh oysters, langoustine, smoked salmon and smoked kippers sell all over the world.

ABOVE
The baronial austerity of Arkinglas's exterior was belied by the interior, equipped with every technological luxury. This is one of the shower cages.

ABBOTSFORD HOUSE

Selkirkshire

It is the spirit of Sir Walter Scott which pervades at Abbotsford and makes it, perhaps, the greatest of all our literary shrines. 'So potent is Sir Walter's personality', writes the historian Hugh Massingberd, 'that you feel he might, at any moment, pop his dome-like head around the door.' When Sir Walter's great-great-great-granddaughter, Patricia Maxwell Scott died in 1998, who with her sister had been in charge of his beloved home for over forty years, her obituarist tried to define why Abbotsford was such a particularly strong and moving place to visit, compared to other houses open to the public. 'The real difference was the welcoming spirit the Maxwell Scott sisters bestowed on their house. Seven-day weekly opening, and a warm welcome for each visitor, with a strong parting impression of the importance of Sir Walter himself, became part of a visit to Abbotsford. There were no high-tech resources or modern visitors' aids. The Maxwell Scotts' personal involvement has been a model for other historic house owners.'

The Edinburgh-born Scott had developed an early love for this border country when as a sickly child he used to stay for long stints on his grandfather's farm near Abbotsford. Later as a young lawyer serving as Sheriff Depute of Selkirkshire he travelled around the area, never tiring of hearing traditional stories and local ballads which fired his infinitely romantic soul. When he began writing in earnest, his poems 'The Lay of the Last Minstrel', 'The Lady of the Lake' and 'Marmion' made him enough to finance the beginnings of his dream: to own his own home beside the Tweed, the river he loved so passionately. Despite advice from many quarters to buy elsewhere, Scott saw the potential of the messy, down-at-heel farm of Cartley Hall.

'My dreams about my country cottage go on. My present intention is to have only two spare rooms with dressing-rooms, each of which, at a pinch, will have a couch bed; but I cannot relinquish my Border principles of accommodating all the cousins and duniwassals who will sleep on the floor and in the hay-loft rather than be absent when folks are gathered together.' Thus wrote Scott about his new acquisition. And indeed the world and his wife did gather over the ensuing years in the gradually growing house. Neighbours, relations and an ever-growing fan club from every corner of Britain visited Abbotsford, from Wordsworth and Thomas Moore, to Maria Edgeworth and Washington Irving. Parties of French prisoners-of-war on parole in Selkirk regularly came to dinner and entertained Scott with first-hand descriptions of their Emperor, Napoleon, and when the King visited in 1822 (wearing flesh-coloured tights under his kilt), he exclaimed, 'Sir Walter Scott! The man in Scotland I most wish to see!'

By this time Scott was in literary full sail, his *Waverley* novels feeding the public with the romantic image of Scotland they craved and which, to the English at any rate, had hitherto been hidden in a murky mist of unfortunate history. Because of the success of his writings he had been able to add to his land, and in the end, he pulled down the old farm and built a new house altogether. With its crow steps and turrets, its towers and gables, its battlements and portcullis, it was everything Scott had ever dreamed of – a romance in stone. 'Abbotsford is all I can make it' he said '. . . I look back at the time when there was not a tree here, only bare heath; I look round and see thousands of trees growing up, all of which – I may say, almost each of which – have received my personal attention.'

Scott hung on to his beloved Abbotsford when, with the collapse of the printing firm of which he was a sleeping partner, he was faced with liabilities of £116,000. Honourable to the end, he spent his last years writing nineteen to the dozen to pay off his debts, thus allowing the house to remain intact, which it still is today. It is full to the brim with Scott's squirrel-like selection of historic relics including Bonny Dundee's pistol and Rob Roy's broadsword. The most moving room of all is Scott's study, the scene of his unremitting toil, which was to reward so many. His small desk faces into the room, for he feared that if he looked out on the view he so loved, he would be carried away into a reverie and would not be able to write.

RIGHT

Scott's study, where he wrote his novels. It is connected by a staircase to his bedroom, so he could return to work here at night, unbeknown to his guests.

OPPOSITE

The entrance front and courtyard.

MERTOUN HOUSE

Roxburghshire

East of the small town of St Boswells, Mertoun House stands on a dramatically high bank above the majestic River Tweed. It commands the most spectacular of views to the ornamental park on the opposite bank where artfully positioned trees merge with the fertile farmland of this bold border country all around. Beyond, the distant Cheviot Hills form a beautiful backdrop. A narrow Victorian suspension bridge spanning the wide water is hidden by trees.

The Scotts of Harden, whose domain it was, are one of the oldest families in the Borders. Their early history is scattered with tales of cattle rustling, border forays and colourful wives such as 'Muckle-mouthed Meg' and 'the Flower of Yarrow' who brought her husband, Walter, a pair of spurs on a plate whenever the larder was bare. William Scott bought Mertoun on the 22 September 1641 from the Haliburtons and the records underline the value of the salmon fishing in the Tweed even then. William lived in the old crow-stepped house by the high-walled garden which served the family well, but when his grandson, also William, inherited Mertoun at the age of sixty there were radical changes. Although William's unpleasant wife Dame Jean Nisbet couldn't abide Mertoun or her husband she was a compulsive spender and egged him on to build a new house. She even 'sold the silver Plate with all the other Household furniture & thus accomplished her importunat Desire in liveing in Edinburgh. She would not be persuaded to stay with him att Mertoun but during the last thirteen years of his life kept a separate ffamilie which undoubtedly occasioned a vast Deal of Expences Considering that Sir Wm entertained thirty servants without a mistress'. Scott employed the famous architect, Sir William Bruce, the founder of classical architecture in Scotland, to build their elegant house at Mertoun, in the palest pink sandstone. Bruce had enlarged and remodelled Holyroodhouse for Charles II and built great houses such as Hopetown and his own Kinross House. At Mertoun he employed Tobias Bachop as master mason and the house was begun in 1703 but was still unfinished in 1707 when Scott died with debts of around £11,000.

Dame Jean had successfully ruined him, and the fortunes of subsequent Scotts ebbed through the next two centuries, flowing a little now and then, but never far enough to secure Mertoun for future generations of the family. In 1912 Mertoun was sold to the Duke of Sutherland's father who doubled its size. In 1953 it was reduced back to the original William Bruce house and the Sutherland family still live here today. The Duchess is a keen gardener and there is much new planting of rhododendrons and Korean azaleas near the house and artificial lake. In one of her favourite spots, by an ivy-covered wall, she has created a small rock and sandstone terraced garden for spring-flowering alpines.

The old parish church stands in the woods to the west of the house and to the east a path leads above the Tweed down under trees and back to the original Scott house which now looks over the best vegetable garden in Britain. Below it stands a large beehive-shaped dovecote by a little rushing stream with the date of 1567 over the door. Through the garden gate at the bottom of the slope and up through an orchard of 100-year-old apple trees under which a flock of geese graze, the garden spreads over a south-facing slope. The onions are as big as footballs, the lines of sweet peas as high and as wide as Becher's Brook and the rows of parsley like bright green hedges. Here is perfect orderly timelessness. The garden is designed for maximum cropping rather than in some new-fangled interpretation of the famous French *potager* at Villandry in France which set the fashion for myriad kitchen gardens across the land turning into complicated geometric patterns. Here at Mertoun is the everlasting real vegetable garden mixed with pockets of perfect flowers and greenhouses of figs and peaches trained to perfection with white-painted and raffia-bound branches. It is the domain of Mr Breed who has lived all his life at Old Mertoun House. His father was head gardener before him.

OPPOSITE

Mertoun in springtime, framed by azaleas.

BELOW

Fruit, vegetables and flowers in the walled garden.

MELSETTER HOUSE

Orkney Islands

Here amidst silvery walled fields and mild hills, back from the rugged red sandstone cliffs, Melsetter House nestles among some of the only trees on the whole Island of Hoy as though it too is growing in the landscape. Until the fifteenth century the Orkneys had belonged to Denmark and still their place names and much of their language is Scandinavian. They remain suspicious of the Scots who became their landlords but friendlier towards southerners. It was to this remotest of places that the successful Birmingham industrialist Thomas Middlemore felt drawn to retire from the world and build his dream. He was the eighth of thirteen children and on becoming manager of the family leather business made its fortunes escalate. He added a factory at Coventry which supplied bicycle accessories. By the time he finally inherited the business in 1889 he had grown tired of the hurly-burly of industrial Birmingham. His wife Theodosia's family had originally come from Sutherland. She was a great friend of William Morris' daughter, May. The Middlemores mixed with the Birmingham Arts and Crafts set with their high ideals and early socialist leanings. Rather than building a swanky pile somewhere in the Midlands to display the Middlemore money, Thomas opted for 'the simple life' and in 1898, having sold the family firm, he bought the Melsetter estate which comprised the islands of Hoy, Walls, Fara and Rysa.

William Lethaby, whom Middlemore had probably met through his Arts and Crafts connections, was his ideal architect. Brought up on the north coast of Devon, he had worked in the office of the legendary Victorian architect Norman Shaw, and had been singled out by the great spokesman on the Arts and Crafts Movement Hermann Muthesius as the star of Shaw's large stable. 'The number of his houses is not large but all appear to be masterpieces' he wrote, and 'continued the best traditions of English house building.' Lethaby took inordinate trouble with his jobs: at his last at Avon Tyrrell, he had produced 229 working drawings in his own hand – nothing was too much trouble for him. He sought a harmonious perfection using the local styles and materials, and Melsetter remains one of the greatest hymns to the philosophy of the Arts and Crafts Movement.

The site he chose came after much deliberation: 'near the top of the hill which slopes gently away to the south-east . . .' he wrote, 'here it stands protected from Atlantic gales but high enough to command the widest views of the Scapa Flow and across to the rugged coast of Caithness and the mountains of West Sutherland beyond.' Around were the gold, brown and green hills of Hoy and below it the sea of 'a peacock's neck in hue'. Lethaby's house clung to the vestiges of a small and existing dwelling and used the old walls of the garden. Perhaps with the echoes of William Morris' Kelmscott, Melsetter rose with its undulating waves of gables and its perfectly crafted details and finish of traditional harling and red sandstone dressings. It has a clarity and an unsurpassed simplicity which is utterly satisfying, with its stone balls, sedate chimneys, neat crowsteppings and fine elegant brackets holding up the guttering.

Inside, Melsetter exemplifies the ideals of the age, combining terrific practicality with high romance. There were light panelled walls, inglenooks, wonderful friezes of plasterwork laced with wild flowers, furniture by Ernest Gimson and fabrics by William Morris, china displayed on shelves at picture-rail level, cosy fireside chairs, beautifully simple dressers designed by Lethaby, and everywhere a feeling of welcoming warmth. In the chapel across the courtyard with its exaggerated buttresses is the most beautiful piece of stained glass designed by Ford Maddox Brown. Lethaby had woven together the disparate remains of the old steading and made a cosy courtyard at the heart of things. From the courtyard a little glimpse can be had of 'the street' of small outbuildings. The names of Thomas and Theodosia were inscribed on a cornerstone with a heart between them on the completion of this their perfect house – 18 August 1898. They were happy here and the famous Orcadian Jo Grimond, who also loved it here, said, 'The sea ensures that Orkney is never hot. Nor are its colours hot. But the character of all Orkney materials, human, vegetable and mineral, is warm, so that when you get into the courtyard of Melsetter, which with its flagstones and great jars might be a piece of Italy, you feel at once surprise and recognition.'

RIGHT
Melsetter House from Melsetter Hill, at the north end of Longhope Bay, looking south over the Pentland Firth.

OPPOSITE
In this view of the garden front, it is hard to tell what is Wiiliam Lethaby''s work (principally the wing on the right) and what is earlier.

BIDDICK HALL

County Durham

County Durham is set apart from Scotland and England: it is a County palatine, a land of Prince Bishops and the highest waterfalls in England. It has the River Tees on its southern border, the North Sea on its eastern edge, the River Tyne to the north and the most breathtaking cathedral city in its midst. There are villages called Pity Me, Quaking Houses, Shiney Row and Sunnyside, vast built up industrial areas, and sudden unexpected surprises like Biddick Hall, looking as though it had been picked up from the home counties and planted at the eastern edge of Lambton Park. Beneath the latter are a hundred or so disused coal mines, the making of the Lambton family's fortune, and meandering through, the wide and tidal Wear cuts a deep, dramatic cleft. The low moan of far-off motorways sounds like the sea and in the evening the orange glow of Newcastle-upon-Tyne, six miles away, hangs in the middle distance.

Sir William Lambton of Lambton, who commanded the Durham Dragoons for Charles I, bought the earlier house which stood here and was originally owned by the de Biddics. Sir William was killed at Marston Moor in 1644 and left Biddick to his widow Dame Katherine, assuming that she would then leave it to his second son (his eldest would inherit Lambton Castle across the park). She outlived both her eldest and second sons and it was her grandson Freville who built the present Biddick Hall. The bricks were brought back from Holland as ballast after the produce of the Lambton coal mines had been unloaded; the ceilings were almost certainly decorated by the Italian plasterers who were working on Lumley Castle at the time (1723); and perhaps Vanburgh, who was building Seaton Delaval nearby, had an influence on the design of Biddick. He could even have drawn plans for Freville, who visited Seaton throughout the summer of 1721, for certainly the proportions of Biddick are extravagantly grand for such a house.

Freville's new house had been built around the original Pele tower, and its walls were so thick that the present Lord and Lady Lambton were able to install two bathrooms in their width in the 1950s, the time when Biddick was to have its next major addition. During 1954 and 1955 they added a long wing containing a library on the first floor, running back northwards behind the Georgian nucleus from the design of E M Lawson and Partners of Newcastle. On the ground floor, the school and children's rooms gave on to a new formal garden enclosed by hornbeam hedges and clipped may trees.

The Lambtons are a remarkable, fiercely independent family, with a long parliamentary tradition. General John Lambton, MP for Durham, declined a peerage in 1793 and his grandson William, also an MP, was a brilliant Whig. His son John was perhaps the most famous Lambton of all and became the first Earl of Durham in 1833. He was nicknamed 'Radical Jack' and

'King Jog' ('jogging along on £40,000 a year'), and was a hero among the miners in the north of England, setting an example by establishing a Benevolent Association for old and sick miners in his own collieries. He was a cabinet minister, Lord Privy Seal, and was one of the committee of four who drafted the Reform Bill. He became Governor General of Canada in 1838 and produced the celebrated *Durham Report* which laid the foundation of the British Empire. It was he who bought Reynolds' *The Banished Laird*, having heard the tragic story of James Drummond, heir to the Duke of Perth. The latter was believed to have drowned while escaping to France after the battle of Culloden but instead hid in the labyrinth of coal pits beside the river in the park. He worked incognito as a ferryman and lived in Biddick boathouse for more than twenty years. A terrible flood robbed him of his few possessions and his proof of identity. His grandson enlisted Lord Durham's help to prove his claim to the Earldom of Perth, which ultimately failed. The tale inspired Macaulay to write *Epitaph on a Jacobite*.

> ...*To my true King I offered, free from stain,*
> *Courage and faith – vain faith and*
> *courage vain...*

LEVENS HALL

Cumbria

There could hardly be a more familiar or loved image of England than the gables of Levens Hall poking up behind the giant lumpy topiary shapes. When Colonel Grahme came to live at Levens at the end of the seventeenth century, he was already interested in gardening and was a great friend of the diarist and gardener John Evelyn who encouraged him to recognize that the beauty of nature could be enhanced by planting and by opening vistas. Colonel Grahme appointed the garden designer Monsieur Guillaume Beaumont to reconstruct the garden and park at Levens. The correspondence between them still exists and described the laying out of this famous topiary garden, still intact in its original design. Grahme and Beaumont together made a garden of such wonder that, even in their day, parties came out from Whasset, Row and Kendal over rough terrain and along terrible roads to see it.

Although this period saw the last gasp of formality in grand gardens, and by the eighteenth century radical steps were being taken by the rich to sweep away their parterres and encourage 'nature' instead, the garden at Levens mercifully survived the fickleness of fashion. Grahme's daughter, the Countess of Suffolk and Berkshire, refused to do away with the parterre because she wanted to preserve every item of her childhood memory. When she died the widow of her eldest son came to live at Levens until her death at a great age. Her gardener, who was called Mr McMillan, was as old as she was and let the garden go to seed. The descriptions of it in the early 1800s are of tangled and trailing honeysuckle, mignonette and roses.

When Colonel Grahme's line ran out, Levens was inherited by an Upton and then a Bagot, the great-grandfather of the present owner. Levens remains utterly romantic – its park is speckled with black fallow deer and a small herd of Bagot goats, a rare breed that the present owners are trying to maintain and encourage. Today there

are only four gardeners, while in the nineteenth century there were dozens. The clipping of the giant beech hedge starts in the middle of August and usually takes until mid-October to finish. The yew is then clipped and this takes until December.

The house has been a family home for 700 years – it began first as a peel tower built in the thirteenth century by the Redman family, then their cousins – the Bellinghams turned the fortified tower into a gentleman's residence at the end of the sixteenth century. The last Bellingham, Alan, described by a contemporary as 'that ingenious but unhappy young man', lost the whole of the Levens estate through gambling and it was bought (or possibly won) by his cousin, Colonel Grahme. There is a tradition that Levens was won with the turn of the ace of hearts and certainly there are the most beautiful decorated down spouts on the front of the house with gilded hearts and the initials of James and Dorothy Grahme. The Grahmes added the south wing and the brew house and brought a dash of fashion and elegance to Levens.

Inside, panelling and tapestries abound, the plasterwork, the hallmark of the Bellinghams, is brilliant. Mrs Howard, a Suffolk descendant and heiress, had commissioned much furniture from the famous cabinet maker, Mr Gillow of Lancaster, who had also designed a water closet. The agent wrote to Mr Gillow, 'of course I have no experience of such conveniences'. There is a portrait by William Orpen of a rather disdainful-looking Sir Charles Bagot – a Regency buck, who was known as 'Beauty Bagot' and who had a distinguished career in the Diplomatic Service.

Stories of hauntings are bound to be rife at Levens. The 'Grey Lady' is supposed to be the ghost of a gipsy woman who was refused admission to the house. She died of starvation saying that no son should inherit the house until the River Kent ceased to flow and a white fawn was born in the park. The 'Pink Lady', more benign, walks about in a pink print dress and a mob-cap and the 'Black Dog' is a little woolly dog who runs in front of peoples' legs and up the stairs with unwary guests who then hunt in vain for him in their bedrooms.

BROADLEYS

Cumbria

Charles Francis Annesley Voysey, who designed Broadleys, often repeated his view that 'we cannot be too simple'. By the end of the nineteenth century much Victorian architecture had reached a peak of complication. Like a breath of fresh air Voysey created a stylized adaptation of English country tradition which, along with Charles Rennie Mackintosh in Glasgow, relied on simplicity of composition for greatest effect. Their influence was revolutionary and echoes of their look later swept through the mushrooming suburbs of the early twentieth century. Voysey's interiors were almost puritanically plain. He designed every detail himself and, unlike his hero Morris, he designed his own furniture. His small neat office in Marylebone had two intercommunicating rooms and so methodical was his routine that he only had two articled pupils at any one time. One of them, Noel Sheffield remembers 'there was no typist, no typewriter, no telephone', and Voysey wrote all his letters by hand in the most elaborate script.

The nineteenth century had seen artists and poets flocking to the Lake District. Wordsworth was one of the instigators and the final seal of approval came with Ruskin, the great architectural influence of the nineteenth century, who built a house on Coniston Water. As has often been the case, it is the artists who are the forerunners of fashion, and soon the world and his wife craved the romance of its bold scenery and Lake Windermere in particular.

'Owing to its natural beauty, protected situation and other attractive features, Windermere is popular not only as a holiday resort but as a permanent summer and winter residence. It is entirely modern and in its environs are many residential villas embowered in trees and shrubs and surrounded by beautiful gardens', reads a guide to the Lakes of the 1900s. In 1897 Mr and Mrs Currer Briggs

bought the most idyllic site they could lay their hands on and wrote to Voysey the architect. They were influenced by the new aesthetic movement and wanted for their new house that combination of romance and practicality which the Arts and Crafts Movement promised. Voysey did not disappoint them.

He explained about his building of houses in his essay 'Ideas in things': 'So you will gather your flues together, and collect the rooms in such a sequence that will enable you to cover them with one roof, or as few roofs as possible. Varying planes at varying angles catch and cut up the lights and shades and add to complexity, to the utter destruction of repose and breadth.' Broadleys is all repose and breadth.

Travelling south along the lakeside road, through the village of Bowness, the scenery becomes more dramatic, the villas more sparsely spaced and hidden among the maturity of their Edwardian planting. At Gill Head, where Cartmel Fell looms huge to the south and the road is dark with overhanging trees, a hidden drive turns sharply towards the lake and suddenly one of the

crown jewels of the Arts and Crafts Movement is before you.

The main block of the house faces west towards the lake above terraced gardens designed by Mr Mawson. The service block comes off at a right angle at the back and forms a sort of court where you arrive. Here on this east side are the exaggerated sweeping gables, the cottage-style front door with its hinges forged with heart-shaped ends (a trademark of Voysey), the elaborate gutters, the pebble-dash over the two-foot-thick stone walls, and the cosy, comforting scale of the whole, so nice to come home to on a wet and windy evening. On the west side the great grey Westmorland slated roof dominates the three two-storey bay windows. The hall takes up the central bay through the two storeys; the dining- and drawing-rooms are on either side. Above these are the two main bedrooms with their spectacular views up and down the lake. It is an extremely practical house, having seven bedrooms, two bathrooms, a playroom, a kitchen and the usual domestic offices.

177

BELOW

*Blackwell was designed in 1898 by the sophisticated Hugh
Baillie Scott, a precursor of the Modern Movement, who echoed
the traditional style of the neighbourhood.*

BLACKWELL

Cumbria

Blackwell was built as a holiday home for Edward Holt, a brewery owner and a former Lord Mayor of Manchester. Its setting, a little above the shores of Lake Windermere, is as romantic as its architect, Hugh Baillie Scott. The latter's epitaph on his grave in Edenbridge churchyard in Kent reads, 'Nature he Loved, and, Next to Nature, Art'. He did wonderful watercolours of his proposed and often imaginary interiors – all pale mauves, pale greens and whites in the drawing-rooms or dark wood grained brown and orange in the dining-rooms – which graced the pages of the magazine *The Studio*, essential reading for followers of the latest advanced styles in fine and applied arts. From there Baillie Scott got his commissions. In 1896 Queen Victoria's grandson, Ernest Ludwig, Grand Duke of Hess, commissioned Baillie Scott to decorate two rooms in his palace at Darmstadt in his new style. His friend C R Ashbee's Guild of Handicraft, the already flourishing Arts and Crafts community in the Cotswolds, provided the furniture and metalwork. Through this job Baillie Scott gained more commissions in Germany where, at the time, English architects were set on a pedestal. Blackwell was his first big house in England.

Baillie Scott, the eldest of fourteen children, was sent to agricultural college at Cirencester because his father intended him to manage the family business of sheep farming in Australia. However Baillie Scott insisted on becoming an architect. He was articled to Major Charles Ely Davis who had a practice in Bath and who had been the pupil of Sir John Soane. After he married in 1889 he moved to the Isle of Man where he built many houses in its capital, Douglas.

Baillie Scott was the progenitor of open-plan living in England and he illustrated this at Blackwell in a huge double-height hall from which a single-height inglenook leads off, where you can have a private conversation and yet still feel part of the main company. The ceiling drops again where a bay window breaks to form a space for the billiard table. 'Having arrived at the central idea of a hall being the living-room as the keynote of a home it follows naturally that one must group round this the various other rooms' wrote Baillie Scott about his ideal country house. 'First the "ladies' bower", the "drawing-room" as we now call it. This is a recess in the hall which is set apart for tea and music and is characterized by a certain daintiness of treatment which bears a feminine relation to the masculine ruggedness of the hall . . . at the opposite end is the "refectory". . . Here one catches a glimpse of a table bright with silver, glass, and flowers against the dark background of the seating which runs round three sides of the table . . . one must not omit to mention the obvious adaptability of the hall to festive occasions. The underlying idea of the central focus with its grouped dependencies here exactly meets the requirements of the case, and one need not hesitate as to whether the drawing-room or the dining-room carpet should be taken up for dancing.'

The dining-room at Blackwell is designed to be dark and voluptuous, and has a deep ingle each side of the fireplace lit by two little windows. The drawing-room, in contrast is light and delicate with a bay window looking across Windermere. The tree motif is used as a decoration throughout the house on screens and in carvings. 'It was especially desired that the Mountain Ash should form the subject of the decoration', he wrote. 'In the carved trees, which appear in the staircase screen and on the hall ingle, birds' nests are interwoven in the branches and birds flutter amongst the leaves and fruit. In the brackets to the lower beams and in the bosses to the ceiling various local plants are represented. One is entwined with bryony, another shows the blooms of the wild guelder-rose while the bloom and berries of the hawthorn and the wild rose are amongst the features of the carving. The same variety of carving occurs in the white drawing-room, where, in the capitals to slender columns, the foliage and branches of various trees are represented. Two of the most important features in the metal work are the drawing-room grate and the electric light pendant in the hall. In each of these the ironwork is brightened by white enamelled and scarlet berries.'

BELOW

A progenitor of the open-plan in England, Baillie Scott often created an inglenook as an intimate sitting area to relieve a large space.

LEIGHTON HALL

Lancashire

Climbing up Peter Hill from Yealand Conyers, the road winds between sudden outcrops of silver stone and grows alarmingly steeper and steeper. At the very top, a modest lodge and gateposts herald the first breathtaking view of Leighton Hall. It lies halfway down the great wide slope of Utopian park. The whole scene is like a painting of some fantastic and imaginary landscape. Over to the west, a mile or two away across wooded hills, the sea sparkles in Morecambe Bay. Behind the house the great lakeland hills rise in the most dramatic backdrop high into the sky and further on down at the bottom of the valley lies Leighton Moss, a huge marshy mere, the home of a quarter of Britain's bittern population.

The façade of the house, built using the silvery white limestone quarried from nearby, is in the castellated and theatrical neo-Gothic style of the nineteenth

BELOW

The hall Gothicized in the early nineteenth-century for Richard Gillow. The 'daisy table' stands at the foot of the stairs.

century. On the south side is a small turreted wing built in the 1870s by the famous architectural firm Austin and Paley of Lancaster. Behind the façade is a symmetrical eighteenth-century house built in 1763 on the ruins of a still earlier house. The famous cabinet-making Gillow family of Lancaster are inextricably woven into Leighton's history, and Gillow descendants live here still. For five centuries the owners of Leighton have nearly all been Roman Catholic. The property passed through the Middleton family to Albert Hodgson who was captured at Preston in the 1715 Jacobite rising. Leighton was sacked and burned by government troops, and when Hodgson was eventually released from prison he retired to a ruined and heavily mortgaged home.

The situation was saved when his daughter Mary married a rich local Catholic called George Towneley of Towneley Hall. He wasted no time in rebuilding the house in the latest Adam style in 1763 and in laying out the spectacular park and replanning the woods. Towneley had commissioned a distant Catholic cousin named Gillow to design the house (whose family was to inherit the house a century later). The Towneleys had no children and Leighton was eventually sold to a Lancaster banker whose mother was a Gillow but by 1822 the property was sold again to another cousin, Richard Gillow, the grandson of Robert Gillow, the founder of the famous furniture business Gillow and Company of Lancaster.

By the 1800s Gillow and Company was the biggest furniture company in Europe and in 1810 the firm's accountant performed in effect a management buy-out from the three brothers, Robert, George and Richard, who had inherited it. (By the end of the nineteenth century Gillows was fitting out many large Atlantic liners and joined forces with the Liverpool upholsterer, Mr Waring. Thus the famous firm Waring and Gillow was born.)

Free from the shackles of the firm, the Gillow brothers – with their perfect Catholic pedigree and huge bank accounts – were ripe fodder for the impoverished Catholic aristocracy and they all in turn married grand wives. Richard married a Miss Stapleton of Carlton Towers in Yorkshire and together they had fourteen children and added the fashionable Gothic façade to their house. Inside the hall they made a delicate curving cantilevered stair and the whole effect was light and graceful. The family chapel has an eighteenth-century Gillow altar front and the dining-room chairs are also early Gillow. The famous 'daisy table' stands in the hall with its eight petal-shaped edges which turn down on individual flaps. Their eldest son, Richard, who lived until he was 99, was known as 'Old Squire'. He drained the Leighton Moss and made it into corn fields. He also built on the wing to house a billiard room which, during the next century, became the music room where the great opera singer Kathleen Ferrier gave her last recital in a

BELOW

Few houses are so beautifully sited as Leighton. In this distant view of the entrance front. Austin and Paley's picturesque additions of 1870 are on the left.

MEOLS HALL

Lancashire

There have been many 'new Georgian' houses built since the Second World War but one of the most exceptional is Meols Hall. It springs bold and confident from an earlier and adjoining architectural muddle. The new Meols fits into its half-enclosed landscape in an easy and comfortable way. It stands on the very skirt of the grand seaside town of Southport which its owners, the Heskeths, had helped to develop. Where the saltings and mud flats of the Ribble estuary give way to open Lancashire coast, a long stretch of firm flat sand stretches down towards Merseyside and here Southport has retained a dignified separateness, still proud of its days as a smart Victorian and Edwardian watering place. It was an innkeeper called William Sutton from the tiny village of Churchtown who used driftwood from the beach to build the very first bathing house here in the eighteenth century and gradually his village became engulfed by the ever-growing town. Its solid stone eighteenth-century church sports monuments to the Fleetwood family and the Hesketh family who were in the end to inter-marry. The gates to Meols Hall are right beside the church and the comfortable-looking brick house, with no fancy meandering drive, is close by, very much in the Borough of Southport.

Roger Hesketh and his brother Peter who were the architects of the new Meols loved the view from the garden side of the house across the wide lawn, between the two gazebos they had built, to the Moss – a small uninhabited marshy wilderness scattered with stumpy trees and the odd red brick barn. On spring and autumn evenings they watched the skeins of wild geese over Meols. It was and still is very much an urban site with a rural outlook – the best of both worlds. A house had stood on the site of Meols since the beginning of the twelfth century and the Heskeths have always owned and lived in the houses which came and went. In the early eighteenth century Roger Hesketh of Meols married Margaret Fleetwood, the heiress of nearby Rossall Hall, and the couple chose to live at the latter. Meols was reduced in size and turned into the agent's house. In the nineteenth century Sir Peter Hesketh-Fleetwood came unstuck over his involvement in the development of the town of Fleetwood and sold most of the Lancashire estates. Meols Hall, however, was saved by Sir Peter's younger brother Charles who was rector of the parish. In

1938 Roger Hesketh inherited what was then still the small muddly agent's house and determined to restore it to a house he could be proud of.

Roger and his brother Peter had both studied architecture at the Architectural Association and Peter had gone on to work under Professor Richardson at London University. They had both travelled extensively in England, Europe and America looking at buildings with friends such as Christopher Hussey and John Summerson. Both unmarried at the time, they moved in to Meols and began to plan what should happen. In the same year a completely unexpected windfall in the form of the contents of a house in Hampshire which comprised the Fleetwood-Hesketh family collection, came back to Lancashire after nearly 100 years. All plans were obviously halted at the outset of war and it was not until the 1960s that the new Meols was begun, using only local craftsmen and builders. By this time Peter had married and was living at Hale near Liverpool and was thus on hand to help his brother who carried out all his own supervision. 'A contractor is bound to add something to his tender to cover contingencies which may never arise' he had said. 'Similarly if one changes one's mind when building is already in progress and things do not always look quite the same in reality as they do on paper, the additional cost can be accurately gauged from the time sheets, while there is no means of precisely assessing the "extras" on a contractor's account which in consequence tend to increase disproportionately.' Because of the time lapse between inheriting the old house and building the new one together with the unexpected inheritance, the house was planned very much from the inside out even down to where the furniture should stand and pictures should hang. Roger Hesketh, by this time MP for Southport, was meticulous and organized. He and his brother both felt strongly that the new Meols should continue the eigtheenth-century Palladian ideals reinterpreted to fit their particular needs. The beautiful dressed stonework was rescued from Liverpool where it was about to be dumped into a disused dock and the eighteenth-century red bricks came from the demolished Tulketh Hall near Preston. Inside an enfilade of drawing-room, hall and dining-room faces out to the garden. Meols remains a deeply comfortablefamily house where the new generation of Heskeths continue to look out over the same view of the Moss that their twelfth-century forebears had themselves enjoyed.

OPPOSITE

Meols from the east, built in the 1960s in the manner of James Gibbs, by the owner Roger Hesketh, aided by his brother Peter.

BELSAY
Northumberland

Northumberland is vast, archaic and more feudal than anywhere else in England. There is still an air of anarchy about the place and its houses remained fortified long after those in the south. Belsay's great fourteenth-century tower stands as a reminder of its warring past, with the new modern hall beside. Belsay Hall is as pure, plain, austere and masculine as a house could be. It has no fancy trappings and stands as a monument to one extraordinary man's singular vision. The visionary was Sir Charles Monck, so called on inheriting a fortune from his maternal grandfather. His original name was Middleton and it was here at Belsay that the Middletons had lived since the 1200s.

The first recorded Sir Richard de Middleton, was Henry III's Lord Chancellor. The house was briefly vacated when Gilbert, the Lord Chancellor's nephew, raised an army of men and held two cardinals to ransom and extorted a large sum of money from the bishopric of Durham and then plundered on southwards to Yorkshire. He was captured and executed and his land confiscated. However the Middletons regained Belsay in 1371 and thereafter the estate was occupied continuously by the family who eventually transformed their defensible tower into a formal, conventional Elizabethan house. When Charles Monck took over Belsay, backed by the enormous wealth from his mother's side, he extended the park and razed the old village of Belsay to the ground, building a new row of houses and shops with an arcade in a plain style and grey stone a suitable distance away. Then on a virgin site he decided to build a modern mansion for himself and his new young Yorkshire bride, Louisa.

In the autumn of 1804 he had taken Louisa on a two-year honeymoon during which they travelled through Europe looking at Berlin, Dresden, Prague, Vienna and Trieste, Venice, then they finally stayed on in Greece. They spent the summer of 1805 in Athens where their son Charles Atticus was born. For months Monck sketched statues and made measured drawings of temples and it was here that he met Sir William Gell, who helped him with designs for a new house with its Grecian set of rules.

Monck was an obsessive character, meticulous to a degree, and he ended by making over 300 architectural drawings for Belsay. The foundations of the new house were dug on 25 August 1807. He was his own clerk of works and supervised every detail, even training some of the craftsmen to carry out exactly what he wanted. Much of the detailing of the house can be sourced to Athens; the stable belfry is based on the Tower of the Winds, oak bookcases in the library are detailed from the Erechtheion and the two columns on the front of the house are modelled on those of the Theseion. The house is exactly 100 feet square and took exactly ten years to build.

John Mordaunt Crook, in his book *The Greek Revival*, describes Belsay as 'the most dramatic English performance' of the style in which the three major factors of the Greek Revivalist Movement are clearly represented. 'The Anglo-French cult of the antique; the Franco-Italian rationalist tradition; and the empirical philosophy of the Picturesque . . . the setting of the house is essentially Romantic. Nowhere else in Britain is the Romantic basis of neoclassicism so clearly expressed . . .' Sir Charles was clearly captivated by the romance of Greece and although he replicated a temple he was able to combine symmetry and perfect geometry with the domestic lifestyle of a Northumbrian squire. However his neighbours, though recognizing his upright character, 'paid little attention to anything he said'.

The outside of the house was ever more perfected by the precise cutting of its stone from a quarry in the grounds – which Monck later made into one of the most spectacular 'quarry gardens' in the country. It is redolent of the Picturesque style, and today lush with ferns and exotic plantings, added to by his successor Sir Arthur Middleton. The stables beside the house present the same perfection and the same high-grade symmetry. Inside, the hall is double-height with towering pillars around it like the grandest of Roman baths; lit by a blaze of light from the lantern it forms a perfect circulation area.

Monck faced his house eastwards into the park where already his forebears had enhanced the landscape. William Middleton, third baronet, had planted substantial belts of woodland along the crags, including Bantam Wood where his wife planted great drifts of snowdrops. Today it is all looked after by English Heritage.

CRAGSIDE

Northumberland

William Armstrong, one of the greatest inventors of the Victorian age, thought nothing of his own brilliance. 'Mere conception of primary ideas in invention is not a matter involving much labour and it is not a thing . . . demanding a large reward; it is rather the subsequent labour which the man bestows in perfecting the invention . . .' he said. Through his very modesty and calmness of temperament he was able to bring about enormous industrial innovations at the peak of Britain's golden industrial era. Cragside displays all his originality, sense of romance, free spirit and pride in his country. It was the first house in the world to be lit by water-generated electricity – of his own invention – and is fitted throughout with the latest machine-made textiles, and decorated and adorned by the greatest modern craftsmen and artists of the time.

Today the house rises like a Wagnerian fairy-tale castle clinging to a steep ravine above the River Coquet and surrounded by some of the 7,000,000 trees which Armstrong planted to clothe the once barren boulder-strewn hillside. On the skyline at Nellie's Moss, he created lakes to act as reservoirs for the main power-house situated 340 feet below.

Armstrong's family always joked that he had 'water on the brain'. As a child he had holidayed often with the Donkins who were family friends at the village of Rothbury in Coquetdale. 'My earliest recollections consist of paddling in the Coquet, gathering pebbles on its gravel beds, and climbing among the rocks on the crags', he remembered towards the end of his life. The son

of a Newcastle corn merchant, he trained to be a lawyer at his father's behest and became a partner of Donkin, Stable and Armstrong. While out fishing during his honeymoon in Yorkshire, he noticed how a nearby water wheel was using a tiny part of its capacity, and became ever more obsessed with the idea of harnessing columns of water. Armorer Donkin, Armstrong's benevolent mentor, recognized a budding genius in the latter's constant experiments as an amateur scientist and allowed him time off. Armstrong's innovative ideas coincided with the transformation of Tyneside after the Napoleonic Wars, into one of the most industrially advanced centres of the world using coal, iron, steam and water, and the navigability of the Tyne as its key factors. Armstrong was inspired by this heroic era of Newcastle's history and together with his mechanical genius and legal training he became a vital contributor to the country's new and confident surge of energy. He abandoned the law firm and began his own company, W G Armstrong, which was to make him a millionaire.

Norman Shaw, a little-known architect whose talent Armstrong spotted, was employed by him to enlarge his modest villa. Armstrong had built it as a weekend retreat in the 1850s on land he had bought in Coquetdale. Shaw wrote to his wife about the 'wonderful hydraulic machines that do all sorts of things you can imagine'. Shaw never had *carte blanche*, neither did he ever have a cross word with his employer in the fifteen years it took him gradually to add to and enhance this magical place. He created a deeply comfortable house, full of nooks and corners, panelling and bay windows and in the dining-room an inglenook to beat all.

By the time Armstrong decided to live at Cragside, he was also using it as a shop window for potential customers, fitting it out with every sort of device, from a kind of inverted lawn spray which converted hydraulic pressure into rotary motion for the kitchen spit, to a hydraulically powered lift. By the time the Prince and Princess of Wales visited Cragside in 1884 it was the true 'palace of a modern magician', made even more incredible by 10,000 small glass lamps hanging amongst the rocky hillsides and lining the myriad winding paths. A description of the time went on, . . . 'The château itself was a blaze of light. From every window the bright rays of the electric lamps shone with purest radiance, and the main front was made brilliant by a general illumination.' Cragside remains a celebration of this great man who was the catalyst for and the predictor of the worldwide use of hydroelectricity, and is still, through his house and its spirit, an inspiration for future generations. In 1997 the house passed to the Treasury as past payment for death duties and was transferred to the National Trust whose Northumbrian representative Sheila Pettit, worked on its restoration and made it appear that William Armstrong had only just left the room.

OPPOSITE

The house beetles above steep slopes clad in rhododendrons.

BELOW

The drawing-room: 'Renaissance at its fruitiest, Elizabethan at its most exuberant, are gaily mixed together,' wrote Mark Girouard of this room in Country Life *in 1969.*

BELOW

John de Markenfield's house and farm buildings within the
moat have hardly changed since the fourteenth century. The
gatehouse is sixteenth-century.

MARKENFIELD HALL

Yorkshire

The old grey Hall stands lost at the end of a track in the middle of meadows and cornfields, beyond small woods and well away from the world. Once it had dominated the old road south from Ripon but was bypassed and left stranded long ago. Markenfield is one of the most romantic medieval survivals in all England. It has not changed, it is still moated and is still the working farm it always was. There has been no aggrandizement but for the battlements, built in 1310 by John de Markenfield. He was a cleric and Chancellor of the Exchequer to Edward II and, due to his station and his close friendship with Piers Gaveston, was granted a licence to crenellate. A small bridge leads across the moat under the arch of a gatehouse to face John de Markenfield's 'L'-shaped house standing within the moat. The farm buildings and a small chapel with a turret and spire are placed around the little courtyard. It is here the local tenantry would have been mustered for their march to the Battle of Flodden where Sir Ninian Markenfield held a command. Here, two generations later, troops gathered to see off hundreds of northern warriors clad in glowing colours, the banners of their leaders waving above them, in the great Northern Rebellion. Fountains Abbey nearby, one of the greatest Yorkshire monasteries, was dissolved by Henry VIII and myriad local people lost their jobs. For centuries the monks at Fountains had cultivated and farmed the lands around Markenfield, Dawley, Grantley and Ripon. They had fostered the wool trade and helped people in sickness. They had received gifts from neighbouring landowners and as a result had become extremely powerful which made Henry uneasy.

Unlike most great families in the south who had, after a while, sailed with the wind, Markenfield stood firm, pledged to the 'older faith'. By 1569, twenty years after the dissolution, the ground swell was such in the neighbourhood and far beyond, that the Rebellion of the North was born – this time against Henry's daughter, Queen Elizabeth I. In Yorkshire Thomas Markenfield and Richard Norton of Norton Conyers were the leaders. The grandson of Sir Ninian of Flodden fame and a direct descendant of Sir Thomas, young Thomas who was 'rash, daring and too wildely yonge' set forth to bring Mary Queen of Scots to the throne of England. They joined the Earl of Northumberland at Toxteth on the banks of the River Swale but the Earl, having received news of the arrest of many prominent supporters of the rebellion, wanted to call a halt. Neither Norton nor Markenfield would support him; they marched to Durham Cathedral where they made a bonfire of the new prayer books and then marched south once more to Ripon. It was in Ripon marketplace that, upon a cold day in December, hundreds of local farmers ruined by the closure of Fountains Abbey and by grasping southern courtiers came surging in to join the rebels, and the entire rabble

army swept further south. Meanwhile the advisers of Queen Elizabeth encircled the rebels who in the end turned and fled. The Earls of Westmorland and Northumberland fled to Scotland and young Markenfield lost the hall for ever. He fled abroad, never to return. He had staked his home and possessions by riding off at full tilt against Elizabeth I who neither pardoned nor forgot.

By the 1750s this sad moated manor had been abandoned and became the haunt of bats and owls. It was Sir Fletcher Norton a descendant of the Norton Conyers who bought Markenfield Hall and saved it from ruin. A rich lawyer who had risen to become Attorney-General, he was nicknamed Sir Bullface Double Fees. Although he preferred to live at his nearby home of Grantley, he made Markenfield structurally sound and when raised to the peerage, he took the title of Lord Grantley of Markenfield. In the 1950s a descendant moved back to this ancient haunt of bygone struggles and the family live here still.

BELOW

Markenfield Hall is one of the most romantic surviving medieval houses in all England.

SLEDMERE

Yorkshire

In 1812, John Bigland wrote, 'Sledmere may be considered as the ornament of that bleak and hilly district. The circumjacent hills are adorned with elegant farmhouses . . . in summer the waving crops in the fields, the houses of the tenantry elegantly constructed and judiciously dispersed, the numerous and extensive plantations skirting the slope of the hills, and the superb mansion with its ornamental grounds in the centre of the vale, form a magnificent and luxuriant assemblage little to be expected in a country like the Wolds; and to a stranger on his sudden approach the *coup d'oeil* is singularly novel and striking.' Over 150 years later Sledmere shines out as an exemplary kingdom – well loved and well cared for.

Along the street you travel between plum and orange brick farm and stud buildings and the park wall is overhung with high beech trees. On down a gentle slope and across from the Tritton Inn are richly detailed Victorian estate houses with deep bargeboards, grand rainwater hoppers bearing fleur-de-lis designs and red-painted crisscross gates in low garden walls under neatly clipped holly hedges. The postbox, set in the leaded lattice window of the Post Office, still bears the letters GR. On past the creeper-clad eighteenth-century rectory stands a dignified domed rotunda on raised columns above a well. It was built by a previous Sir Tatton Sykes in memory of his father, Sir Christopher Sykes, '. . . who by his assiduity and perseverance', the inscription reads, 'in building and planting and inclosing on the Yorkshire Wolds, in the short space of thirty years, set such an example to the other owners of land, as has caused what once was a bleak

ABOVE
The house from Castle Farm, looking across the Wolds landscape, enclosed and forested in 1770–1800.

Most of the local inhabitants' families have lived here for generations and the feeling of local pride is almost tangible.

The wide chalk uplands of the Wolds are crossed by open roads edged with wind-bent hedges giving views to bare sweeping horizons and glimpses of blue distant country. Sometimes you can see long dark woods and coppices, half hidden in hollows, or small villages set in shallow valleys lying low against the ever-bracing winds. If there are clouds, more often than not they are scudding fast, but on some days a sea fret comes in from the coast and obliterates every feature with a thick mist.

The village of Sledmere is in a mild vale in the hills.

and barren tract of country to become now one of the most productive and best cultivated districts in the county of York. AD 1840'.

Across the road, lodges and majestic gates herald the entrance to the park, and the drive curves and sweeps gently away up to Sledmere, the elegant house of the Sykes family, with its faintly raised eyebrows, arched above windows. Around it spectacular beech trees are anchored to the ground by huge spreading skirts, some of them eighty feet across. Each generation of Sykes has planted trees so that there is a never-ending succession to come.

It was Richard Sykes who laid the first foundation stone for the house in 1751, and despite a disastrous fire in 1911 which necessitated an almost total reconstruction, the long arch-shaped library with its plasterwork by Joseph Rose, remains one of the greatest rooms in England. Although Richard planted avenues and woods, his son Christopher, who took possession from his ageing father in 1770, had far more grandiose schemes. First he employed Thomas White and subsequently Capability Brown to lay out pleasure grounds and rides and to draw up proposals for improvements, but it was Sykes who was the main driving and designing force. By 1779 he had planted 177,210 trees – mostly beech, Scots pine and larch. He built strategically placed farms and other buildings – eye-catchers at the end of wooded views to be seen from the house – like the mile-distant and castellated Castle Farm designed by John Carr of York.

As if the Wolds had not been justly rewarded by Christopher's planting, his grandson Tatton became even more of a legend. He restored or built afresh sixteen churches in the neighbourhood and according to Gordon Home writing on Yorkshire in 1908 Tatton was '. . . the sort of man that Yorkshire folk came near to worshipping. He was of that hearty, genial, conservative type that filled the hearts of the farmers with pride. On market days all over the Riding one of the always fresh subjects of conversation was how Sir Tatton was looking . . . So great was the conservatism of this remarkable squire that years after the advent of railways he continued to make his journey to Epsom, for the Derby, on horseback'. The Sledmere stud started in 1800, and became world famous in the twentieth century producing, amongst other celebrated horses, Muntaz Mahal, the foundation mare for the late Aga Khan, whose line produced Derby winners.

LEFT
Sir Tatton Sykes at the age of eighty, painted by Francis Grant in 1853.

191

BURTON AGNES HALL

Yorkshire

The village of Burton Agnes is irresistible. It presents the perfect ensemble with its church reached from the street under a long canopy of yew trees, its ancient manor house beside and, beyond, the perfect mellow red brick Hall. The Hall is reached through one of the most satisfactory gatehouses in all the land with its four octagonal turrets – the whole looking for all the world like a miniature Jacobean mansion. Its date is 1610, nine years later than the glittering house itself, designed by the grand master, Robert Smythson. He put all his efforts into the swaggering multi-windowed entrance façade which is such a breathtaking sight from this main thoroughfare between York and Bridlington. Its undulating and varied projections of square, rounded and five-sided bays and its gabled and high-chimneyed roofline remain unaltered and all that has changed is the fenestration in the central block which was modernized at the beginning of the seventeenth century.

The estate of Burton Agnes has never changed hands since the original Norman manor house was built by Roger de Stuteville. One of his daughters was called Agnes which may have been responsible for the name Burton Agnes. The lower chamber of the stone manor with its massive piers supporting a vaulted roof still survives. It was clad in its brick shell in the seventeenth century when it was used as a laundry. Burton Agnes passed through the female line to the Griffiths who had emigrated from Wales to Staffordshire. They didn't take much interest in Burton Agnes until Sir Walter Griffiths came to live in the old manor house in the fifteenth century. His great-grandson, Sir Henry, was appointed to the Council of the North based in York and, although he had started to build a new home in the Midlands, abandoned it in favour of his strategically sited Yorkshire property and proceeded to build the hall in all its glory.

Anne Griffiths, the youngest of his three daughters, watched the building of the new house and believed it to be the most beautiful ever built. When it was almost finished she went one afternoon to visit the St Quintins at Harpham about a mile distant and on her way was attacked and robbed. She was brought home but died a few days later. From her death-bed she told her two sisters that unless some part of her could remain in 'our beautiful home as long it should last' she would never rest. She made them promise that when she was dead they would sever her head and preserve it in the Hall. They did not dare and she was buried in the churchyard. Her ghost then terrorized the household, the sisters confided in the vicar, and his advice was that the grave be opened and their promise be kept. The skull thus came to the house and the ghost was seen no more.

Sir Henry's great hall, designed to astound his visitors, contains some of the most elaborate and extraordinary carving and plasterwork of its age. The screen is an overcrowded mass of myriad allegorical figures, depicting unending stories of knights, apostles, tribes of Israel and evangelists. The massive chimneypiece represents yet more elaborate allegory in finely carved alabaster depicting the wise and foolish virgins. The shallow oak staircase in the inner core of the house has continuous newel posts which stretch to the ceiling above up to the full height of the stair, giving generous scope to the Elizabethan woodcarver to display his talents. The long gallery on the top floor runs the full length of the house. Until the 1950s it contained a mass of bedrooms put there in the 1810s when the stupendously carved barrel-vaulted ceiling had collapsed. Luckily a small piece remained and the local architect Francis Johnson of Bridlington, was employed to supervise a Leeds firm of craftsmen to reconstruct it. The newborn gallery now houses the family collection of French impressionists and the work of modern British designers. Kaffe Fassett's tapestry of flowers and vegetables is inspired by the magnificent garden where 100 clipped yews stand sentinel along formal patios between great swards of lawn, and a voluptuous vegetable garden lies hidden behind high brick walls.

CASTLE HOWARD

Yorkshire

'If our first parents, after being turned out of the Garden of Eden, had been immediately placed upon this spot of ground, they would have concluded that they had only exchanged one Paradise for another', wrote John Tracy Atkyns soon after Castle Howard was built in the first years of the 1700s. It is the whole ensemble of Castle Howard's enormous domain with the house in its midst that is its glory. Castle Howard commands the landscape for miles around and if you live within a five-mile orbit of its magic centre, in Welburn, Slingsby or Thornton le Clay, Castle Howard is part of your life. You drive through its park this way and that, you catch glimpses of its pyramids, its domes, its obelisks, its columns from so many miles away. The five-mile-long avenue which skirts the house and leads straight as a die from near Whitwell-on-the-Hill to a mile short of Slingsby, is the grandest road in Britain, triumphally punctuated, every so often, with some gigantic piece of architecture. First the Flats Gate, then the Exclamation Gate, followed by the Carrmire Gate, a great long battlemented wall in a low hollow dip with two little castles at either end, and at its centre a Triumphal Arch topped by a grand pediment. On up between extravagantly wide verges edged by gigantic groups of beech trees the road rises and falls again and again and every so often provides a tantalizing glimpse of a far-away pyramid or temple. Next comes the Pyramid Gate, its arch under a huge solid pyramid right on the brow, and as you come through the arch you look down the next fall of road and up to a towering obelisk which bears the inscription written by Castle Howard's creator, the third Earl of Carlisle:

> *If to perfection these plantations rise,*
> *If they agreeably my heirs surprise*
> *This faithful pillar will their age declare*
> *As long as time these characters shall spare*
> *Here then with kind remembrance read his name*
> *Who for posterity performed the same*
> *Charles the III Earl of Carlisle*
> *Of the family of the Howards . . .*

Because the great hills which stretch away in all directions are on a grand northern scale, so too are the buildings which if, perhaps, placed in a southern county would dwarf the landscape. From Easthorpe on a northern hill a mile from Castle Howard the view across the valley to its mausoleum is perhaps the most spectacular of all. 'I do design to build a burial place near my seat of Castle Howard, where I desire to be laid', wrote the third Earl in his will. It was designed by Nicholas Hawksmoor and began in 1729 but not finished until the 1740s after the deaths of both its architect and its commissioner, and has been celebrated as the noblest invention of all Castle Howard's glories. It rises ninety foot into the sky supported by a collonade of twenty pillars like an acropolis. Not unnaturally Horace Walpole had his say about Castle Howard. 'Nobody . . . had informed me that I should at one view see a palace, a town, a fortified city, temples on high places, woods worthy of being each a metropolis of the Druids, vales connected to hills by other woods, the noblest lawn in the world fenced by half the horizon, and a mausoleum that would tempt one to be buried alive; in short I have seen gigantic places before, but never a sublime one.'

The house crowning the hill above the wide lake, fits beautifully in to its setting. It is everything that the third Earl wanted and it was the playwright Vanburgh who had never built anything before in his life whom the young Carlisle commissioned. Vanburgh had already had two hits with his plays *The Relapse* and *The Provok'd Wife*, and was a lively member of the Kit-Cat Club – a group of Whigs, Carlisle among them, at the cutting edge of London life. It had a handful of dukes among its members as well as Sir Robert Walpole the first Prime Minister and many writers including Congreave. Carlisle, who had inherited these Yorkshire acres through his ancestors and had climbed the ladder of social success to become the First Lord of the Treasury, wanted a house to show off his grandeur. He had already discarded some designs by William Talman and gradually between the years of 1699 and 1702 the design of the present house evolved. Although it was never finished completely and was added to subsequently over the next 100 years, it remains chiefly the work of the third Earl and Vanburgh, the playwright-turned-architect, Britain's most theatrical of all who loved above everything to be in the limelight. Towards the end of his life, however, Vanburgh said, 'I have grown more and more of the opinion that the less one has to do with what is called "the World", the more quiet of mind; and the more quiet of mind the more happiness'.

TREASURER'S HOUSE

York

Treasurer's House overlooks the gigantic awe-inspiring and wonderful York Minster which fills every inch of sky and every view from every front window. The survival of the house is largely due to the single-minded and eccentric Frank Green who saved it from its sure decline in the 1890s and restored it to his unwavering antiquarian ideal. In 1897 when he bought it, it was, according to the daughter of his architect Temple Moore, 'a bug-ridden slum'. His desire to save the house was an altruistic one for he never married; he saw Treasurer's House as a public show-piece and a place of display and of antiquarian interest rather than as a cosy home. 'The house is one of the few which exhibits architecture from the time of the Romans through the eleventh, twelfth and fifteenth centuries down to George III' he wrote in 1900 in the Yorkshire Philosophical Society Annual Report. Indeed, it was Green's workmen who unearthed the base of a Roman column in the cellars when they began work on the restoration and who also discovered a section of Roman road. In 1953 an apprentice plumber who was working in the basement saw a bedraggled troop of Roman legionnaires coming through the wall at a level, unknown to him, of the original Roman road.

The Treasurer controlled the finances of the Minster and had to entertain important guests but inevitably after the dissolution, his job became redundant and the house was seized by the Crown. Treasurer's House was next owned by two post-Reformation archbishops and then by Thomas Young who was Archbishop of York from 1562 to 1568. He played an important role in policing the still insecure Protestant Church throughout the north of England where Catholic uprisings were two a penny. He pulled down a lot of the Archbishop's Palace and with the stone built himself a new residence which is the present Treasurer's House. Young and his descendants didn't enjoy their new mansion for long, and thereafter its history is chequered with noble Yorkshire families. The house was refitted time and time again, perhaps most radically in 1725 when it was divided in two between the Morritt family and the Robinsons. By the end of the nineteenth century the house was rapidly going down hill and had become five separate properties occupied by what Dickens would have described as a 'shabby genteel' collection of widows, doctors and teachers.

Frank Green, its saviour, was the grandson of a successful Wakefield industrialist and engineer who had invented 'Green's Fuel Economizer', a device which used the waste gases in the steam boiler to preheat the water fed into it thus saving energy and cutting costs. Frank's father had taken a short cut into the social élite by buying a shooting estate in Norfolk adjoining Sandringham and building Ken Hill, a brand-new slap-up house there, in which to entertain the Prince of Wales and his son.

Frank's mother was already a great patroness of the arts and had employed many of the great names of the day to decorate and enhance Ken Hill. She bought De Morgan pottery, Frank Brangwyn paintings and commissioned the architect Thomas Jeckyll to design much of the furniture. Frank Green therefore was brought up in an artistic atmosphere and perhaps because he had already lived through the building of a new house from start to finish was all the more keen to do his bit for England by restoring an ancient one.

While Frank's elder brother, a skilled fox hunter, was expected to 'ride the family into society', Frank, the industrious one, was expected to run the family business. He excelled. A perfectionist in all ways and not least in his restoration of the house, Frank collected furniture and pictures to fill the house on the back of Green's Fuel Economizers, and commissioned textiles and wallpapers from the firm of Bodley, Garner and Scott (later Watts & Co.). He was so meticulous about the arrangement of the furniture in each room that he nailed studs into the floors to show exactly where it should stand. They are still there to this day. He was fanatical about cleanliness and would often get up in the middle of the night and inspect the kitchens for any speck of dirt. He slept in clean linen sheets every night of his life and although the household laundry was done in York, his own was sent all the way to London once a week. He was always impeccably dressed, wore dazzling waistcoats, floppy silk bow ties and correspondent shoes. He had a fleet of Rolls-Royces especially adapted to his needs which he took touring on the Continent, writing two books about his travels which he had privately printed. In the family tradition he was passionately keen on hunting and bought up large tracts of land around York for the benefit of the York and Ainsty Hunt of which his brother was master. In July 1930 he gave Treasurer's House and its contents to the National Trust and moved to Dulverton in Somerset where he died in 1954 at the age of ninety-three.

MOUNT IEVERS

County Clare

County Clare – stony and weatherbeaten – was one of the worst devastated areas of all Ireland during the potato famine of the mid to late 1840s. Traces of the county's chaotic upheavals through the last few centuries are everywhere. Myriad defensive towers, built between the fifteenth and early seventeenth centuries still stand solid amid the small gorse-edged fields, where occasional Ayrshire cattle graze and oddly placed white pebble-dashed bungalows, built yesterday, are scattered at random. There are old abandoned tractors and 'Community Alert Area' notices and everywhere the ghosts of O'Briens, the once fighting-strong family of Clare, whose private army is still heard marching on the parade ground at Carrigahalt.

The square tower of the old castle at Mount Ievers once stood where the present house stands now, high and mysterious, encompassed by trees and in its simple and unassuming way the most beautiful house in Ireland. Not many houses have the power to stop you in your tracks, and when they do hit some inner heart string, it is more often than not inexplicable. As Mark Girouard writes, 'Magic is an overworked word, but there is undoubtedly a magic about Mount Ievers . . . One can analyse points . . . but the house has an aura about it that is harder to explain . . . It gives one an extraordinary shock of delight and surprise to see it, rising high, thin and ghostly among the trees.'

The south front of Mount Ievers was built for show in the local stone, but it is the north face which today is more beautiful. Its brick has weathered into the softest pale pink over which is a patina of silvery lichen which only the soft air of County Clare could produce. The brick had come on the cheap from Holland when it was used as ballast on the return journey of boats which had probably been exporting oil produced from the local oilseed rape. Certainly there are other walls in County Clare which have been built through this method – the great ruined walled gardens of Carrigahalt to mention

one. The meticulously kept accounts for the building of Mount Ievers in 1731 display extraordinary frugality, for the whole house cost £1,478 7s 9d in all, plus some small extras such as £15 for providing two horses to the architect-builder who was called John Rothery. The limestone face of the house was provided from the estate quarry, and the timbers were floated down the River Shannon from Portumna to Killaloe and then hauled for the remaining twenty miles. The slates came from Broadford eight miles away and cost 9s 6d per 100. The forty-eight labourers who worked on the house were paid ten pence a week but they were supplied with shoes and coarse linen woven at Mount Ievers and also with food. The eleven masons were paid five shillings a week.

It was Henry Ievers who had pulled down the old castle and built the present house. His father, John, had been Colonel-in-Chief of the Clare Militia Dragoons and the county MP. The house Henry built could well have been built fifty years before but it is evidently what Henry wanted for its tall and haunting appearance befits the place and though it could have been loosely copied from a drawing in *Vitruvius Britannicus* of Chevening in Kent, to which it bears some relation, it is none the less completely and utterly Irish. At every string course the house diminishes in size by six inches and it was the builder's art rather than a textbook which produced Mount Ievers' perfection of scale.

Inside, the house has been decorated modestly compared to most Irish interiors of the time. Its elegant staircase is its chief glory, and set into the panelling above the drawing-room chimneypiece is an oil painting of the house at the time it was built with formal avenues leading off from a grand main avenue, and all around in the hills the towers of County Clare. The O'Briens' Bunratty Castle, near the skyline, is the largest of all and beyond it boats sail along the Shannon. In the late 1960s Squadron Leader Norman Ievers restored the fish ponds which are shown in the painting and put back the original glazing bars on the south side of the house which had been changed in the 1850s.

OPPOSITE

The tall, narrow proportions of Mount Ievers at once mark it out as distinctively and inimitably Irish.

FLORENCE COURT

County Fermanagh

After the small fields of County Leitrim the country around Florence Court in Fermanagh grows bigger and bolder. The long road from Enniskillen to Sligo, which the builder of the house had originally engineered and constructed with his partner Owen Wynne, winds on between silver birches, sudden outcrops of bungalows, and one-street villages with rainbow-coloured houses, until nearer to the Court, the signs of expensive husbandry begin. High trees rise from the hedgerows near the entrance lodges and the drive leads into one of the most wonderful parks in the world. Black wellingtonias jut above great belts of beech which flank this wide bowl of parkland. It seems as if this is an archaic wilderness untouched by the hand of fashion and into which this beautiful house has been dropped. To the north in the half distance rises the strange rocky height of the Cuilcagh mountain and all around there are more mountains on every horizon. Florence Court stands on a small hill with the ground sloping away from it in every direction. It is a bravely sited house built by a valiant and good man, Sir John Cole. His family had risen to pre-eminence during the seventeenth century and had made their money from plantations in the West Indies and bought huge tracts of County Fermanagh land with the proceeds.

It seems highly likely that it was Sir John Cole who began to build Florence Court in the early eighteenth century in memory of his beautiful Cornish wife, Florence Wrey from Trebitch, who died in 1718. There is a great Irish tradition of naming your house after your wife. The next three generations of Coles continued to build up this rare beauty of a house. Sir John the first Baron Mount Florence, tried to complete the house and did finish the main block, and his son, the first Earl of Enniskillen, finished off the house with its flanking arcaded wings ending in pavilions, in the 1770s.

The Coles loved this house and have made it unusually beautiful with its rusticated corners and window surrounds, pediments, brackets and keystones. Many architectural historians are bemused by it perhaps because it fits no historical pattern – they call it 'unscholarly' and 'endearing rather than fine'. The Coles were a laudable and interesting family who were passionate about this bit of the land, and did endless good works. They employed Irish craftsmen to produce some of the most beautiful rococo plasterwork ever seen in Ireland.

Hens and grandly plumed cockerels strut about the plain, stylish stables and farm buildings to the north of the house – cut from huge blocks of granite stone. A grey granite gravelled drive leads down through deep banks of moss and hart's-tongue past the old ice house to the third Earl of Enniskillen's magnificent sawmill at the little valley bottom. The water from the stream is collected in a leat and runs along a wooden viaduct which crosses above the drive and then works a gigantic iron wheel which still turns and tumbles the water and drives the circular saw. The third Earl was also an enthusiastic amateur scientist and assembled one of the largest collections of fossil fish in the world comprising around 10,000 specimens. He made a museum for it in one of the pavilions and it was sold to the British Museum in 1883; the museum was then made into a billiard room.

A mile to the east of the house stands the Florence Court yew which was raised from a seedling found on the slopes of Duilcagh by the Cole's tenant farmer in the 1760s. It can only be propagated from cuttings and so all Irish yews are descended from this one or its sibling which the farmer planted in his own garden but which died in the nineteenth century. The father or mother of every Irish yew is still growing here at Florence Court.

In the 1950s Viscount Cole, the son of the fifth Earl of Enniskillen, gave Florence Court to the National Trust and sadly two years later an electrical fault caused an enormous fire to break out outside the Venetian room. By the evening two-thirds of the interior had been destroyed. However the foresight of the firemen saved the ceiling of the dining-room. They made holes in it so that

the water that was being poured on top of it by the fire hoses didn't break it down completely. It survives as a breath-taking canopy of swirling acanthus foliage as the centrepiece of Zeus in the form of an eagle surrounded by the four winds. The National Trust has rebuilt the interior and repaired the exterior beautifully. In the 1970s the sixth Earl transferred nearly all the surrounding land to the Northern Ireland Ministry of Agriculture to make a forest park before his death in 1989. Florence Court stands as an elegant and moving monument to the great family of Cole.

CASTLE COOLE

County Fermanagh

Castle Coole is a neoclassical ideal of a country house put down exactly like an architect's model in a romantic park on the outskirts of Enniskillen. One side is frostily serene and overlooks the ice-cold lake, while the other is a grandly monumental columned mausoleum. Its stone is crisp, its air austere. There is no softening planting around it but just its perfect symmetrical presence, detached from its surroundings: detached from the huge spreading chestnut trees whose limbs touch the ground and are covered with bright green moss. The drive curves like a stream and then straightens out along an avenue of oaks beside the lake where the oldest non-migratory flock of greylag geese in the whole of the British Isles still lurk, having been introduced by Colonel James Corry in the early 1700s. If they leave the lake at Castle Coole, legend has it that the Lowry-Corrys will leave too.

In 1797, when the owner of Castle Coole, the first Earl of Belmore, had just moved in, he showed it to a French visitor, Bougrenet de la Tocnaye. 'A superb palace,' said the Frenchman, '. . . temples are only fit for the gods.' Lord Belmore might well have thought he was one. His speedy escalation up the social ladder over the last two decades of the eighteenth century was as wildfire. He had inherited the estate from his mother who married into the prosperous Belfast merchant family of Corry, the owners of the estate for a century. Armar Lowry-Corry who eventually became Lord Belmore thought the modest house of his mother's family was far too mean for his new social status. He had married Lady Henrietta

Hobart in 1780 who was the daughter of the Earl of Buckinghamshire and a year later Armar was elevated to the peerage as Baron Belmore. He swiftly became a viscount a few years later and then an earl. His evident determination to outdo his brother-in-law and neighbour, the Earl of Enniskillen at Florence Court, drove him on to order the very finest house he could muster.

Although he had first asked the Dublin architect Richard Johnston to draw up plans, he was then persuaded to dismiss him and to employ the very latest fashionable architect of the day, James Wyatt. He had already built houses in Ireland by remote control and had cornered the house mail-order business to perfection. Using the same layout as Richard Johnston had originally drawn up, Wyatt designed this perfect essay in geometry. He never visited the site, nor saw the house built. Lord Belmore, ever determined to outdo his neighbours and to own the smartest house in Ireland, ordered the white Portland stone from the Purbeck Quarry in Dorset to be cut to perfection to face his new palace. He only considered the very latest London plasterers. Joseph Rose, who was a stuccoist whom Wyatt was fond of using, was responsible for most of the ceilings in the state rooms at Castle Coole. The sculptor Richard Westmacott carved several of the state rooms' chimneypieces and shipped them to Ireland together with many of the decorative details, not to mention the enormous bills.

Lord Belmore didn't appear to mind that Wyatt never visited the house as many of the latter's clients in England had done. There his reputation was decidedly mixed. William Beckford, who had employed Wyatt during the building of Fonthill Abbey, wrote to him, 'where, infamous beast, where are you? What putrid inn,

RIGHT
The entrance front, which faces south: one of Ireland's most coolly accomplished pieces of neoclassicism.

what stinking tavern or pox-ridden brothel hides your hoary and glutinous limbs?' Wyatt became Surveyor-General of the Office of Works in 1796 and apparently spent so little time at his post that his cleaning lady ran a successful girls' school in his office. When Wyatt died the Office of Works was in such a muddle that the whole system had to be reorganized. The remoteness of Wyatt seemed to suit Lord Belmore who, however, after paying some of Wyatt's bills, began to back down on the more recent proposals. By June 1795 the house had cost around £54,000, without Wyatt's fee included. When Lord Belmore died in 1802 he left debts of £70,000. His son (a suave dandyish figure with fine legs for a boot and an elaborate hairstyle) seems somehow to have overcome the debts and began to spend even more money on furnishing Castle Coole in the bold masculine style of the Regency period. He employed John Preston, the foremost Dublin upholsterer, who lavished the house with tassels, fringes, door hangings and gilded furniture. The records of every detail of Castle Coole's building and furnishing have survived and there are many tiny details such as Preston's supply of 'soft shamois for preserving covers of all built furniture' and that the State Bed made by Preston for the imminent visit of George IV was hung with scarlet silk curtains and the material alone, including the curtains at the windows, cost over £1,000. The King never came.

The stables and farm buildings, themselves an essay in minimalism, lie low under the hill out of sight from the house. A huge arch with closed doors and a grille leads into the hill and up to the house through a long underground tunnel. This was the means by which servants and tradesmen entered and left the house so that they were never seen. Thus Castle Coole could remain, on its haughty rise, pure and unencumbered, as though serviced by magic.

ABOVE
*The serenely
magnificent entrance
front of Ireland's
largest and earliest
Palladian house.*

The small town of Celbridge has a wide main street of inns, hardware shops, bookmakers and bike shops. At its eastern end a pair of sphinxes top the grand gate piers which mark the entrance to Ireland's finest Palladian house. A splendid lime-tree avenue, where Celbridge Sunday-afternoon lovers stroll, leads up what must have been merely a back drive for suddenly the house is upon you with its fine central block flanked by two curved colonnades which end in two high-chimneyed wings. Castletown's scale and gentle feel is far friendlier and more intimate than any photograph can convey. Its builder 'Speaker' William Conolly, was a man of enormous wealth and power who started from humble origins, amassed a huge fortune by dealing in forfeited estates, was elected Member for Donegal and wanted to own the grandest house in all Ireland.

He commissioned the Italian architect, Allessandro Galilei, to build this house of perfect classical proportions. The front hall which rises for two storeys is lit by eleven south-facing windows and is designed to overwhelm. The windows look on to the Irish yews and the level park across the lake, the River Liffey, and the Wicklow Hills. The long gallery on the first floor looks up to a vista of the Conolly folly and is one of the most beautiful in all Ireland 'Speaker' Conolly died in 1729 but his widow, Katherine, lived on at Castletown for another twenty-three years and never left the estate. Mary Delaney, a contemporary, wrote at her death in 1752, 'We have lost our great Mrs Conolly. She died last Friday, and is a general loss; her table was open to all her friends of all ranks, and her purse to the poor. She was, I think, in her ninetieth year. She has been drooping for some years, but never so ill as to shut out company; she rose constantly at eight, and by eleven was seated in her drawing-room, and received visits till three o'clock, at which hour she punctually dined, and generally had two tables of eight or ten people each; her own table was served with seven courses and a dessert, and two substantial dishes on the side table; and if the greatest person in the kingdom dined with her, she never altered her bill of fare. As soon as dinner was over she took the ladies to the drawing-room, and left the gentlemen to finish as they pleased. She sat down in her grey cloth great chair and took a nap, whilst the company chatted to one another, which lulled her to sleep. Tea and coffee came exactly at half an hour after five; she then waked, and as soon as tea was over, a party of whist was made for her till ten, then everybody retired. She had prayers every day at twelve, and when the weather was good took the air, but has never made a visit since Mr Conolly died. She was clever at business, wrote all her own letters, and could read a newspaper by candlelight without spectacles. She was a plain and vulgar woman in her manner, but had very valuable qualities.'

CASTLETOWN
County Kildare

Katherine Connolly built a folly to the memory of her husband which remains to this day one of the most extraordinary pieces of architecture in all Ireland – an obelisk rising above a series of arches. It was built as an eye-catcher at some distance from the house and stands 140 feet high on a small hill. The electricity pylons which now stride across County Kildare are mere ghosts in comparison. Katherine's sister, Mary Jones, was appalled at her extravagance and wrote to a friend in March 1940: '. . . it will cost her £300 or £400 at least, but I believe more. I really wonder how she can dow so much, and live as she duse.' The Irish Georgian Society set up a fund to save the obelisk in the 1960s and a firm of steeplejacks from Belfast were employed to secure its top. The vast stone pineapples were reinstated and two new ones carved. Desmond Guinness, the founder of the Irish Georgian Society also saved Castletown itself from certain dereliction when he bought it as an empty and abandoned house with 100 acres in 1967. The estate had been bought up by property speculators and much of it developed. Today the house belongs to the State and is being restored by the Office of Public Works, a vast and worthy undertaking.

GLIN

County Limerick

West of Limerick along the banks of the wide River Shannon there are oak-filled inlets with the wrecks of old castles looming above, there are desolated homes of vanished families with brambles growing around them and everywhere a suggestion of past calamities. At the village of Glin the ruined castle, an early stronghold of the Knights of Glin, serves as a forlorn reminder of lost battles against the English. The wide village street of painted houses – red, pink, terracotta, green, cream, apricot, grey, mustard yellow and duck-egg blue, with quoins and keystones picked out in contrasting shades – slopes gently uphill towards high pastures, where a track leads past ivy-clad stone walls, gorse and fuchsia bushes. From here a huge view of the Shannon opens out to the remote hills of County Clare on the opposite banks and below is the tall battlemented house of Glin looking like a run-aground ship on its mild sweep of lawn. A herd of Friesian cows ambles down towards lichen-covered farm buildings, past the enormous walled garden sloping into the sun which is full of apple trees, chickens, beehives, rhubarb, huge artichoke plants, fig trees, urns, stone heads, rustic summer houses and vine-filled greenhouses.

Glin is the latest dwelling of the Fitz-Gerald family. Originally Norman knights, their various branches arrived here in the thirteenth century – including the White Knight, the Knight of Kerry, and the Knight of Glin who is sometimes known as the Black Knight or the Knight of the Valley. It is the descendants of this last who are still here today. Desmond Fitz-Gerald, the great scholar of Irish

architecture, furniture and paintings, is the twenty-ninth Knight of Glin.

The present house was built in the 1780s by the heroic Colonel John Fitz-Gerald who at the age of twenty, had formed the Glin Cavalry. During this brief period of national independence a great deal of house building and tree planting went on among Ireland's ruling classes and Glin was no exception. Colonel John used the very best masons and carpenters who were doing work in Limerick at the time. The hall has a screen of Corinthian columns beyond which the most elegant flying staircase in Ireland rises at the back of the house. The rooms are high and light and everywhere decorated with the most delicate plasterwork. Colonel John ended his life with enormous debts, mostly incurred by wild extravagance and by 1802, 5,000 acres of the Glin lands were sold. He died the following year leaving the family almost bankrupt. But the Colonel's son, also John, was to become the family's saviour who despite marrying a clergyman's daughter, became an extremely successful gambler and made enough money to crenellate the house and make it look like some sort of romantic castle – in reverence to his medieval ancestors. He was a famous womanizer, a poet and much loved locally, but in 1854 'the Knight of the Women' as he became known, died of cholera caught in the Glin poorhouse where he officiated as Chairman of the board of guardians. His son, the 'Cracked Knight' took over the reins. He had suffered concussion after a fall and there are still tales told to this day in the village of his riding his horse up the back stairs at Glin.

Next came the 'Big Knight' who took to the whiskey bottle. The twenty-seventh Edwardian Knight was a crack shot and a good golfer but became tragically paralyzed by a stroke in 1910. He continued to live at Glin as a recluse through the 'Troubles'. When the Sinn Fein came to burn his house down in 1923 he roared at them from his wheelchair 'Well you'll have to burn me in it, boys', whereupon they left and the house was saved. His son, the present knight's father, died young leaving his widow and her twelve-year-old son to hold Glin together and set it to rights. Her second husband, Ray Milner a rich Canadian businessman, helped his wife to overhaul the entire house and decorate the bedrooms. The present knight with his beautiful wife Olda continue to maintain this fragile and unique entity, through their tireless and unending hard work and take pleasure in sharing the wonder of Glin with visitors, scholars and friends and run it as a country house hotel. When she married the twenty-ninth Knight of Glin, Olda discovered that 'this house on the banks of the River Shannon would always be my greatest rival for my husband's affections. Some living force from the past has been carried through without a break to the present, and it seems to bring back things – and people – that belong'.

BELOW
The entrance hall, with part of the Knights of Glin's collection of Irish art and furniture. The large portrait shows Richard Fitz-Gerald, famous as a duellist.

OPPOSITE
Glin Castle and the Shannon beyond.

LISSADELL

County Sligo

When the Irish poet William Butler-Yeats was twenty-nine years old he stayed at Lissadell. He wrote to his sister that he found the house 'an image of aristocratic elegance . . . an exceedingly impressive house inside with a great sitting-room high as a church and all things in good taste'. The most beautiful thing of all about Lissadell is its slow, winding two-mile drive along the edge of Sligo Bay where low woods, shaved diagonally by Atlantic winds, grow right down to the edge of the beach, Hart's-tongue grows along the way and after the ruins of a great walled garden choked by thick ivy, the house is suddenly there set back from the shore on a rise and with its central bay looking out to the sea. Here at this library window a young Yeats pictured the sisters Constance and Eva Gore-Booth in their imagined youth. In October 1927 he wrote:

> The light of evening, Lissadell
> Great windows open to the south,
> Two girls in silk kimonos, both
> Beautiful, one a gazelle,
> But a raving autumn shears
> Blossom from the summer's wreath;
> The older is condemned to death,
> Pardoned, drags out lonely years
> Conspiring among the ignorant,
> I know not what the younger dreams —
> Some vague Utopia — and she seems,
> When withered old and skeleton-gaunt,
> An image of such politics,
> Many a time I think to seek
> One or the other out and speak
> Of that old Georgian mansion, mix
> Pictures of the mind, recall
> That table and the talk of youth,
> Two girls in silk kimonos, both
> Beautiful, one a gazelle.

When Yeats stayed, Eva Gore-Booth was by then a fairly well-known poetess and her sister, Constance, a heroine. She had been a friend of James Larkin, the Labour leader and had taken part in the Easter Rising of 1916. She was imprisoned and at one point sentenced to death but was later elected to the House of Commons in the 1918 General Election as an MP for Sinn Fein. She was the first woman to gain a seat in Parliament. She was married to the Hungarian Count Markievicz who was a famous portrait painter of his day. The dining-room at Lissadell is painted by him with the standing figures leaning against columns representing himself, the butler, the gamekeeper and his father-in-law Mordaunt Gore-Booth. There is one blank column reserved for the head housekeeper who was too shy to pose for the Count.

It was the Gore-Booth girls' grandfather, Sir Robert, who built the house in this romantic place. It sits under the awe-inspiring mountain Ben Bulben, with its lower slopes of steep emerald fields where Yeats imagined the Gore-Booth girls riding to hounds as they had done when they were young and impetuous. The gentle curve of Sligo Bay unfurled its shoreline and half guarded the house from the infinite view to America. In the late 1820s Sir Robert Gore-Booth commissioned the English architect, Francis Goodwin, who had just finished the town hall in Macclesfield. The house, built in big chiselled blocks of Ballysodare stone from Sligo, is as plain as could be, in the Greek revival style; practical and full of light giving on to the southern and sometimes sunny aspect. There was no evident back door but instead a long tunnel led from the outside to a sunken inner courtyard where a pet seal was kept for a time in a little pond. Soon after the house was finished in the 1830s, a famine swept Ireland; the house was mortgaged and Sir Robert insisted that no rents were accepted for any properties.

The enfilade as you enter the house is 120 feet long and stretches across the music room whose organ is pumped by bellows in the basement. This opens on to the central bay and the immortalized window. One night when Yeats was staying in the house he crept out to the top of the stairs and shouted that he had seen the ghost of Lissadell. Mordaunt Gore-Booth, his host, was furious at being woken and shouted back, 'Would you ever go to hell'.

THE FOLLOWING HOUSES ARE OPEN TO THE PUBLIC

EH indicates English Heritage Property;
NT indicates National Trust Property.

ABBOTSFORD HOUSE, Melrose, Roxburghshire, TD6 9BQ, 01896 752043. Open: 16 Mar.-31 Oct. Daily (July-Sept.) 10am-5pm, Sun. (Mar.-May & Oct.), 2-5pm.

ARBURY HALL, Nuneaton, Warwickshire, CV10 7PT, 024 7638 2804. Open: Easter-Sept. Bank Holiday Sunday and Monday 2-5pm.

AUDLEY END HOUSE, Audley End, Saffron Walden, Essex, CB11 4JF, 01799 522399, EH. Open: 1 Apr.-31 Oct., Wed.-Sun. & Bank Holidays (Apr.-Sept.) 11am-6pm,. Wed.-Sun. (Oct.) 10am-3pm.

BELSAY HALL, Belsay, Nr. Ponteland, Northumberland, NE20 0DX, 01661 881636, EH. Open: Daily, (Apr.-Sept.) 10am-6pm, (Oct.) 10am-5pm, (Nov.-Mar.) 10am-4pm.

BELTON HOUSE, Grantham, Lincolnshire, NG32 2LS, 01476 566116/592900, NT. Open: 27 Mar.-31 Oct. Wed.-Sun. & Bank Holiday Monday 1-5.30pm (not Good Friday).

BLICKLING HALL, Blickling, Norwich, Norfolk, NR11 6NF, 01263 738030, NT. Open: 27 Mar.-31 Oct. Wed.-Sun & Bank Holiday Monday 1-4.30pm.

BURTON AGNES HALL, Driffield, Yorkshire, YO25 0ND, 01262 490324. Open: Apr.-Oct. daily 11am-5pm.

CANONS ASHBY, Daventry, Northamptonshire, NN11 3SD, 01327 860044, NT. Open: 27 Mar.-31 Oct. Sat.-Wed. 1-5.30pm.

CASTLE COOLE, Enniskillen, Co. Fermanagh, BY74 6JX, 028 6632 2690, NT. Open: Apr.-Sept. Sat.-Sun. (Apr. & Sept.) 1-6pm, daily (May-Aug.) 1-6pm.

CASTLE HOWARD, York, North Yorkshire, YO60 7DA, 01653 648444. Open: 12 Mar.-31 Oct. daily 11am-4.30pm.

CASTLETOWN, Celbridge, Co. Kildare, Ireland, 00 353 1 628 8252. Open: closed for renovation at time of press - call for information.

CHATSWORTH, Bakewell, Derbyshire, DE45 1PP, 01246 582204/565300. Open: 17 Mar.-31 Oct. daily 11am-4.30pm.

CHISWICK HOUSE, Burlington Lane, London, W4 2RP, 020 8995 0508, EH. Open: Apr.-Sept. daily 10am-6pm.

COTEHELE, St Dominick, Saltash, Cornwall, PL12 6TA, 01579 351346, NT. Open: 27 Mar-31 Oct. 11am-5pm daily except Fri. (4.30pm in Oct.). Open Good Friday.

CRAGSIDE, Rothbury, Morpeth, Northumberland, NE65 7PX, 01669 620150, NT. Open: Apr.-Oct. daily except Mon. 1-5.30pm.

DORNEY COURT, Windsor, Berkshire, SL4 6QP, 01628 604638. Open: July-Aug., May Bank Holidays Mon.-Thurs. 1-4.30pm.

DUFF HOUSE, Banff, AB45 3SX, 01261 818181. Open: Apr.-Sept. daily 11am-5pm.

ELTON HALL, Nr. Peterborough, PE8 6SH, 01832 280468. Open: June-Aug. Weds. (June) 2-5pm, Weds., Thurs. & Sun. (July-Aug.) 2-5pm.

FIRLE PLACE, Firle, Nr. Lewes, East Sussex, BN8 6LP, 01273 858335. Open: July-Sept. Weds., Thurs. & Sun. 2-5.30pm.

FLORENCE COURT, Enniskillen, Co. Fermanagh, BT92 1DB, 028 6634 8249, NT. Open: Apr.-Sept. Sat., Sun. & Bank Holidays (Apr. & Sept.) 1-6pm, daily except Tues. (May-Aug.) 1-6pm.

FORDE ABBEY, Nr. Chard, Somerset, TA20 4LU, 01460 221290. Open: Apr.-Oct. Sun., Weds. & Bank Holidays 1-4.30pm, also Thurs. (June-Aug.).

FRAMPTON COURT, Frampton-on-Severn, Gloucestershire, GL2 7EU, 01452 740267. Open: by arrangement.

GODOLPHIN HOUSE, Breage, Helston, Cornwall, TR13 9RE, 01736 762409. Open: 1 May-30 Sept. Thurs. (May-June) 2-5pm, Tues. & Thurs. (July & Sept.) 2-5pm, Tues. (Aug.) 10am-1pm, 2-5pm. Open Bank Holiday Monday (not Christmas).

GLIN CASTLE, Glin, Co. Limerick, Ireland, 00 353 68 34173. Open: May-June, daily 10am-12noon, 2-4pm.

HONINGTON HALL, Shipston-on-Stour, Warwickshire, CV36 5AA, 01608 661434. Open: Jun.-Aug. Weds., Bank Holiday Monday, 2.30-5pm.

HOUGHTON HALL, Houghton, Kings Lynn, Norfolk, PE31 6UE, 01485 528569. Open: 4 Apr.-26 Sept. Sun., Thurs., Bank Holiday Monday 2-5.30pm.

IGHTHAM MOTE, Ivy Hatch, Sevenoaks, Kent, TN15 0NT, 01732 811145, NT. Open: 28 Mar.-Oct. Mon., Weds., Fri., Sun. 11am-5.30pm.

KELMSCOTT MANOR, Kelmscott, Nr. Lechlade, Gloucestershire, GL7 3HJ, 01367 252486. Open: Apr.-Sept. Wed. 11am-1pm, 2-5pm, Sat. (3rd in Apr.-Sept., 1st in July-Aug.) 2-5pm.

KNEBWORTH HOUSE, Knebworth, Hertfordshire, SG3 6PY, 01438 812661. Open: 27 Mar.-26 Sept. daily (27 Mar.-11 Apr., 29 May-5 Sept.) 12-5pm, (17 Apr.-23 May, 11-26 Sept.) 12-5pm weekends & Bank Holidays only.

KNIGHTSHAYES, Bolham, Tiverton, Devon, EX16 7RQ, 01884 254665, NT. Open: 27 Mar.-Dec. daily except Fri. (27 Mar.-31 Oct., closed Thurs. in Oct., open Good Friday) 11am-5.30pm, Sun. (Nov.-Dec.) 2-4pm (pre-booked groups only).

KNOLE, Sevenoaks, Kent, TN15 0RP, 01732 450608, NT. Open: 27 Mar.-31 Oct. Wed.-Sat. 12-4pm, Sun., Bank Holiday Monday & Good Friday 11am-5pm.

LACOCK ABBEY, Lacock, Chippenham, Wiltshire, SN15 2LG, 01249 730227/730459, NT. Open: 28 Mar.-31 Oct. daily except Tues., 1-5.30pm.

LEIGHTON HALL, Carnforth, Lancashire, LA5 9ST, 01524 734474. Open: daily, not Mon. & Sat. (May-Sept., open Bank Holiday Monday) 2-5pm, (Aug.) 11.30am-5pm, (Oct.-Apr.) booked groups only.

LEVENS HALL, Kendal, Cumbria, LA8 0PD, 01539 560321. Open: 1 Apr.-14 Oct. Sun.-Thurs. 12-5pm.

LINCOLN'S INN FIELDS, Sir John Soane's Museum, 13 Lincoln's Inn Fields, London, WC2A 3BP, 020 7405 2107. Open: Tues.-Sat. 10am-5pm, (1st Tues. of month) 6-9pm, closed Bank Holidays and 24 Dec.

LISSADELL HOUSE, Drumcliffe, Co. Sligo, Ireland, 00 353 71 63150. Open: June-mid Sept. Mon.-Sat. 10.30am-12.30pm, 2-4.30pm.

LITTLE MORETON HALL, Congleton, Cheshire, CW12 4SD, 01260 272018, NT. Open: 20 Mar.-19 Dec. Wed.-Sun. & Bank Holiday Monday (20 Mar.-31 Oct.) 11.30am-5pm, (6-28 Nov., 4-19 Dec.) Sat. & Sun. 11.30am-4pm.

LONGLEAT HOUSE, Warminster, Wiltshire, BA12 7NW, 01985 844400. Open: daily, (13 Mar.-31 Oct.) 10am-5pm, (Nov.-Mar.) 10am-4pm.

LOWER BROCKHAMPTON MANOR HOUSE, Bringsty, Worcestershire, WR6 5UH, 01885 488099, NT. Open: Apr.-Oct. Weds.-Sun. & Bank Holiday Monday (Apr.-Sept.) 12.30-5pm, closed Good Friday, Weds.-Sun. (Oct.) 12.30-4pm.

MADRESFIELD COURT, Madresfield, Malvern, WR13 5AU, 01684 573614. Open: Pre-booked guided tours on specific dates.

MAPPERTON, Beaminster, Dorset, DT8 3NR, 01308 862645. Open: Mar.-Oct. Mon.-Fri. 2-6pm, by appointment only.

MARKENFIELD HALL, Hell Wath Lane, Ripon, Yorkshire, HG4 3AD, 01609 780306. Open: closed at time of press - call for information.

MEOLS HALL, Churchtown, Southport, Merseyside, PR9 7LZ, 01704 228326. Open: 14 Aug.-14 Sept. daily, 2-5pm, coach parties by appointment all year.

MONTACUTE HOUSE, Montacute, Somerset, TA15 6XP, 01935 823289, NT. Open: 24 Mar.-31 Oct. daily except Tues., 12-5.30pm.

MOTTISFONT ABBEY, Mottisfont, Nr. Romsey, Hampshire, SO51 0LP, 01794 341220, NT. Open: 27 Mar.-31 Oct. Sat.-Weds., 1-5pm.

NEWSTEAD ABBEY, Newstead Abbey Park, Nottinghamshire, NG15 8GE, 01623 455900. Open: Apr.-Sept. 12 noon-5pm.

OWLPEN MANOR, Uley, Nr. Dursley, Gloucestershire, GL11 5BZ, 01453 860261. Open: Apr.-Oct. Tues.-Sun. & Bank Holiday Monday, 2-5pm.

PLAS MAWR, High Street, Conwy, LL32 8EF, 01492 580167. Open: Mar.-Oct. daily (except Mon.), 10am-6pm.

PLAS NEWYDD, Llanfairpwll, Anglesey, LL61 6DQ, 01248 714795, NT. Open: 27 Mar.-31 Oct. Sat.-Weds., 12 noon-5pm.

PRIDEAUX PLACE, Padstow, Cornwall, PL28 8RP, 01841 532411. Open: Easter Sunday-7 Oct. Sun.-Thurs., 1.30-5pm.

ROUSHAM HOUSE, Nr. Steeple Aston, Bicester, Oxfordshire, OX6 3QX, 01869 347110. Open: Apr.-Sept. Weds., Sun., Bank Holiday Monday, 2-4.30pm.

SEZINCOTE, Moreton-in-Marsh, Gloucestershire, GL56 9AW. Open: May-July & Sept., Thurs. & Fri. 2.30-6pm.

SLEDMERE HOUSE, Sledmere, Driffield, East Yorkshire, YO25 3XG, 01377 236637. Open: May-Sept., Tues.-Fri. & Sun. 11.30am-4.30pm, open Bank Holiday Saturday and Monday.

SPENCER HOUSE, 27 St. James's Place, London, SW1A 1NR, 020 7514 1964. Open: all year except Jan. & Aug., Sun. 10.30am-5.30pm.

STANDEN, East Grinstead, West Sussex, RH19 4NE, 01342 323029, NT. Open: 24 Mar.-7 Nov. Weds.-Sun. & Bank Holiday Monday, 12.30-4pm.

STANFORD HALL, Lutterworth, Leicestershire, LE17 6DH, 01788 860250. Open: Easter-Sept. Sat. & Sun. 2.30-5.30pm, Bank Holiday Monday and following Tues. 2.30-5.30pm.

STANTON HARCOURT MANOR, Stanton Harcourt, Nr. Witney, Oxfordshire, OX8 1RJ, 01865 880117. Open: Apr.-Sept. Thurs., Sun. & Bank Holiday Monday, 2-6pm.

STANWAY HOUSE, Stanway, Cheltenham, Gloucestershire, GL54 5PQ, 01386 584469. Open: tours by arrangement.

STRAWBERRY HILL, St. Mary's University College, Waldegrave Road, Twickenham, TW1 4SX, 020 8240 4114/4224. Open: Easter-Oct. Sun. by appointment.

SUDBURY HALL, Ashbourne, Derbyshire, DE6 5HT, 01283 585305, NT. Open: 27 Mar.-31 Oct. Weds.-Sun. & Bank Holiday Monday, 1-5.30pm.

THRUMPTON HALL, Thrumpton, Nottingham, NG11 0AX, 01159 830333. Open: 10.30am-7.30pm by appointment.

TRAQUAIR, Innerleithen, Peeblesshire, EH44 6PW, 01896 830323. Open: 3 Apr.-Oct.. daily (Apr.-May, Sept.), 12.30-5.30pm, (Jun.-Aug.) 10.30am-5.30pm, (Oct.) Fri.-Sun., 12.30-5.30pm.

TREASURER'S HOUSE, Minster Yard, York, North Yorkshire, YO1 7JH, 01904 624247, NT. Open: 27 Mar.-31 Oct. daily except Fri., 10.30am-5pm.

TREDEGAR HOUSE, Newport, NP1 9YW, 01633 815880. Open: Weds.-Sun. & Bank Holidays (Easter-Sept.), 11am-4pm, Sat. & Sun. (Oct.), 11am-4pm, (Nov.-Mar.) groups by appointment.

WENLOCK PRIORY, Much Wenlock, Shropshire, TA3 6HS, 01952 727466, EH. Open: daily (Apr.-Oct.), 10am-6pm (5pm in Oct.), Weds.-Sun. (Nov.-Mar., not 24-26 Dec. or 1 Jan.), 10am-4pm (closed 1-2pm in winter).

WIGHTWICK MANOR, Wightwick Bank, Wolverhampton, WV6 8EE, 01902 761108, NT. Open: Mar.-Dec. Thurs. & Sat., 2.30-5.30pm, Bank Holiday Sunday & Monday, 2.30-5.30pm.

WILTON HOUSE, Wilton, Salisbury, SP2 0BJ, 01722 746720. Open: 27 Mar.-31 Oct. daily, 10.30am-5.30pm, rest of the year parties by prior arrangement.

For more information, contact:

ENGLISH HERITAGE,
23 Savile Row, London, W1X 1AB,
020 7973 3000.

THE NATIONAL TRUST,
36 Queen Anne's Gate, London, SW1H 9AS,
020 7222 9251

THE FOLLOWING HOUSES ARE *NOT* OPEN TO THE PUBLIC

ARDKINGLAS, Argyllshire

ASHDOWN HOUSE, Berkshire

BADMINTON HOUSE, Gloucestershire

BAGGY HOUSE, Devon

BIDDICK HALL, County Durham

BLACKWELL, Lancashire

BROADLEYS, Cumbria

BRYMPTON D'EVERCY, Somerset

CAME HOUSE, Dorset

CASTLE HILL, Devon

COMPTON WYNYATES, Warwickshire

CREEK VEAN HOUSE, Cornwall

DEANERY GARDEN, Berkshire

DRAYTON HOUSE, Northamptonshire

EASTON NESTON, Northamptonshire

ENDSLEIGH, Devon

HELMINGHAM HALL, Suffolk (gardens are open to the public)

HEYDON HALL, Norfolk

THE HOMEWOOD, Surrey

MELSETTER HOUSE, Orkney Islands

MELTON CONSTABLE, Norfolk

MERTOUN HOUSE, Berwickshire (gardens are open to the public)

MILTON ERNEST HALL, Bedfordshire

MOUNT IEVERS, County Clare

PITCHFORD HALL, Shropshire

PORT ELIOT, Cornwall

PORT LYMPNE, Kent

RAMSBURY MANOR, Wiltshire

WADHURST PARK, Sussex

AUTHOR'S ACKNOWLEDGEMENTS

I would like to thank Nell Arran
Susie Bagot
Bruce Bailey
David Beaufort
Jan Beckett
John Blackley
John Brandon-Jones
Lady Braye
Sebastian Bulmer
Sarah Bulwer Long
Mike Bushell
Grania Cavendish
David Cholmondeley
Henrietta Clifford
Susan Cunliffe-Lister
Rose Daventry
Debo Devonshire
Olda Fitzgerald
Nicky Gage
Oliver Garnett
Susie Gascoigne
Christopher Gibbs
Richard Gillow Reynolds
The Knight of Glin
Diedre Grantley
Richard Halsey
Alexander and Clare Hesketh
Rob Hesketh
Janey Heynes
Nicholas Howard
Simon Howard
John Hoyes
Richard Ingrams
Haidee Jackson
Russell Jackson
Amabel Lindsay
Christopher Lloyd
David Lytton Cobbold
Nicholas Mander
Dame Jean Maxwell-Scott

Flora and Catherine Maxwell-Stuart
Meave Melvin
Rosalind Morrison
Grace Nagel
Dr Arthur Naylor
Jamie Neidpath
Johnny Noble
The Marquess and Marchioness of Northampton
Tory Oaksey
Amanda Packford-Garrett
Jill Palmer
Andrew Parker Bowles
Henry Pembroke
Roselle Pope
Alan Powers
Cathy Powers
Mr and Mrs Proby
Mr and Mrs Hans Rausing
Mr and Mrs R G Reynolds
Jane Rick
Chris Ridgway
Mark Roper
Jacob Rothschild
Caroline Sandwich
Mary Schofield
Ann Somerset
Anthony Spink
Peregrine St Germans
Christopher Sykes
Tatton Sykes
Peter Thornton
Henry Thorold
Tim and Xa Tollemache
Rosamand Treave
Rick Turner
Frances Watkins
Alexander Weymouth
Sarah Wiggin
Heathcote Williams
for their help.

I would also like to thank
Desmond Guinness and Mary Brown of the Irish
Georgian Society
Fiona MacCarthy, Katie Harris and Elizabeth Walker
of Foster and Partners
Alan Bell, Mr Stephenson and all the brilliant staff
of the London Library
Emily Brooks, Warren Davis and Penny Woollams
of the National Trust
Richard Hewlings and Cathy Philpotts of
English Heritage
Camilla Costello and Olive Waller of the
Country Life Picture Library
Richard Adams
Mrs Carmal
Bridget Cherry
Penny Guinness
John and Eileen Harris
Rupert Hildyard
Nickie Johnson
Nicky and Suzannah Johnston
Anthony Lambert
Hugh Massingberd
Toby Motley
Nick Peto
Lionel and Mary Stopford Sackville
Judy Swire
Emma and Toby Tennant
Jenny Whittaker
for their inordinate kindness,
Douglas Keen and Desmond Elliott as always
Louisa Morrison for calm and steady research
Emma Mann for her hard work
Michael Hall for scholarly support
and Rupert Lycett Green for inspired help

BIBLIOGRAPHY

Amory, Mark, *The Last Eccentric*, Chatto and Windus, 1998

Aslet, Clive, *The Last Country Houses*, Yale University Press, 1982

Automobile Association, *Book of the Seaside*, Drive Publications Ltd, 1972

Betjeman, John, *Pictorial History of English Architecture*, John Murray, 1970

Brown, Roderick (Editor), *The Architectural Outsiders*, Waterstone, 1985

Burke's and Savills, *Guide to Country Houses, Volume II*, Burke's Peerage Ltd, 1980

Burke's and Savills, *Guide to Country Houses, Volume III*, Burke's Peerage Ltd, 1981

Cecil, David, *Some Dorset Country Houses – A Personal Selection*, Dovecote Press, 1985

Cheetham, J H and Piper, John, *A Shell Guide: Wiltshire*, Faber & Faber, 1968

Clifton-Taylor, Alec, *The Pattern of English Building*, Faber & Faber, 1972

Clifton-Taylor, Alec (Edited by Denis Moriarty), *Alec Clifton-Taylor's Buildings of Delight*, Victor Gollancz Ltd, 1986

Coats, Peter, *Great Gardens of Britain*, Weidenfeld and Nicolson Ltd, 1967

Colvin, Howard, *A Biographical Dictionary of British Architects 1600–1840*, Yale University Press, 1995

Cook, Olive and Smith Edwin, *The English House Through Seven Centuries*, Penguin Books, 1984

Crookston, Peter (Editor), *Village England*, Hutchinson, 1980

De Figueiredo, Peter and Treuherz, Julian, *Cheshire Country Houses*, Phillimore & Co. Ltd, 1988

Delderfield, Eric R, *West Country Historic Houses and their Families – Volume 2: Dorset, Wiltshire and North Somerset*, David & Charles, 1970

Dictionary of National Biography (published in 21 volumes), Oxford University Press.

Downes, J K, *English Baroque Architecture*, A Zwemmer Ltd, 1966

Drabble, Margaret, *A Writer's Britain – Landscape in Literature*, Thames & Hudson Ltd, 1979

Dutt, William A, *Highways and Byways in East Anglia*, Macmillan & Co., 1914

Dutton, Ralph, *The English Country House*, B T Batsford Ltd, 1935

Dutton, Ralph, *The English Garden*, B T Batsford Ltd, 1937

Evans, Herbert A, *Highways and Byways in Oxford and The Cotswolds*, Macmillan & Co., 1905

Fedden, Robin and Joekes, Rosemary (Compiled and Edited by), *The National Trust Guide*, Jonathan Cape, 1984

Firth, F B, *Highways and Byways in Derbyshire*, Macmillan & Co., 1905

Forman, Sheila, *Scottish Country Houses and Castles*, Collins, 1967

Foster, Norman, *Team 4 and Foster Associates – Buildings and projects 1964–1973*, Watermark Publications (UK) Ltd, 1991

Garnham, Trevor, *Melsetter House*, Phaidon, 1995

Girouard, Mark, *Life in the English Country House*, Yale University Press, 1978

Girouard, Mark, *National Trust Guide Book: Hardwick Hall*.

Girouard, Mark, *Robert Smythson and the Architecture of the Elizabethan Age*, Country Life Ltd, 1966

Girouard, Mark, *The Victorian Country House*, Yale University Press, 1979

Gradidge, Roderick, *Dream Houses – The Edwardian Ideal*, Constable & Co., 1980

Gray, A Stuart, *Edwardian Architecture*, Gerald Duckworth & Co. Ltd, 1985

Grigson, Geoffrey, *Wiltshire*, Thames and Hudson, 1957

Hadfield, John (Editor), *Shell Guide to England*, Book Club Associates with Michael Joseph, 1973

Hall, Michael, *The English Country House (From the Archives of Country Life 1897–1939)*, Mitchell Beazley, 1994

Hardwick, Michael & Mollie, *Writers' Houses – A Literary Journey in England*, Phoenix House, 1968

Harrod, Wilhelmine and Linnell, The Rev C L S, *A Shell Guide: Norfolk*, Faber & Faber, 1957

Highman, Douglas, *Shell Guide: Warwickshire*, Faber & Faber, 1979

Hope Moncrieff, J J, *Essex painted by L Burley Bruhl*, Adam & Charles Black, 1909

Hudson's, *Historic Houses and Gardens including Historic Sites of Interest*, 1998 Edition

Hutton, Edward, *Highways and Byways in Wiltshire*, Macmillan & Co., 1917

Ingrams, Richard (Compiler), *England: An Anthology*, Collins, 1989

Jellicoe, Ann and Mayne, Roger, *A Shell Guide: Devon*, Faber & Faber, 1975

Lees-Milne, James, *Some Cotswold Country Houses: A Personal Selection*, The Dovecote Press, 1987

Lucas, E V, *Highways and Byways in Sussex*, Macmillan & Co., 1904

Lycett Green, Candida, *England: Travels Through an Unwrecked Landscape*, Pavilion Books, 1996

Lycett Green, Candida, *The Perfect English Country House*, Pavilion Books, 1991

Lytton Cobbold, Chryssie, *Board Meetings in the Bath: The Knebworth House Story*, Methuen, 1986

Macaulay, James, *The Classical Country House in Scotland 1660–1800*, Faber & Faber, 1987

Maclean, Charles and Sykes, Christopher Simon, *Scottish Country*, Thames & Hudson, 1992

Marr, J E, *Westmorland*, Cambridge University Press, 1909

Massingberd, Hugh and Sykes, Christopher Simon, *Great Houses of Scotland*, Lawrence King Publishing, 1997

Mitchell, W S, *A Shell Guide: East Sussex*, Faber & Faber, 1978

Montgomery-Massingberd, Hugh, *The Field Book of Country Houses and their Owners. Family Seats of the British Isles*, Webb & Bower Ltd, 1988

Mordaunt Crook, J, *The Greek Revival*, John Murray, 1972

Muir, Richard, *The Coastlines of Britain*, Macmillan London Ltd, 1993

Nicholson, Nigel, *The National Trust Book of Great Houses of Britain*, Book Club Associates with Weidenfeld and Nicolson, 1978

Norwich, John Julius, *The Architecture of South England*, Macmillan London Ltd, 1985

O'Brien, Jacquiline and Guinness, Desmond, *Great Irish Houses and Castles*, Weidenfeld and Nicolson, 1992

Pevsner, Nikolaus, *Cumberland and Westmorland*, Penguin, 1970.

Pevsner, Nikolaus (Revised by Elizabeth Williamson with Geoffrey K Brandwood), *Leicestershire and Rutland*, Penguin Books, 1992

Pevsner, Nikolaus (Revised by Elizabeth Williamson), *Nottinghamshire*, Penguin Books, 1979

Pevsner, Nikolaus, *Shropshire*, Penguin Books, 1989

Pevsner, Nikolaus and Nain, Ian, *Sussex*, Penguin Books, 1996

Pevsner, Nikolaus and Neave, David, *Yorkshire: York and the East Riding*, Penguin Books, 1997

Pevsner, Nikolaus and Wilson, Bill. *Norfolk 1: Norwich and North East*, Penguin Books, 1997

Piper, John and Betjeman, John, *A Shell Guide: Shropshire*, Faber & Faber, 1948

Robinson, John Martin, *The Latest Country Houses*, The Bodley Head, 1984

Sager, Peter, *East Anglia*, Pallas Athene, 1996

Sherwood, Jennifer and Pevsner, Nikolaus, *The Buildings of England: Oxfordshire*, Penguin Books, 1996

Shortt, Hugh (Editor), *Salisbury: A new approach to the City and its neighbourhood.* 1972.

Smith, Juliet, *A Shell Guide: Northamptonshire*, Faber & Faber, 1968

Steele, James, *Architecture Today*, Phaidon Press Ltd, 1997

Thompson, Paul, *William Butterfield*, M.I.T. Press, 1972

Thomson, Hugh, *Highways and Byways in the Borders*, Macmillan & Co., 1913

Thorold, Henry, *The Ruined Abbeys of England, Wales and Scotland*, Harper Collins, 1993

Thorold, Henry, *A Shell Guide: Derbyshire*, Faber & Faber, 1972

Thorold, Henry, *A Shell Guide: Lincolnshire*, Faber & Faber, 1965

Thorold, Henry, *A Shell Guide: Staffordshire*, Faber & Faber, 1978

Turnor, Reginald, *The Smaller English House 1500–1939*, 1952

Verey, David, *A Shell Guide: Herefordshire*, Faber & Faber, 1955

Verey, David, *Gloucestershire, The Vale and the Forest of Dean*, Penguin, 1970

West, Anthony (revised by David Verey), *A Shell Guide: Gloucestershire*, Faber & Faber, 1952

Wiltshire, Kathleen, *Ghosts and Legends of the Wiltshire Countryside*, Venton educational, 1991

COUNTRY LIFE ARTICLES

BAGGY HOUSE, DEVON – The Home of Mr & Mrs Gavyn Davies by Marcus Field (Country Life – September 26, 1996)

BORDERS BRIGHT by William Tait (Country Life – April 18, 1996)

CASTLE HILL – I, DEVON – by Christopher Hussey (Country Life – March 17, 1934)

CASTLE HILL – II, DEVON – by Christopher Hussey (Country Life – March 24, 1934)

EASTON NESTON I by H. Avray Tipping (Country Life – November 7, 1908)

EASTON NESTON II by H. Avray Tipping (Country Life – November 14, 1908)

EASTON NESTON I by H. Avray Tipping (Country Life – August 20, 1927)

EASTON NESTON II by H. Avray Tipping (Country Life – August 27, 1927)

EASTON NESTON RECONSIDERED by Howard Colvin (Country Life – October 15, 1970)

ENDSLEIGH HOUSE, DEVON – I by John Cornforth (Country Life – October 9, 1997)

ENDSLEIGH HOUSE, DEVON – II by John Cornforth (Country Life – October 16, 1997)

FRAMPTON COURT I – GLOUCESTERSHIRE by Christopher Hussey (Country Life – October 8, 1927)

FRAMPTON COURT II – GLOUCESTERSHIRE by Christopher Hussey (Country Life – October 15, 1927)

GEORGIAN ARCHITECTS AT BADMINTON by Howard Colvin (Country Life – April 4, 1968)

GLIN CASTLE, CO. LIMERICK by John Cornforth (Country Life – June 11, 1998)

HEYDON HALL, NORFOLK – I by John Cornforth (Country Life –July 22, 1982)

HEYDON HALL, NORFOLK - II by John Cornforth
(Country Life - July 29, 1982)
HEYDON HALL, NORFOLK - III by John Cornforth
(Country Life - August 5, 1982)
THE HOME OF DR AND MRS HANS RAUSING by
Clive Aslet (Country Life - July 17, 1986)
THE HOMEWOOD, SURREY by Neil Bingham
(Country Life - July 22, 1993)
HOUSES NEWLY OPENED TO THE PUBLIC I by John
Cornforth (Country Life - April 7, 1977)
THE IMAGINATION OF HAWKSMOOR by Mark
Girouard (Country Life - September 20, 1962)
INEPT OR INNOVATIVE - *The Tredegar House Mystery* by
Giles Worsley (Country Life - February 4, 1988)
MELTON CONSTABLE, NORFOLK (Anonymous
author, Country Life - September 16, 1905)
MELTON CONSTABLE - NORFOLK I by Christopher
Hussey (Country Life - September 15, 1928)
MELTON CONSTABLE - NORFOLK II by Christopher
Hussey (Country Life - September 22, 1928)
MERTOUN, BERWICKSHIRE I by John Cornforth
(Country Life - June 2, 1966)
MERTOUN, BERWICKSHIRE II by John Cornforth
(Country Life - June 9, 1966)
MOUNT IEVERS, COUNTY CLARE, EIRE by Mark
Girouard (Country Life - November 8, 1962)
OWLPEN OLD MANOR, GLOUCESTERSHIRE - I by
Christopher Hussey (Country Life - November 2, 1951)
OWLPEN OLD MANOR, GLOUCESTERSHIRE - II by
Christopher Hussey (Country Life - November 9, 1951)
PITCHFORD HALL, SHREWSBURY (Anonymous
author, Country Life - February 2, 1901)
PITCHFORD HALL, SHROPSHIRE by Gervase Jackson -
Stops (Country Life - June 22, 1992)
PITCHFORD HALL I by H. Avray Tipping (Country Life -
April 7, 1917)
PITCHFORD HALL II by H. Avray Tipping (Country Life
- April 14, 1917)
A PUBLIC FUTURE FOR TREDEGAR by Richard
Haslam (Country Life - October 5, 1978)
RAMSBURY MANOR, WILTSHIRE (Anonymous
author, Country Life - August 10, 1907)
RAMSBURY MANOR - I - WILTSHIRE by H. Avray
Tipping (Country Life - October 2, 1920)
RAMSBURY MANOR - II - WILTSHIRE by H. Avray
Tipping (Country Life - October 2, 1920)
RAMSBURY MANOR, WILTSHIRE - I by Christopher
Hussey (Country Life - December 7, 1961)
RAMSBURY MANOR, WILTSHIRE - II by Christopher
Hussey (Country Life - December 14, 1961)
RAMSBURY MANOR, WILTSHIRE - III by Christopher
Hussey (Country Life - December 21, 1961)
ROBERT HOOKE AND RAMSBURY MANOR by
Howard Colvin (Country Life - January 23, 1975)
STANFORD HALL, LEICESTERSHIRE I by Arthur
Oswald (Country Life - December 4, 1958)
STANFORD HALL, LEICESTERSHIRE II by Arthur
Oswald (Country Life - December 11, 1958)
STANFORD HALL, LEICESTERSHIRE III by Arthur
Oswald (Country Life - December 18, 1958)
TREDEGAR HOUSE, GWENT by Giles Worsley
(Country Life - March 24, 1994)
TREDEGAR PARK I - MONMOUTHSHIRE by H.
Avray Tipping (Country Life - December 5, 1908)
TREDEGAR PARK II - MONMOUTHSHIRE by
H. Avray Tipping (Country Life - December 12, 1908)
THRUMPTON HALL, NOTTINGHAMSHIRE I by
Arthur Oswald (Country Life - May 21, 1959)
THRUMPTON HALL, NOTTINGHAMSHIRE II by
Arthur Oswald (Country Life - May 28, 1959)
THRUMPTON HALL, NOTTINGHAMSHIRE III by
Arthur Oswald (Country Life - June 4, 1959)
THRUMPTON HALL, NOTTINGHAMSHIRE by
Christopher Hussey (Country Life - August 11, 1923)
WENLOCK ABBEY, SHROPSHIRE
(Country Life - August 20, 1907)
WENLOCK ABBEY, SHROPSHIRE - I by Christopher
Hussey (Country Life - December 1, 1960)

PHOTOGRAPHS

All photographs copyright Country Life Picture Library:
P. Barker p57, Great Dixter; p127, Haddon Hall. *C. Boursnell*
p26&27, Baggy House; p132&133, Chatsworth; p175, Levens
Hall. *J. Buck* p63, Ightham Mote. D. Davison p204&205,
Castletown. *J. Easten* p126, Haddon Hall. M. Fiennes
p52&53, The Homewood; p60&61, Wadhurst Park;
p138&139, Tredegar House. *J. Gibson* p20&21, Castle Hill;
p22, Endsleigh; p24&25, Knightshayes; p46&47, Ashdown
House; p76, Knebworth; p148&149, Madresfield; p170&171,
Melsetter House; p172&173, Biddick Hall; p186&187,
Cragside; p188&189, Markenfield Hall; p200&201, Florence
Court; p208&209, Lissadell. *A. Gill* p14&15, Cotehele;
p96&97, Dorney Court. *Gunn* p23, Endsleigh; p32, Came
House; p117, Arbury Hall. *A.E. Henson* p34&35, Brympton
D'Evercy; p36 (main), Montacute House; p50&51,
Mottisfont Abbey; p54&55, Firle Place; p66&67, Port
Lympne; p84&85, Melton Constable; p88&89, Blickling
Hall; p90&91, Houghton Hall; p92, Harlaxton Manor; p103,
Rousham House; p108, Canons Ashby; p110&111, Easton
Neston; p128&129, Sudbury Hall; p150, Owlpen Manor;
p154&155, Sezincote; p158&159, Frampton Court;
p190&191, Sledmere; p196&197, Treasurer's House;
p202&203, Castle Coole. *A. Hyde* p131, Hardwick Hall. *T.*
Imrie Tait p68&69, 13 Lincoln's Inn Fields; p78&79, Audley
End; p80&81, Elton Hall; p192&193, Burton Agnes Hall;
p194&195, Castle Howard; p206&207, Glin. *J. Nieman*
p40&41, Longleat House; p70&71, Spencer House; p94&95,
Belton House; p100&101, Kelmscott Manor; p166&167,
Abbotsford House. *A. Ramsay* p144&145, Pitchford Hall. *A.*
Reeve p162&163, Duff House. *Scarbro* p44, Ramsbury Manor.
F. Sleigh p36 (top), Montacute House. *A. Starkey* p28, Forde
Abbey; p30&31, Mapperton; p42&43, Wilton House; p56,
Great Dixter; p59, Standen; p72&73, Strawberry Hill; p83,
Helmingham Hall; p86&87, Heydon Hall; p93, Harlaxton
Manor; p98&99, Milton Ernest Hall; p106&107, Drayton
House; p114&115, Honington Hall; p118&119, Stanford
Hall; p120, Newstead Abbey; p142&143, Wenlock Abbey;
p152&153, Badminton House; p156, Stanway House;
p182&183, Meols Hall; p199, Mount Ievers. *S. Upton*
p124&125, Wightwick Manor. *Ward* p38&39, Lacock Abbey;
p122&123, Thrumpton Hall. *F.W. Westley* p12, Port Eliot;
p136&137, Plas Newydd; p180&181, Leighton Hall. *S.*
Witney p168&169, Mertoun House. G. Wright p10&11,
Godolphin. *Anonymous* p16&17, Prideaux Place; p29, Forde
Abbey; p48&49, Deanery Garden; p64, Knole; p77,
Knebworth; p102, Rousham House; p104&105, Stanton
Harcourt Manor; p112&113, Compton Wynyates; p116,
Arbury Hall; p134&135, Plas Mawr; p140&141, Little
Moreton Hall; p151, Owlpen Manor; p157, Stanway House;
p160&161, Traquair House; p164&165, Ardkinglas.

For further information, please contact the Librarian, Camilla
Costello, Country Life Picture Library, King's Reach Tower,
Stamford Street, London, SE1 9LS, 020 7261 6337.

Other Sources

© Abbot Hall Art Gallery p179, Blackwell. © English
Heritage p176&177, Broadleys. English Heritage
Photographic Library p74&75, Chiswick House; p184&185.
Belsay Hall. © Lucy Sclater, Abbot Hall Art Gallery p178,
Blackwell. National Trust Photographic Library/Nick Meers
p147, Lower Brockhampton. Richard Einzig/Arcaid
p18&19, Creek Vean.

POETRY

In Memory of Eva Gore-Booth and Con Markiewicz by W.
B. Yeats reproduced by kind permission of A. P. Watt Ltd. on
behalf of Michael B. Yeats. (Lissadell)
Poem by John Betjemen reproduced by kind permission of
Candida Lycett Green. (Sezincote)
Poem by Rudyard Kipling reproduced by kind permission of
A.P. Watt Ltd. (Firle Place)

INDEX